Twayne's Evolution of Modern Business Series

SERIES EDITOR
Kenneth Lipartito
FLORIDA INTERNATIONAL UNIVERSITY

OTHER TITLES

The American Aerospace Industry
Roger E. Bilstein

Curtiss-Wright
Louis R. Eltscher and Edward M. Young

The American Amusement Park Industry
Judith A. Adams

A History of Black Business in America
Juliet Walker

E. H. Harriman
Lloyd J. Mercer

Wal-Mart
Sandra S. Vance and Roy V. Scott

INVISIBLE FUEL

Manufactured and Natural Gas in America, 1800–2000

Christopher J. Castaneda

California State University, Sacramento

TWAYNE PUBLISHERS • NEW YORK

Invisible Fuel: Manufactured and Natural Gas in America, 1800-2000
Christopher J. Castaneda

Twayne Publishers
1633 Broadway
New York, NY 10019

Library of Congress Cataloging-in-Publication Data
Castaneda, Christopher James, 1959–
    Invisible fuel : manufactured and natural gas in America,
1800–2000 / Christopher J. Castaneda.
        p. cm. — (Twayne's evolution of modern business series)
    Includes bibliographical references and index.
    ISBN-13: 978-0-8057-9830-2
    ISBN-10: 0-8057-9830-7
    1. Gas industry—United States—History. 2. Offshore gas industry—
United States—History. 3. Gas companies—United States—History.
4. Liquefied natural gas industry—United States—History. 5. Liquefied
petroleum gas industry—United States—History 6. Gas appliances—
United States—History. 7. Gas—lighting—United States—History.
I. Title. II. Series.
HD9581.U5C29   1999
338.2'7285'0973—dc21   99-427714
                                                                              CIP

Printed in Mexico
4 5 6 7 8 9 19 18 17 16 15

For
Terri Aline Alford Castaneda, and our children,
Courtney Lynn Castaneda and Ramsey Harris Castaneda

CONTENTS

ILLUSTRATIONS

TABLES

MAPS

FOREWORD

FOR A MAJOR source of energy, gas has been nearly invisible to the public, in more ways than one. Yet its commercial history goes back nearly two centuries. In fact, from ancient times, people have noticed boiling springs and remarked on lakes of flammable water. By the early nineteenth century, scientists, inventors, and amateur explorers began to harness the BTUs of this clean-burning fuel. As this book shows, transforming natural gas into usable energy was a long struggle against the resistance of both nature and human institutions.

Even before natural gas became a major energy source, American cities were manufacturing and distributing synthetic gas through intricate pipe systems. Derived from coal, manufactured gas provided heat, light, and cooking fuel for residents in New York, Boston, Philadelphia, and other urban centers during the nineteenth-century gaslight era. It was gas lighting that gave Broadway its nickname, the Great White Way, well before electricity arrived on the scene. Perhaps because oil and electricity have often supplanted gas as a fuel, we have tended to forget about it, but in fact gas has remained a viable energy option throughout the electric era. Gas entrepreneurs successfully negotiated a competitive struggle with alternative fuel sources by moving from illumination to heating and cooking. The competition between gas and electricity was never so one-sided as we might suppose. For a time, Americans not only cooked and heated with gas but even cooled with gas-powered refrigerators.

Competition as well as regulation has shaped the gas industry throughout its history. Gas competed both with other mineral fuels and with itself, as natural sources began to supplant artificial ones early in this century. Huge coal gasification plants, usually located in poor and undesirable neighborhoods because of their noxious odors, were rendered obsolete by giant interstate gas pipelines that shipped fuel thousands of miles from Southwestern fields. The building of these pipelines, over opposition from entrenched coal gas interests, domestic oil companies, and powerful coal lobbies and unions, is a major part of this story, as Castaneda shows. It is a history of technological innovation and business entrepreneurship every bit as thrilling as the giant Alaska oil pipeline of later decades. Much of the gas industry's history was played out under regulation. From the same measures that created the Federal Power Commission and broke up the giant power utility combines in the 1930s, gas came under government mandates that shaped its boundaries and set its prices. Through the 1950s and 1960s, regulation tended to limit gas supplies, which in turn restricted availability for major energy users. But with the deregulation of the 1980s, gas once again has become a competitive industry. It now constitutes a quarter of America's energy supply. New "gas majors," such as the Houston-based Enron corporation, have positioned themselves to become the dominant suppliers of this fuel. They are also using diversification strategies to move into a wide range of energy products as deregulation restructures electricity and opens new markets to competition. As *Invisible Fuel* demonstrates, this latest round of competition harkens back to the earlier, dynamic struggles that made gas a major resource and contributor to American energy needs.

Christopher Castaneda has for the first time told this story in a single volume. We are pleased to have his contribution to the history of modern American business in the series.

Kenneth Lipartito

PREFACE

THIS BOOK IS a concise narrative of the U.S. gas industry placed within a historical context. It is not an encyclopedic compendium, but it does identify and describe significant themes and developments in the production, transportation, distribution, and consumption segments of this industry's history. Supplemented with quantitative data and illustrations, the narrative traces the gas business from its earliest years through the twentieth century. The chronology, notes, and selected bibliography should help guide readers to sources that might more fully explain particular topics and issues. While this book is an overview of the industry's history, it does focus on entrepreneurship, particular technological and organizational innovations, competitive challenges from other fuels, and public policy (including environmental) issues.

I begin this study with a brief overview of the gas industry's European origins. Subsequent chapters examine separately the early development of manufactured coal gas and natural gas production and utilization in the United States. By the late nineteenth century, independent gas distribution firms (most of which produced coal gas) began to merge as competitive pressures from kerosene and particularly electricity forced gas companies to market their fuel more for heating and cooking than for lighting. Innovations in gas-lighting technology sustained the gaslight business into the late nineteenth century, but gas lighting quickly declined as electric power became available.

By the early twentieth century, gas and electric firms consolidated into large public utility holding companies that together composed the "power trust." These large organizations combined manufactured and natural gas production, transmission, and distribution business functions as well as the same for electrical power. In the mid-1920s, urban distributors of manufactured coal gas sought access to abundant Southwestern natural gas reserves. With the development of new pipeline manufacturing and welding technologies, long-distance pipelines were able for the first time to transport gas from fields located 1,000 miles distant, or more, to urban utilities.

The Wall Street stock market crash of 1929 and the onset of the Great Depression exposed anticompetitive practices and monopolism in the utility industry. The Federal Trade Commission launched an investigation of the nation's public utilities, and its work culminated in New Deal legislation that imposed federal regulations on gas and electric businesses. These regulations did not constrain industry growth during the post–World War II era, as numerous pipeline firms organized to build lines connecting gas supply with local distribution companies. Natural gas transported by these pipelines to Midwestern, Northeastern, and Western utilities allowed them to convert their distribution systems from manufactured to the more efficient natural gas. After World War II, natural gas consumption in the United States ranged from about 20 to 30 percent of total national energy utilization.

Strong demand for natural gas continued in the 1950s and 1960s, and natural gas shortages first appeared in the late 1960s; economists almost uniformly blamed the shortages on gas-pricing regulations instituted by the 1954 Phillips decision. The 1973 OAPEC (Organization of Arab Petroleum Exporting Countries) oil embargo exacerbated the problem as factories switched boiler fuels from petroleum to natural gas. Cold winters further strained the nation's gas supply. The resulting energy crisis compelled consumer groups and politicians to call for changes in the regulatory system, which seemed to be strangling gas production.

Apparent industry dysfunction in an era of environmental awareness and loud calls for conservation prompted policy makers to begin the process of deregulating the gas industry. Deregulation meant removing price controls on gas production dedicated for interstate commerce, transforming interstate pipelines into virtual common carriers, and allowing gas utilities and end users to contract directly with producers for gas purchases. By the 1990s, market forces rather than complex government regulations guided much of the industry's business.

As in the insurance, telecommunications, and banking industries, deregulation spawned a new generation of combines in the natural gas industry. Whether this new era of corporate combination is evidence of the cyclical nature of history, suggesting that these new large utility firms will one day be broken apart again by federal mandate, is a question for the future.

ACKNOWLEDGMENTS

THIS BOOK IS the result of many years of gas industry research, and there are many people and organizations who deserve thanks. I apologize to those whose names I have unintentionally neglected to include here. Kenneth Lipartito first suggested that I undertake this work. I thank him for this and his subsequent encouragement and useful comments on the manuscript. Joel Tarr and Brian Nicholson read earlier versions of the manuscript and provided useful and insightful suggestions. At Twayne Publishers, Michelle Kovacs skillfully guided the manuscript through production; thanks also to Jill Lectka. The staff at Impressions Book and Journal Services provided very professional services. Others, who over the years have directly contributed to my understanding of the gas business through their comments on conference papers and publications, include Joseph Pratt, Lou Galambos, Richard H. K. Vietor, Martin Melosi, Alan Anderson, James Castaneda, Tony Turbeville, and James W. Hart. Skip Horvath, Martin Edwards, Vipul Srivastava, and Ronald Lewis helped answer specific questions late in the project. Others, who helped in less tangible but no less important ways, include Nancy Boothe, J. Brian McCauley, Donald McCauley, Dallas McCauley, and Kenneth Owens.

My gas industry research at various times has been supported through projects for Texas Eastern Corporation and Panhandle Eastern Corporation (both of which are now owned by Duke Energy) and a generous summer fellowship and assigned time from the California State University, Sacramento (CSUS). The CSUS history department also generously supported this work and provided funds enabling me to employ two graduate students, Jeffrey Crawford and Robert Hull, both of whom excelled at assisting in the research for this book. Brian Emerson engaged in a hectic last-minute research venture to help tie up loose ends. Lauretta Frost and Kathryn King, interlibrary loan staff at CSUS, helped me find books and articles not easily accessible. The Business History Group also deserves thanks for supporting my natural gas research. But of course, all errors and omissions are my responsibility alone.

Many individuals and businesses also contributed substantial time and effort in helping me locate and acquire photographs. These persons include Lewis Stewart (Pacific Gas & Electric), Richard Bonney (Baltimore Gas & Electric), John Pepper, Keith Schmidt, and John Barnett (Duke Energy), James O'Neill (Enron), Robert Cox (American Philosophical Society), Mindy Gunter and Jeff Korman (Enoch Free Pratt Library), John Petralia (National Archives), Nancy Perlman (Baltimore Museum of Industry), Mark Severts and Roger Dudley (Public Service Company of Colorado), Kevin Belford (American Gas Association), and Jane Applegate (Dayton Power & Light).

My family has patiently endured many years of my gas industry research and dinnertime discussion of the same. For this, I am eternally grateful, and I dedicate this book to Terri, Courtney, Ramsey, and Susie, the dog.

PART 1
Introduction

1

Origins of Gas

"I call this Spirit, unknown hitherto, by the new name of Gas."
—Jean Baptiste van Helmont, *Van Helmont's Works* (1664)

DURING THE LAST half of the twentieth century, natural gas became an increasingly popular fuel, providing approximately one-fourth of the nation's energy. It has been used to power metropolitan buses in cities such as Sacramento, to generate electricity for electric utilities in Texas and other states, and to cook food and heat homes and businesses across the country. While there is a limited amount of natural gas in the United States and the world, it is the most clean-burning fossil fuel and for this reason appeals to the environmentally conscious.

In contrast, the mid-nineteenth-century manufactured coal gas industry was substantially one-dimensional. Manufactured gas (as opposed to natural gas) was a fuel used predominantly for lighting. Thus, from a broad historical perspective, the history of the United States gas industry is a study of the conversion from coal gas lighting to a more diversified natural gas–based industry.

The early gas industry therefore includes two related yet distinct gases, natural and manufactured. Natural gas is composed primarily of methane, a hydrocarbon that has the chemical composition of one carbon atom and four hydrogen atoms, or CH_4. As a "fossil fuel," natural gas flowing from the earth is rarely pure. It is often associated with petroleum and may contain other hydrocarbon gases and liquids, including ethane, propane, and butane. In the United States, significant natural

3

gas utilization did not begin until after the discovery of large quantities of oil and natural gas in western Pennsylvania during 1859.

Manufactured coal gas (once commonly referred to as town gas) was used for lighting throughout most of the nineteenth century; it was also used for cooking and heating from the late nineteenth through the mid-twentieth century.[1] Generally, a technologically simple process of heating coal, or other organic substance, will produce manufactured gas. The resulting flammable gas (a combination of carbon monoxide and hydrogen and other gasses depending on the exact process) was stored in a "holder" or "gasometer" for later distribution. Coal-based gasworks produced manufactured gas from the early nineteenth century through the mid-twentieth century.

This history of the gas industry examines these two related gases, their origins, and development. In this chapter I give a brief overview of their history from discovery through early utilization and commercialization. The earliest history is shrouded in folklore. There are references in literature to burning springs, burning bushes, or perpetual lights that suggest natural gas was used, albeit rarely, for heating. In ancient China, burning gas springs heated brine water to extract salt, and observers noted flaming gas springs in Greece and Rome. There are recorded observations of burning springs in France, Italy, and Russia as well. The philosopher Plutarch and theologian St. Augustine described lights that may have been the result of burning natural gas.[2]

It was scientific experimentation, however, that yielded the first clues about the origins of "inflammable gas," later referred to as flammable gas. During the late sixteenth century, Jean Baptiste van Helmont, a Belgian physician and chemist, became the first scientist to identify the differences between gases and air. In about 1609, he filled a "vessel" with 62 pounds of oaken coal and placed the vessel in a furnace. He burned the coal, which "necessarily belch[ed] forth a wild spirit or breath." Ultimately, the coal was reduced to one pound of ashes. Helmont proclaimed that the remaining 61 pounds "are the wild spirit, which also being fired, cannot depart, the vessel being shut." Helmont wrote, "I call this Spirit, unknown hitherto, by the new name of Gas, which can neither be constrained by vessels, nor reduced into a visible body, unless the seed being first extinguished."[3] Gas is diffuse and without form, and it appeared wild, chaotic, and even ghostly to him.

Van Helmont's experiments became the basis for the first published account of coal gas production. However, there were numerous other accounts of experimentation with flammable gas vapors during the seventeenth century.[4] A French scientist, Jean Tardin, observed an ancient gas spring near Grenoble, France. In 1618, he published his observations that these flames were similar to those created from the gas emanating from burning coal and oil. In Munich, Johann Joachim Becher made reference to a gas from heated coal.

The English clergyman John Clayton conducted and recorded the earliest significant scientific experiments with coal gas. In about 1683, Clayton observed a well-known gas spring located in a ditch at Wigan in Lancashire. The spring's flame, Clayton wrote, "was so fierce that several strangers have boiled eggs over it."[5] Clayton constructed a dam and removed the water from the ditch. A workman dug into the source of the spring and discovered coal. Clayton took some of this coal for use in an experiment. He burned the coal and discovered that "a *Spirit* arose which I could no ways condense."[6] Subsequently, Clayton filled ox bladders with the gas, and

> when I had a mind to divert strangers or friends I have frequently taken one of these bladders & pricking a hole therein with a pin & compressing gently the bladder near the flame of a candle till it once took fire it would then continue flaming until all the spirit was compressed out of the bladder.[7]

Jean Pierre Minckelers (1748–1824) took Clayton's playful flammable gas experiments one step further. A professor of natural philosophy at the University of Louvain, Minckelers in 1785 illuminated his classroom with light from a gas flame. For this early practical utilization of gas lighting, he is sometimes referred to as the "inventor of gas-lighting."[8]

These experiments contributed to the work of several men who installed and promoted the first European public gas-lighting systems. In France, the engineer Philippe Lebon developed the "thermolampe" for producing manufactured gas from wood. The French government issued him a patent for this process in 1799 and renewed it in 1801. Although he was unable to interest the government in providing financial support for his efforts, Lebon recognized the commercial possibilities for gas lighting. He staged the first public demonstration of gas lighting and heating at the Hotel Seignelay in Paris on October 1801. The demonstrations of interior lighting and heating, as well as an outdoor gaslit water fountain, continued for several months. Afterward, Lebon continued to promote gas lighting, but he had little success. His own life ended tragically in 1804 when he was robbed and stabbed to death on the Champs Elysees. In France, Lebon's death ended, for a time, further gas-lighting developments.[9]

In England, the mechanic and engineer William Murdock was more successful in developing a practical gas-lighting process. Murdock was chief engineer for the Matthew Boulton and James Watt engineering firm (Boulton, Watt & Company); Watt achieved renown for developing the first practical steam engine. Murdock worked at their Soho factory in Birmingham, which produced steam engines and became "the prototype for the modern factory."[10]

Murdock spent a great deal of time developing a process to create and store gas produced from heated coal; he also experimented with gases manufactured from peat and wood as well as coal. First, Murdock developed a portable gaslight system for use as headlights on a steam-powered carriage. Next, in 1792, he adapted this method for his home in Redruth, Cornwall. He produced and transported coal gas approximately 70 feet through copper and tin pipes to light a room in his house. He also developed a portable gasworks to provide illumination for a factory at Old Cumnock, Ayrshire.[11]

When Murdock heard of Lebon's gaslight demonstration in Paris, his own interest in gas-lighting technology intensified. Gregory Watt, a son of English inventor James Watt, had seen the gaslights at the Hotel Seignelay and informed his brother, James Jr., of Lebon's demonstration. (Both of the elder Watt's children were partners in Boulton & Watt.) James Jr. relayed the information to Murdock. Chastened with a competitive spirit, Murdock proceeded more intensely with his own gaslight projects and subsequently installed gaslights at the Soho Foundry initially to celebrate the Treaty of Amiens (March 27, 1802), which marked the end of the War of the Second Coalition between Britain and France.[12]

Gas lighting found its first commercial use in British cotton mills, where the mill owners recognized its several advantages. Gaslights were relatively inexpensive and produced comparably bright light, yet they were safer than oil lamps. On January 1, 1806, George Lee of Phillips and Lee, co-owner of a large cotton mill, was Murdock's first big customer. Samuel Clegg, one of Murdock's engineers, installed the coal gasworks built by the Soho factory. The mill burned gas in 50 gas lamps that evening. By the next year, the works provided 1,250 cubic feet of gas per hour to light 271 argands and 633 cockspurs equivalent to 2,500 candles. An argand was a typical wick oil-burning lamp with a glass chimney modified to burn gas; a cockspur was a burner with three small holes at the end of a closed pipe. Murdock calculated that the cost of lighting the mill with gas (less the sale of the coke by-product) was 600 English pounds, compared to 2,000 pounds for candles producing an equivalent amount of light. These projects allowed the Boulton, Watt, & Company to develop a standard gasworks model, but the firm retreated from the business after 1814 as competition intensified.[13]

William Murdock's most important contribution to gas history was his systematic investigation of the characteristics of various types of coal subjected to different temperatures and heating times.[14] Murdock also studied the efficiency of different retort designs (the container in which coal was burned), lamps, and the relative costs of candles versus gaslights. His interest in coal gasification was not merely pecuniary; he was an engineer more interested in technological innovation than commercialization.[15]

Samuel Clegg, once Murdock's assistant, emerged as Murdock's chief rival. Unlike Murdock, Clegg was more interested in the chemistry of gas manufacture than the mechanics. Like Murdock, Clegg had worked as an apprentice for Boulton, Watt at the Soho Foundry. He left the foundry in 1805 to form his own firm, which manufactured gas-producing apparatuses for various customers, including cotton mills. Clegg was especially interested in developing methods to remove the impurities from gas, and he is credited as the first person to begin purifying coal gas by passing it through limewater.[16]

While Murdock and Clegg worked on technical problems, Friedrich Albrecht Winzer began promoting commercial gas lighting first in Germany and then in Britain. A German national, Winzer had previously worked with Lebon in France. He held four patents for "extracting inflammable air from all kinds of fuel" and conducted public gas-lighting demonstrations in London during late 1804.[17] Winzer's greatest contribution was recognizing that a large centralized gasworks station could produce enough gas, distributed through buried pipelines, to supply many lights within a large urban area. He offered to provide residential light and heat in the same manner as some were then supplied with water. He discussed his ideas with persons in Germany, who were not enthusiastic about the prospect of tearing up streets to install piping for the new and unproved gaslights. Winzer decided to promote his plan in England, but he feared that the English public might misconstrue his plan to rip up city streets as a devious charade instigated by Napoleon Bonaparte to destroy London's streets. So Winzer anglicized his name to Frederic Albert Winsor in an attempt to eliminate the stigma associated with his foreign appellation.

Winsor actively promoted gas lighting in London. At the Lyceum Theatre in 1804, he presented lectures about gas and staged gas-lighting demonstrations using a variety of fixtures; he also displayed gas cooking appliances. Winsor's demonstrations met with intense curiosity but little financial support. The Prince of Wales did request that Winsor install gaslights on the wall separating Carlton House and Pall Mall to celebrate King George III's birthday on June 4, 1805. Winsor produced the gas at 97 Pall Mall and transported it through half-inch tinned iron pipes to an assortment of open-flame and glass-enclosed burners.[18]

Winsor also sought from the English Parliament an act allowing him to incorporate the National Light and Heat Company. Murdock successfully opposed Winsor's application, claiming the right of priority; Murdock wanted to gain broad acceptance of his gas-lighting process first through industrial application before offering it to residential customers.[19] Winsor reapplied to Parliament in 1810 for a joint-stock limited-liability charter, and he received one on April 30, 1812, for the renamed London and Westminster Gas Light and Coke Company. He had succeeded in chartering the company, but he had great difficulty in constructing a plant and distribution system. Because Winsor lacked both management and engineering skills, the new board of directors quickly forced him out of the very business he had established. Samuel Clegg, who had joined the company as engineer in 1812, soon took over and got the firm going. Clegg also patented a "wet" gas meter (1815) and gas governor. By the end of 1815, the company had 26 miles of gas mains in London. The small diameter (three-quarters of an inch) cast-iron pipe for these mains was manufactured by the same method used to produce rifle barrels, and old rifle barrels frequently were recycled as gas mains. Clegg left the firm in 1817 after a dispute over his compensation.[20]

Friedrich Christian Accum, a lecturer in chemistry, and one of England's most knowledgeable experts on gas lighting, worked for the new firm. He had previously served as a technical witness for Winsor's incorporation application to Parliament, and he joined the gas company soon after it was formed. Although Accum left three years later, he remained active in the gaslight business. He authored the first textbooks on gas lighting, which described in detail, for example, the equipment Clegg had installed earlier at the residence of the engraver and printer Rudolf Ackerman on London's strand in 1811. Accum's description of this and other gas-lighting equipment and processes became the basis of his first text, *A Practical Treatise on Gas-Light* (London, 1815).

Europeans and Americans interested in this new industry studied Accum's book. Indeed, it became essential reading for those planning to build and operate their own gasworks. Along with this book, English gasworks technology was for years recognized as state of the art. When Americans became interested in gas lighting, they often sent representatives to England to study operating plants and to purchase English equipment, despite the successful development by Americans of manufactured gas-lighting systems well before Accum wrote his book.

The commercial gas industry, based on a relatively simple process of collecting and distributing the vapors of heated coal, began first in Europe and then quickly appeared in the United States. Scientists and engineers first developed gas-lighting systems, but entrepreneurs and

Gaslight fixtures.

Friedrich Accum, *A Practical Treatise on Gas-Light* (London, 1815).

promoters created the commercial industry. Central systems that could supply gas to multiple light fixtures and burners in various locations demanded rigorous management and administration of accounting and engineering in order to operate profitably. The coordination of new gas manufacturing, distribution, and burning methods and technology eventually made gas lighting more widely available. But, as we will see in the following chapters, for much of the nineteenth century, gas lighting literally illuminated the differences between wealthy and poor; it was an expensive urban luxury.

PART 2

Creating an Industry, 1800–1890

2

American Enlightenment

"WITH TWO LIGHTS of the vapor," one observer stated, "I could distinctly read small print at a distance of thirty feet, and one blaze gave considerably more light than two candles."[1] This description of Benjamin Henfrey's 1802 demonstration in Baltimore was perhaps the earliest documented gaslight venture in the United States. Henfrey, of Northumberland, Pennsylvania, used a "thermo-lamp," reportedly based on European design, presumably that of Lebon. The lamp consisted of a 12-inch cylinder, 6 inches in diameter. Henfrey placed about two pounds of coal and an equal amount of wood in the cylinder. A tin tube extended from this cylinder into an adjoining room, which connected to a fixture consisting of four openings, each one-half inch in diameter. When all the equipment was in place, Henfrey placed the cylinder above a small fire. A vapor emanating from the heated wood and coal progressed from the cylinder through tin piping to a lamp, whereupon the vapor was lit. The lamp produced a "beautiful and brilliant light," equivalent to between five and eight candles (measured as 5–8 candlepower). During the same demonstration, Henfrey used a chandelier with six orifices, which produced even better results. In 1803, he placed a gas burner atop a 40-foot tower to light part of a main street in Richmond, Virginia. Despite Henfrey's success, he was unable to attract the financial support needed to develop his gaslight endeavors in either Maryland or Virginia.[2]

David Melville was more successful in promoting this new form of lighting. A pewterer and hardware merchant, Melville began experimenting with gas lighting early in the nineteenth century. In 1806, he installed a gas-lighting system in his house, and he received a patent in 1813 for a coal gas plant design in which coal was heated in a cast-iron retort set in a furnace. The vapors from the heated coal progressed through a tube into a "pneumatic cistern filled with water." The gas was purified as it flowed through the water, and then it was stored in a holder, or gasometer, until needed. A system of weights and pulleys provided a means to pressurize the gasometer by lowering it into a vat of water and thereby forcing the gas through tubing that lead to lamp fixtures. Melville installed gasworks for lighting at cotton mills in Watertown, Massachusetts, and Providence, Rhode Island, during the years between 1813 and 1817. Melville also installed a gaslight in the Beavertail

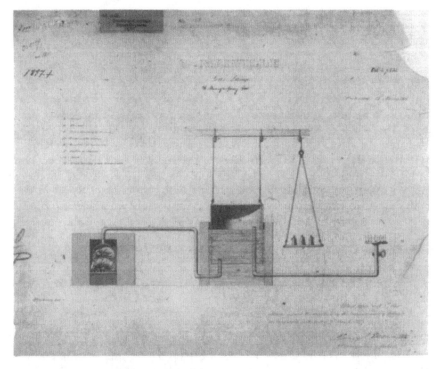

Diagram of David Melville's 1813 gas-manufacturing patent.

National Archives.

Lighthouse in Rhode Island. This light was particularly notable because it could be seen for a distance of 40 miles.[3]

Melville clearly understood the practicality of gas lighting. In announcing one of his gaslight demonstrations, he wrote:

> Gaslights will be found extensively useful in any situation where much light is required, most especially in the growing manufactories of our country, in as much as they are less expensive than those from tallow and oil, and free from the inconvenience and danger resulting from sparks, and frequent snuffing of lamps and candles—circumstances tending greatly to diminish the hazard of fire and proportionately to diminish the rate of insurance on buildings and material subject to that devouring element. . . . [Gaslight is] a discovery that holds out so brilliant a prospect of extensive and permanent usefulness to the country.[4]

Melville recognized the commercial potential of gaslights, but like Henfrey he was ultimately unable to profit from this new technology.

The Peale Family and Gas Lighting

Melville's gaslights and developments in European gas lighting attracted the attention of the Peales, a family of talented artists and natural scientists. Charles Willson Peale, the patriarch, had grown up in Maryland, where he taught himself to paint while engaging a number of other jobs. He later studied painting in London with the American-born historical painter Benjamin West. As a colonel in the Philadelphia militia, he fought in the American Revolution and subsequently became active in local politics. He painted portraits of American Revolutionary War leaders, including 14 of George Washington.

In 1786, Peale founded what may well have been the first museum in America. Located in Philadelphia in the building that housed the American Philosophical Society, this was also the first "national" museum, even though it was not officially recognized as such. Calling it a "Great School of Nature," Peale intended his art and natural history museum to stimulate further inquiry of the natural world. He sought to instill in the new nation a spirit of the European Enlightenment. He did instill this spirit into the lives of at least 2 of his 11 children, Rubens and Rembrandt.[5]

The Peale children grew up in a household heavily influenced by Enlightenment principles. Charles Peale's painting room was filled with portraits of American Revolutionary War heroes. Peale encouraged his children to develop their talents in art and their intellectual curiosity about the natural world. Philadelphia's active intellectual and cultural ambience revolved around scientists, philosophers, craftsmen, and doctors, who actively supported the organization of cultural institutions. The elder Peale, like his friend Thomas Jefferson, believed that scientific inquiry into "natural law" leads to an educated citizenry and social progress.

Several of Peale's children followed in his footsteps. Charles was magnanimous with his talented children, and he actively sought to promote their careers. In publicly announcing his retirement from portraiture in 1794, the elder Peale recommended the talents of two of his sons, Rembrandt and Raphaelle.[6] Not only did Peale recommend his sons to take his place as Philadelphia's leading portraitist, but he also arranged for George Washington to sit for Rembrandt in 1795. Subsequently, Rembrandt made 10 copies of his "harshly realistic portrait of the aging President."[7]

Talented and bored, Rembrandt needed new challenges to engage his ambition. Recognizing his son's situation, Charles devised a plan to finance a trip to England for Rembrandt. In 1801, Peale and several of his sons excavated two mastodon skeletons from swampland in Orange County, New York. The Peales assembled a skeleton from bones and exhibited them in the Philadelphia museum. The money raised from admissions financed Rembrandt's trip to England in 1802 to study with Benjamin West. While in London, Rembrandt and Rubens, who accompanied his brother, saw gaslights for the first time, and they were intrigued.[8]

In Philadelphia, Charles Peale successfully used oil-burning lamps in his museum beginning in 1805. He used the lamps one evening in conjunction with the celebration of Thomas Jefferson's second inaugural. The elder Peale was not entirely pleased with the oil lamps, as they not only illuminated the exhibits but heated the room to an uncomfortable temperature, particularly during the spring and summer months.[9]

By 1810, Charles had decided to retire from his museum and handed management duties over to Rubens, who needed to attract enough fee-paying visitors at $.25 each to pay his own salary as well as his father's annuity. He began to investigate the possibility of using gas lighting at the museum. Not only would gaslights provide superior illumination of the art and exhibits, but the lights themselves would attract curious visitors.

In 1814 Rubens proceeded with plans to install gaslights in the Philadelphia museum, now located in Independence Hall. David P. Erlick, who has studied the Peales' involvement in gas lighting, suggests that the Peales modeled their gasworks after David Melville's design. Rubens paid two Bostonians $600 to set up a coal gas system at the museum. Because the equipment was installed in a large closet located underneath a stairway, it created a fire hazard that Rubens did not initially recognize. To produce the needed gas, workmen fed coal into the retorts, and more coal had to be added before the fuel already in the retorts had completely burned. Opening the retort doors to add more coal allowed substantial volumes of noxious and otherwise odorous fumes into the air. Patrons objected vehemently to the smell. The prevalence of noxious fumes prevented the gas-lighting system from being put into regular operation. Rubens then "settled with the [installers] after numerous complaints of offensive odors and the threats of prosecution."[10]

Rubens continued searching for a partner with whom he could develop a more successful gas-lighting system. Dr. Benjamin Kugler, a family friend who had earlier suggested using gaslights at the museum, was anxious to assist. Kugler had experimented with various gas-lighting methods and had designed one for his own home. Rubens also studied Friedrich Accum's *A Practical Treatise on Gas-Light* (1815), the first "text-book" on manufactured gas lighting, which described English gasworks.[11]

Although Rubens preferred that a gasworks for the museum use bituminous coal, Kugler argued persuasively in favor of pine tar. In fact, coal mined in western Pennsylvania was not easily accessible outside of the Pittsburgh area due to difficulties in crossing the Allegheny Mountains. Although bituminous coal was available from Virginia fields, it was only after new rail connections were established in the late 1840s that abundant quantities of high-quality bituminous coal became available to eastern gasworks.[12] So, Rubens and Kugler proceeded to build a gas-lighting system that utilized pine tar. For a cost of nearly $5,000, they installed a gasworks in the Independence Hall steeple and placed 500 feet of soldered tin pipe throughout the building to carry the gas. On May 16, they invited the public to witness the new illumination system. They placed another system at the Peale family's residence in Philosophical Hall on Fifth Street. Kugler subsequently installed gas lighting at the Chestnut Street Theater and another residence. Although the Philadelphia City Council inspected these lighting systems and appointed a committee to consider gas lighting, they did not take any supportive actions.[13]

Rubens continued expanding the museum's lighting system until he was able to proclaim that the building was the first in the United States to be illuminated entirely with gas. For a $.25 admission fee, a visitor could observe artwork, objects of natural science, and gaslights. Charles Peale informed his daughter, Angelica, that "the whole expence has been nearly made up by a great concourse of Visitors in two weeks." The initial expense of installing the gasworks was not the Peales' only cost. Maintaining the system and purchasing fuel contributed to a substantial operating budget. The elder Peale wrote Thomas Jefferson that while the "gas lights having brought much company together on the evenings of illuminations, [they have also given] the semblance of bringing me immense wealth, especially by those who cannot calculate the cost of my labours and expences." Rubens operated and maintained the gasworks for the next four years until a "fear of fire or explosion," which could have destroyed Independence Hall, forced him to disassemble the equipment.[14]

In the meantime, Kugler patented his pine tar–, or "pitch–," based gas manufacturing process, which produced what he described as carbureted hydrogen gas. Kugler agreed to install gasworks at Philadelphia's New Theatre and at other buildings as well. Although Kugler's few gaslighting systems worked, local government officials offered no strong support or even encouragement. Kugler knew that gas lighting had great potential, but Philadelphia society was not quite ready to embrace this new technology.

By 1814 Rembrandt Peale was anxious to assert his independence. A successful portrait artist, he was 36 years old and the father of nine children. His magnanimous father's undying support notwithstanding, Rembrandt wanted to make his own way even if it meant following in his father's footsteps, but in another city. He moved to Baltimore and began plans for a new Peale Museum. Rembrandt hired architect Robert Cary Long to design the building for $5,000. Rembrandt proceeded with the project, although its actual cost of $14,000 placed a considerable financial burden of debt on the painter.[15]

The Baltimore museum was similar to the Philadelphia museum in that it contained both works of art and specimens of nature, including the second of the two mastodons collected in 1801. Unlike his father's museum, though, Rembrandt's emphasized artworks and manufactured products more than exhibits of natural history. Rembrandt advertised his museum as "an institution devoted to the improvement of public taste and the diffusion of science."[16]

During the War of 1812, Baltimore came under British attack, and under these circumstances Rembrandt's museum did not attract large crowds of enthusiastic visitors. Rembrandt was particularly concerned that if the British attempted to sack the city, his museum would be destroyed. He had already proclaimed a personal commitment to nonviolence, thereby exempting himself from either having to join the local militia or helping to build fortifications. Peale moved his family into the museum so that it would have residential status and hopefully would not be subject to destruction by the British. After repelling the British navy at Fort McHenry (September 12–14, 1814) and Wellington's force at North Point, there was renewed confidence among the citizenry of Baltimore and the new nation. Peale participated in the patriotic cause by donating all museum receipts on October 18 to the widows and orphans of soldiers who died in battle.

Rembrandt knew very well that his museum's success depended upon its ability to attract paying visitors. Peale's artwork and specimens might draw some people, but gaslights would transform his museum into a technological feat itself worthy of the price of admission. Rembrandt received Kugler's permission to install his pitch-based gas production equipment, and Rubens assisted Rembrandt by sending John Pendleton, a young man who had helped Rubens install the Philadelphia museum's gasworks. Pendleton helped Rembrandt erect a small gasworks behind the museum. Dr. Kugler himself, anxious to participate in any new gasworks venture based on his patent, personally assisted.[17]

Rembrandt was convinced both by his father's experiences and by Dr. Kugler that pitch was the best feedstock for producing gas. He knew that a coal gas system produced the by-product coke, which could be resold, but bituminous coal was scarce in Baltimore. Rembrandt wrote in 1816 that pitch "furnishes a purer light, produces no offensive smell, requires no separation or purification through lime water, [and] can be procured at less expense." He was sold on pitch.[18]

The first advertisement for the museum's new attraction appeared in the *American and Commercial Daily Advertiser* on June 13, 1816. Rembrandt's ad illustrated what might be called an early form of marketing talent:

> Gas Lights—Without Oil, Tallow, Wicks or Smoke. It is not necessary to invite attention to the gas lights by which my salon of paintings is now illuminated; those who have seen the ring beset with gems of light are sufficiently disposed to spread their reputation; the purpose of this notice is merely to say that the Museum will be illuminated every evening until the public curiosity be gratified.[19]

Controlled by a valve attached to the wall in a side room on the second floor next to the lecture hall, Rembrandt dazzled onlookers with his "magic ring" of 100 burners. The valve allowed Rembrandt to vary the luminosity from dim to very bright. The successful demonstration of gas lighting at the museum underscored to Rembrandt the immense potential for the widespread application of gas lighting, particularly in that visitors were more interested in the lights than mastodon bones or portraits of Revolutionary War heroes.

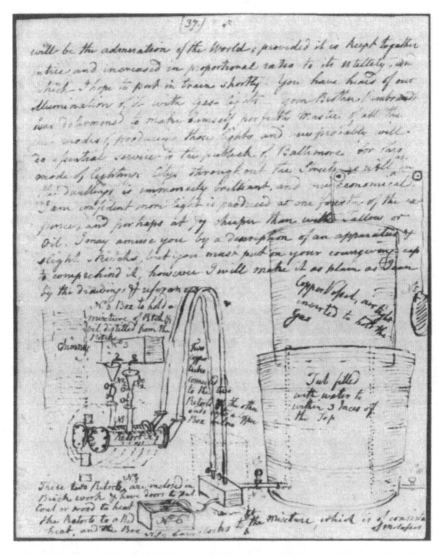

Diagram of the Kugler gasworks shown in a letter from Charles W. Peale to his daughter, Angelica, May 5, 1816.

Courtesy, American Philosophical Society.

The gas-lighting demonstration not only attracted museum visitors but also provided Peale with increased income. The cost of operating Peale's museum was approximately $3,527 per year. His highest annual profit came in 1816, the year he introduced gas lighting, when the museum's income reached $7,000. Except for this one year, however, the Peale museum never earned more than $5,000 per annum while Rembrandt operated it.[20]

The Gas Light Company of Baltimore

Rembrandt realized that lighting a museum building with gas need not be an end in itself. He recognized a singular opportunity to develop a commercial gasworks for the city of Baltimore. This more ambitious proposition was not without financial risk, but it offered seemingly unlimited profit potential. Rembrandt had purchased the patent for Dr. Kugler's gaslight method, and he was ready to put it to use. He organized a group of men, including William Gwynn, editor of the *Federal Gazette and Baltimore Daily Advertiser,* William Lorman, a local bank president, James Mosher, a bank executive and builder, and Robert Cary Long, architect of the museum, to join him in a commercial gas-lighting venture. These men became the official board of directors for the first gas-lighting firm in the nation; Mosher agreed to serve as president.[21]

This group established the Gas Light Company of Baltimore (GLCB) on June 17, 1816. Under the terms of the company's official act of incorporation (February 5, 1817), 200 shares, par value $100, were assigned to each of the five directors; it is not known whether the directors actually paid for their allotted shares. The company could issue a total of 5,500 shares, but new stock issues were allowed only after the directors invested a total of $100,000.[22]

Rembrandt received an additional 100 shares "for holding" Kugler's gas-manufacturing patent rights. Although he also received the right to purchase 200 shares at par, Rembrandt apparently decided not to follow through on this opportunity at the time. Rembrandt's financial situation was not particularly healthy, since the museum project had amassed considerable debt despite its popularity.[23]

Peale, Long, and Mosher acted as the new gaslight company's executive committee, making all the important decisions. Long and Mosher, however, often outvoted Rembrandt. For example, the two agreed, despite Rembrandt's dissent, to locate the gas company's first gasworks consisting of a 30 Mcf (thousand cubic feet) gasometer in a swampy area at the corner of Saratoga and North Streets. Construction went forward.

On February 7, 1817, the GLCB lit its first streetlamp at Market and Lemon Streets (now Baltimore and Holliday Streets). Baltimore's mayor explained to a city council member that the company lit only one lamp on this day due to conditions of frost and "obstacles incidental to getting into operation new inventions of such great magnitude." The Belvidere Theater, located directly across the street from the gasworks, became the first building illuminated by GLCB, and J. T. Cohen, who lived on North Charles Street, owned the first private home lit by gas.[24]

The new company's prospects seemed assured when, in a special session on June 17, the Baltimore City Council granted the company a franchise and contract "to open a street or streets for the purpose of laying his pipes for trying the experiment & estimating the expence at which he could contract with the Council for lighting the city."[25] Nonetheless, Baltimore's gaslight company got off to a slow start. After one year, GLCB was providing gas for only 28 lamps. Gas lighting was costly, and it was very expensive for GLCB to expand its service area. In addition, Rembrandt had ongoing disputes with Long and Mosher about operating and financing issues.[26]

Charles Willson Peale had remained very supportive of Rembrandt's participation in the gas company. During the spring and summer of 1817 the elder Peale visited private gasworks in New York, Philadelphia, and Baltimore, and he reported his findings to Rembrandt. All of these plants produced gas from coal, not the pine tar used by GLCB. The coal gas method had several disadvantages, including a greater amount of heating time for the coal to produce substantial gas. Also, if the coal was not completely consumed, it produced a foul odor; the limewater used in the purification process smelled bad as well. But coal had one clear advantage. The coke by-product could be resold as domestic or industrial fuel and could thereby lower the overall cost of producing coal gas.[27]

Rembrandt's role at GLCB continued to diminish, in large part because he simply did not understand the increasingly complex financial and technological issues related to the business. The nation was then in the midst of the Panic of 1819, and general economic conditions also contributed to the slowness of the firm's growth. In 1820, Rembrandt foolishly accepted five shares of GLCB stock in return for transferring his ownership of Kugler's tar gas patent rights to GLCB. Rembrandt claimed that the five shares were an initial payment only and that he should have received additional stock worth $10,000 when the company's financial situation improved, but he never received the stock. Rembrandt later sued, and in 1834 the Pennsylvania Court of Appeals ruled that Rembrandt was due 195 shares of stock (not including the five already in his possession). However, the court ruled that he had to pay for the stock including principal, dividends, and interest. The total cost of these 195 shares was $14,703.74, and Rembrandt was not financially capable of purchasing this stock; he forfeited the shares. Rembrandt lost on his other claim that he was also entitled compensation for serving as superintendent of GLCB for one year, since he had no direct evidence that he had officially held that position.[28]

Charles Willson Peale, who had taken an active role in helping Rembrandt, later wrote:

> The trouble which Rembrandt has brought on himself in this undertaking had nearly cost him the loss of his health, a neglect of his other business, and nearly his life—such is the folly of a man entering on a precaries [sic] business, or a business of which he had no previous knowledge.[29]

Rembrandt apparently agreed with his father, and he left the gas business. He also agreed to sell his Baltimore museum to Rubens (May 1, 1822), and Rubens took responsibility for managing it until October 31, 1828, when the sale agreement was actually fulfilled. Rubens did well with the museum for a time, but in the 1830s his fortunes reversed. During the Panic of 1837, he decided to sell the museum. Subsequently, none other than P. T. Barnum acquired the Baltimore Peale Museum as well as much of the Peales' Philadelphia collections. Rembrandt thereafter focused his time and energy on his art.[30]

The GLCB expanded slowly. By 1821, the business supplied gas to only 73 customers, most of which were retail establishments, in a city of approximately 63,000 residents. The company's income amounted to approximately $8,000—$3,000 from street lighting and $5,000 from private customers. In order to pay employee salaries, purchase raw fuel and other supplies, maintain and repair its facilities, and pay taxes, the company needed more revenue, which required continued expansion of the system while making the gas-producing process more efficient. The need for increased efficiency led to a reevaluation of the raw fuel stock. The pitch gas method was not efficient.[31]

Coal was more difficult to acquire and more expensive, but the gasworks could sell the coke by-product to offset the increased fuel costs. In 1822, the firm hired an engineer from England to construct a new gasworks that produced gas from bituminous coal. The coal gas method was the standard method used in England, so the firm's decision and ability to hire an English engineer symbolized its commitment to the high standards of current gaslight technology. The company's first coal gas plant was the "Davis Street Works," located at the corner of Saratoga and North Streets. The coal gas facility was successful, and the company later built more gas production plants. By the early 1830s, the GLCB provid-

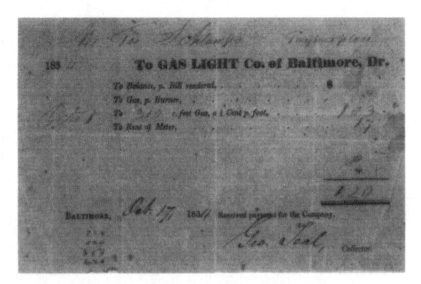

Gas Light Company of Baltimore gas bill, 1834.

Courtesy, Baltimore Gas & Electric.

ed gas for 3,000 private and 100 public lamps, each of which typically produced light equivalent to approximately 15–17 candlepower. The firm's stock was then selling for $135 per share and paying dividends of 8 percent.[32]

One of the new business's most daunting challenges was determining how to charge its customers for gas usage. GLCB did not then have metering devices, so it was not possible to determine exactly how much gas a customer used. Instead, the company billed customers annually per burner based on an estimated amount of time the burner would be lit. Initially, customers were expected to abide by rules that limited flame height, and customers agreed to extinguish all burners by a certain time each day and certainly not to leave lights on all day and night. To enforce these rules, gas inspectors roamed the service area announcing "gas lights out" typically between the hours of 10 and 11 P.M. If the lights remained on, the inspector might turn off the gas valve located outside the house. Even with these soft restrictions, bills were high enough to cover the company's cost of supplying gas to consumers who left their lights on beyond time limits or enlarged the orifices in their burners to produce a brighter light. Thus, typical gas bills were designed for high-volume consumers even though this rate structure made gas lighting extremely expensive for frugal users.[33]

The GLCB issued stock publicly for the first time in 1818. In need of additional capital for general maintenance, improvements, and pipeline extensions, the company advertised 500 shares priced at $100 each, payable in $15 installments. Company records do not indicate the number of shares sold. By 1823, 14 stockholders owned a total of 519 shares of GLCB stock; the largest stockholder was company president William Lorman.[34] By 1826, GLCB stock listed for $106 on the Baltimore Exchange, and the stock price continued to increase. Beginning in 1828, the company paid an extravagant dividend of two dollars per quarter, presumably to attract more stockholders. But the high stock price attracted few new subscribers. To raise funds for the company, the directors borrowed money on their personal credit.[35]

By 1833, GLCB had only about two miles of gas mains in Baltimore, but it was providing gas for approximately 3,000 private and 100 public lamps. Since GLCB was charging a high rate for what was essentially unlimited usage, it was difficult to attract new customers except those who enjoyed high personal incomes. In order to lower the gas charges, the company needed to assess fees for the amount of gas actually consumed, and this meant knowing exactly how much gas each customer used.

On July 19, 1833, the GLCB published an article in the local paper defending its decision to begin metering gas sales. From the company's perspective, being billed only for gas consumed gave customers a financial incentive to turn off their lights and avoid unnecessary charges. But metering evoked considerable upset among the company's customers. One early version of a consumers' group protested at a hotel and sponsored an unsuccessful ordinance to prohibit metered charges. The company responded that metered sales would not only make it possible to measure gas usage but would translate into lower gas costs so that more people could afford gas lighting.[36]

GLCB's first meters were imported from England, as were the majority of the gaslight fixtures. These "wet meters" were simple but accurate. The meter was a metal cylinder that contained a partitioned drum half filled with water. Gas entering the cylinder filled the partitions and forced the drum to rotate. The gas exited the cylinder on the opposite side, and the partitions continued rotating to the input side. An index counted the drum's revolutions, and meter readers calculated the volume of gas used by multiplying the capacity of the partitions by the number of drum revolutions. The accuracy of the meters dropped as water inside the drum evaporated, or froze, depending upon the climate.

To prevent freezing, meter readers sometimes added alcohol, typically whiskey, to the water in the drum. With meters in place throughout its network, the GLCB began charging $.40 per Ccf (hundred cubic feet) along with a monthly rental fee of $.17 for the meter. [37]

Management soon realized that GLCB could manufacture the meters as well as the gas fixtures instead of relying upon imported equipment. The company contracted a local machinist named Samuel Hills to make the equipment. Although Hills discovered that he did not have the necessary knowledge, he hired John M. Slaney Sr., who had worked in London for Clegg & Crosley. The founding partner of that firm was Samuel Clegg, the English engineer who had managed the London and Westminster Gas Light and Coke Company. In the company shop, Slaney oversaw the construction and repair of meters while others built chandeliers, pipes, and fittings.[38] This was the beginning of the vertically integrated utility company.

Gas Lighting in U.S. Cities

The Gas Light Company of Baltimore was the first commercial gaslight company in the United States, and engineers and entrepreneurs in other cities soon formed gaslight firms as well (see table 2.1). A group of businessmen in Boston formed the Boston Gas-Light Company in 1822. Numerous delays in constructing the gasworks prevented the company from actually lighting its first lamp until 1829.

Philadelphia organized the first municipally owned gasworks in the United States when the city established its own firm in the 1830s. Years earlier, Charles Peale had demonstrated the effectiveness of gas lighting at the Philadelphia museum, but local government officials and other prominent citizens remained unimpressed. In a report to the city's common council, a strong case was made against "the filth, the stench, the nuisances . . . and the pecuniary losses" of gasworks.[39] A petition to the council (November 28, 1833) signed by "several hundred excellent people of this city" claimed that gas was "an article as Ignitable as Gunpowder, and nearly as fatal in its effects."[40] This same petition warned against repeating the environmental degradation caused by English coal gas plants, which dumped coal tar and other by-products of gas manufacture into the Thames River:

> The waters of the Delaware and Schuylkill, now considered the most pure and salubrious in the world . . . must soon, we fear, experience the deterioration which has reduced the water of the Thames to the present impure

TABLE 2.1 Introduction of Manufactured Gas to Major Cities

Year	City
1816	Baltimore
1825	New York City
1829	Boston
1832	Louisville
1835	New Orleans
1836	Philadelphia
1843	Cincinnati
1846	St. Louis
1849	Chicago
1854	San Francisco
1867	Kansas City
1867	Los Angeles
1871	Minneapolis
1873	Seattle

Note: The date shown reflects the year manufactured gas was first produced in the city for commercial use. In some cases, the date shown reflects when a city charter was granted, and charters were sometimes granted before or even just after gas service began.

and unhealthy state, for no reservoir will be able to contain the immense fetid drains from such an establishment. . . . Salmon, smelts and other fish, formerly caught in the Thames have nearly all disappeared.[41]

Progress, in the industrial context, persevered over these early environmental concerns.

In the early 1830s, the city government hired engineer S. V. Merrick, "a gentleman of outstanding character and ability," to travel to Europe and investigate gas-lighting systems, and he returned with a favorable report.[42] The council was buoyed by Merrick's report and his determination to build a gasworks, and in 1834 the city began work on a plant located in an outlying section of the city at 22nd and Market Streets. This facility was privately owned, but a Board of Trustees appointed by the common council managed it. The Philadelphia Gas Works (PGW) began operation on February 8, 1836, and initially provided gas for 19 lamps at a price of $.35 per Ccf, and by the end of the year, PGW was selling gas to 670 customers and lighting 301 public street-lamps. In 1841, the common council acquired ownership of the gasworks, although the Board of Trustees remained in charge of management. In 1887, the city's Department of Public Works assumed responsibility for managing PGW.[43]

In New York City, as early as 1812, a group of businessmen ex-pressed interest in forming a gaslight company, although whale oil and tallow candle concerns sought to prevent the city council from awarding a contract. Instead, the New York City Common Council in 1816 formed the "Committee of Arts and Sciences" to investigate the possibility of forming a gaslight company itself. After a successful test using rosin that provided light at Tammany Hall, city officials were satisfied that gas lighting would work and emphasized that such a company should be pri-vately operated.[44]

Subsequently, Samuel Leggett, Thomas Morris, and Josiah Ogden Hoffman sought and received a state charter to build and operate a gas plant. The charter required the company to obtain permission from local government before selling gas in the city. On May 12, 1823, the city granted the New York Gas Light Company (NYGLC) permission to operate. The ordinance contained several stipulations, including one that required the company to be prepared to light houses and public lamps on Broadway from Battery to Grand Streets by May 12, 1825; light any streets, houses, or public lamps south of Grand Street as of May 12, 1828; and that the company should use the "best quality" gas, meaning "of a quality, brilliancy, or intensity to equal the Gas in use for the public lamps in the City of London." In addition, the company was to use cast-iron pipes, rather than gun barrels or hollowed pine logs, to transport gas. Many gaslight companies in the United States had used hollow logs for gas distribution until the mid-1820s, when British-made cast-iron pipes were imported. In the 1830s, American foundries began manufac-turing cast-iron pipe.[45]

NYGLC's state charter limited its capitalization to $1 million and its per share price to $50. Company directors planned on an initial stock offering of 4,000 shares to raise $200,000, enough money to begin con-structing the gasworks. The company's newly formed finance committee hired Timothy Dewey as superintendent at a salary of $1,000 per year. Dewey's job entailed traveling to England and observing both English coal and oil gasworks. He left New York on June 16, 1823, and returned in early 1824. During his 7 1/2-month trip, he purchased $18,500 worth of gas-making equipment, which was not delivered until June 1824. It appeared to Dewey that oil was the best choice since English firms were beginning to build oil gasworks as alternatives to the coal plants, although oil gas plants remained less economical in England because oil was scarce compared to coal. In addition, England had a well-established market for the by-product coke and even coal tar, which was commonly used to coat the wooden hulls of ships. But Dewey recommended that the New York Gas Light Company construct an oil gasworks "on account of its superiority, the smaller extent of the necessary works and the ease with which they can be managed when constructed."[46]

NYGLC built its first gasworks plant at Hester and Rhynder Streets and began producing gas in February 1825. Gas lighting quickly became popular. Within eight months, the company installed approximately 1,700 burners in residences, retail shops, and public buildings. NYGLC also received permission to light without charge the New York City Common Council chambers for one year.

The stupendous view of Broadway illuminated at night evoked the phrase "The Great White Way" and served as a grand advertisement for the successful utilization of gas lighting. Lighting Broadway required that the city purchase lampposts for $24 each and pay $8 per year for the gas for each lamp. While $32 per lamp was expensive, the public's demand for lighting encouraged the common council to budget funds for public street lighting. In 1829, in order to reduce its costs, NYGLC converted its oil gasworks to a rosin (residue from pine tar distillation) gas plant. The switch to rosin allowed the company to reduce its rates.[47]

Lighting on Broadway at night was a technological achievement, but it also exposed social ills otherwise hidden in the darkness. George G. Foster, a reporter for Horace Greeley's *New York Tribune,* was aghast at the nighttime sights illuminated by gaslight. "New York by gas-light!" he wrote in 1850. "To penetrate beneath the thick veil of night and lay bare the fearful mysteries of darkness in the metropolis—the festivities of prostitution, the orgies of pauperism, the haunts of theft and murder, the scenes of drunkness and beastly debauch, and all the sad realities . . . of life in New York." Gas lighting revealed a seamy perspective on urban nightlife.[48]

Gas lighting also allowed people to watch indoor and nighttime theater performances; oil lamps were comparably ineffective. The Chatham Garden Theatre was the first New York theater to be lit with gas. Gas provided a "clear, soft light over audience and stage," and the burners could be hung from the ceiling in the form of chandeliers or attached to the walls, thus leaving room on the sides of the stage that was otherwise used for oil lamp stands.[49]

In subsequent years, other gas companies formed and sought state charters to sell gas in areas outside of the New York Gas Light

Company's service territory. The first of these was the Manhattan Gas Light Company, which organized in 1830 and received a charter from the city government in May 1833. The charter authorized the Manhattan to sell gas north of Grand Canal Street, the border of the NYGLC's service area. Timothy Dewey left the NYGLC to become manager of the Manhattan, which purchased its gasholder and other equipment from England; its first plant was located on 18th Street, and it began delivering gas in November 1834. The Manhattan's authorized capitalization was $500,000, and the firm sold shares priced at $50 each. Its real estate holdings were limited to $100,000.[50]

Although there were initial competitive skirmishes between the NYGLC and the Manhattan in the early 1830s, the two companies soon recognized the business sense in establishing exclusive service areas. Both firms expanded within their respective territories until 1852, when they succeeded in providing gas service to most of the residential and business customers located south of 42nd Street. In 1853, municipal authorities granted the Manhattan Company the right to distribute and sell gas north of 42nd, but the company had little incentive to sell gas in that largely unpopulated portion of the island.

Where the Manhattan saw little profit, another group of businessmen saw opportunity. The 1848 "General Law for the Formation of Gas Light Companies" made it relatively easy to organize a gasworks. Under this law, a group of businessmen formed the Harlem Gas Light Company (February 1855) to provide gas service north of 79th Street, well beyond the Manhattan's established service area. Since the Harlem Company was small, apparently not well organized, and dedicated for gas service so far beyond the Manhattan's market area, neither the Manhattan nor New York companies opposed the Harlem's formation. With a gas plant located between 110th and 111th Streets, the Harlem began delivering gas in 1857. By the end of its first year in service, it supplied gas to approximately 750 public lamps.[51]

The first gas companies in the United States were located along the eastern seaboard, but soon businessmen began forming new gasworks throughout the nation. During the 1840s and 1850s in particular, gasworks appeared in the Midwest and Southwest. Cincinnati was one of the first cities west of the eastern seaboard to operate a gasworks. In 1825, Thomas Lawson, a tin and copper smith, was the first resident of Cincinnati to use manufactured gas. In his storefront, he displayed gas burners shaped as elephant tusks, bird beaks, and peacock tails. Close to his shop, at the corner of Main and Fifth Street, he erected and lit Cincinnati's first gas streetlamp. Over the next few years, he continued experimenting with gas lighting, but a fire in 1831, presumably caused by his gasworks, prompted the city council to order him to "put out his light."[52]

Gas lighting would not return to Cincinnati until the formation of the Cincinnati Gas Light & Coke Company. Incorporated on April 3, 1837, the new gas firm languished for several years, unable to attract investors. In August 1839, the Committee on Lighting the City expressed frustration in a report submitted to the city council:

> Our City has long since reached that point of population, business and wealth to justify the establishment of Works for lighting the principal streets. Not only our Atlantic cities—such as New York, Philadelphia, Baltimore and Boston—but New Orleans, Pittsburgh and Louisville in the West have set us the example of constructing large and liberal establishments for illuminating their respective cities.[53]

To bring gaslights to the city, local government agreed to promote the gasworks. The city passed an ordinance authorizing a $50,000 investment in the company after it first raised $100,000 in private capital. Two more years passed until a local attorney and newspaperman, James F. Conover, offered to invest the required private capital in return for an exclusive gaslight franchise. He received a 25-year franchise on June 16, 1841, but it contained an option for the city to purchase the gasworks at the franchise termination. The company then prepared a prospectus, which appeared in the Cincinnati newspaper on September 26, 1842. It stated that gaslight "over every other species of artificial light is now so generally admitted, and so extensively appreciated, that it might perhaps be considered scarcely necessary for the Company on the present occasion to advert to it."[54]

The Cincinnati coal gasworks commenced operation on January 14, 1843. Customers paid $3.50 per Mcf, but in what became typical practice for gaslight firms, it discounted gas bills by 5 percent if paid within three days. Meters could be rented for as little as $.25 per month or purchased for $19 or more depending upon the meter's size; installation fees began at three dollars for the smallest meters. By the end of 1844, the company had installed 2 1/2 miles of gas mains, served 302 private customers, lit 233 streetlamps, and distributed 5,722 Mcf of gas.[55]

The development of Chicago's coal gasworks took place a few years after the Cincinnati gasworks began operations. Norman B. Judd, an attorney who later nominated Abraham Lincoln for the presidency, led a group of local businessmen in the effort to incorporate the Chicago Gas Light & Coke Company. Illinois Governor Augustus C. French signed the company's charter on February 12, 1849. The charter authorized the company to issue 12,000 shares priced at $25 each, but the firm's real estate holdings could not exceed $50,000. The 10-year charter did not set specific gas rates. George F. Lee & Company of Philadelphia built the company's gas plant; George Lee was also a director of the gas company as well as its engineer. The plant consisted of seven retorts and a 60 Mcf gasholder. In addition, Lee agreed to install 24,000 feet of gas mains and gas meters. The company began operations on August 28, 1850, with five miles of gas mains. Its customer base included 125 private contracts, 99 streetlamps, and one public building. Gas was supplied at a cost of three dollars per Mcf.[56]

Local newspapers covered the advent of Chicago's gaslights. One article described stores that sold equipment necessary for the overland trip to California, which was then in the midst of the Gold Rush. The *Evening Journal* (September 5, 1850) reported that "some of the stores on Lake Street, particularly those devoted to California ware, made a brilliant appearance, and the gas lent an additional glory to refined gold."[57] Apparently, gold flakes in the window displays sparkled in the gaslight.

Chicago Gas grew rapidly. Within 10 years the company's customer base increased from 125 to 2,000, and its distribution system increased in length from 5 to 53 miles. On May 20, 1859, the company's franchise was extended for 10 years, but this franchise agreement set lower rates of $2.00 per Mcf for streetlamps and $2.50 per Mcf for privately owned lamps.[58]

Other entrepreneurs saw an opportunity to sell more gas in the city, and they formed the Peoples Gas Light & Coke Company, which received a signed charter from Illinois Governor Joel Matteson on February 12, 1855. Peoples Gas was prohibited from operating until the conclusion of Chicago Gas's original 10-year charter. The new firm also needed a city franchise and service area agreement with Chicago Gas to operate in the city. In August 1858, the city council granted Peoples Gas permission to lay gas mains. Peoples successfully negotiated an agreement with the city in April 1859 to provide gas for streetlamps, but financial problems plagued the new firm.

In 1861, two wealthy businessmen, Cornelius K. Garrison and Albert Merritt Billings, agreed to finance Peoples Gas in return for complete control. Billings, who had held a patent for a gas-purifying process until he had sold it to Peoples in 1859, became a director of the company. Garrison received the contract to build the firm's gasworks.

In order to stave direct competition, Chicago Gas agreed to sell Peoples 13 miles of its gas lines located on the west side of the Chicago River. Peoples began manufacturing and distributing gas in June 1862. In the meantime, Chicago Gas agreed to operate only in the northern and southern areas of the city. This territorial arrangement remained in effect until 1886. A restrictive law that limited the amount of real estate Peoples could own was eliminated, and the company was allowed to increase its capital stock to $500,000, or higher as necessary. Provisions of an 1865 state law granted the city of Chicago the right to regulate gas prices beginning in 1875, but the price could not be set lower than three dollars per Mcf.[59] By setting a minimum price, the legislature hoped to avert cutthroat rate wars among the gas companies. This strategy seemed to work as the two firms, along with a smaller one, the Hyde Park Gas Company (1871), operated within their respective service areas for several years before a competitive situation erupted, as described in chapter 4.

San Francisco was the first west coast city lit by gaslights. The origins of gas lighting there are related to the Gold Rush. One of the many forty-niners who arrived in California anxious to get rich was Peter Donahue. Born in Glasgow, Scotland, Donahue had worked as an apprentice at a locomotive factory in Paterson, New Jersey. Subsequently, he became an assistant engineer for a Peruvian steamship. In Peru, he learned of the California Gold Rush, and he decided to seek his fortune mining gold. On his way, he contracted malaria in Panama. After recovering from the malady, he joined the crew of the *Oregon* and headed for San Francisco. Like many of the forty-niners, he quickly found that getting rich from gold was not likely. While in the foothills, he heard that his brother James had arrived in San Francisco. Peter returned to the city. A third brother, Michael, joined them. The brothers organized the Union Iron and Brass Foundry and went to work in a business they understood.[60]

Dissatisfied with being a blacksmith, Peter considered other opportunities. He recognized that San Francisco was growing rapidly and that a large city needed a lighting system. Although in 1860 some San Francisco streets were lit with oil lamps, those flickering lamps were not particularly useful. The Donahues investigated the gas-lighting business and decided to form a gasworks. The San Francisco Common Council granted James Donahue a franchise to build a gasworks, lay pipes, and install streetlamps under the name San Francisco Gas Company. After its first full year of operation, the company had 237 customers. Initially, San Francisco Gas charged $.325 for each lamp per night. Residential gas rates were set to be competitive with oil. The first residential rate was $15 per Mcf but was later reduced to $12.50 and then to $10. The gas company's first gas plant was located on a city block enclosed by First, Fremont, Howard, and Natoma Streets. Steamers delivered coal to the plant on the Fremont side, which was a tidewater.[61] The Donahues purchased pipe from R. D. Wood & Company, located in New York, and had this and all other needed equipment shipped to San Francisco. They hired W. W. Beggs, the son of Peter's former employer in New Jersey, as superintendent.

To celebrate the commencement of gas lighting in San Francisco, the company sponsored a banquet at the four-story Oriental Hotel. Company secretary John Crane sent invitations to selected persons "on the occasion of their introducing Gas Light into the Streets of San Francisco." Between 200 and 300 people attended the event on February 11, 1854, commemorating the first public use of gas in San Francisco and the lighting of 84 gas lamps along the company's three miles of mains. A reporter for the *Daily Alta Californian* wrote:

> The good results from the introduction into the city are almost incalcula-
> ble. Beside the greater accommodation, the safety of life and property will
> be very much increased, and when the streets are more generally lighted,
> the frequent midnight robberies and burglaries will materially decrease in
> number.[62]

During the ceremony, someone temporarily turned off the gas flow just as San Francisco mayor Garrison began to speak. Probably shocked at first, the audience apparently broke out in laughter when informed that a prankster had caused the city's first blackout.

By 1850, about 50 cities in the United States had a manufactured gasworks. Generally, gas lighting was available only in medium-sized or larger urban areas, and it was used for lighting streets, stores, and residences. Despite the rapid spread of gas lighting, it was expensive and beyond the means of most Americans. (For a comparison of gas prices across the country, see table 2.2.) "From 1815 to 1855," wrote gas industry historian Louis Stotz, "there was no material increase in the amount of lighting in the homes of people with small means—the great mass of the population." Whale oil and tallow candles continued to be the most popular means to provide lighting. During the same time period, whale oil typically sold for $.80 per gallon, except when prices rose substantially between 1845 and 1855. Tallow candles cost about $.025 each and provided about seven hours of light each.[63]

Developments in portable gas lighting allowed for gas lamp installations in passenger railroad cars. In the 1850s, the New Jersey Railroad's service between New York City and Philadelphia offered gaslight. At the railroad depot, "a strong wrought-iron and brazed cylinder" attached underneath each of six passenger cars received manufactured gas from a retort. Within two minutes all six cylinders could be filled with gas. Each cylinder contained enough gas to light the two burners per car for 15 hours. The gaslights in the cars produced far more light than either whale oil lamps or tallow candles, and they cost less as well.[64]

TABLE 2.2 Manufactured Gas Statistics for Selected Cities, 1859

City	Private Consumers	Public Lamps	Price (Mcf)
Baltimore	8,200	1,800	$2.50
Buffalo	3,300	2,000	3.50
Chicago	4,100	970	2.50
Cincinnati	6,000	1,700	2.50
Louisville	2,539	938	2.70
New York*	15,000	4,000	2.50
Philadelphia	32,000	5,000	2.25
Saint Paul	159	154	6.00
Washington, D.C.	2,500	800	3.50

Source: American Gas-Light Journal (July 1, 1859): 2–3.

Note: Mcf = thousand cubic feet.

*Does not include statistics for all New York City gasworks.

The New Haven Railroad also used gas lighting in the smoking cars of its night express. Each car had two burners that together burned 7 cf (cubic feet) of gas per hour at a cost of about $.015. The two burners provided "very nearly" enough light for passengers to read in all parts of the car. Gas lighting on trains at night allowed passengers "to see each other when the more attractive views through the windows are shut out."[65]

By the end of the 1850s, manufactured gas-lighting systems offered the "most perfect substitute for the light of day." New York City ranked first in manufactured gas consumption, using approximately 600 MMcf (million cubic feet) per year, compared to Philadelphia's consumption of approximately 300 MMcf per year.[66] While manufactured gas utilization for lighting and heating spread rapidly throughout the nation during the 1840s and 1850s, other fuels and technologies soon competed with manufactured gas for the lighting market.

The gaslight experience in the United States during the first half of the nineteenth century was a remarkable episode in American history. First, we have a very clear example of technology that was transferred from England to the United States.[67] A common culture and language facilitated this transfer, but American entrepreneurs made adaptations when necessary. There was no doubt, however, that Americans in the early national period considered English gasworks technology and engineering, from the retorts to the burners, as exemplary. Furthermore, we see how adaptive engineering and technological skill was implemented and then extended geographically from the east to west coasts. Finally, public gaslights most obviously changed life for many people, even those not wealthy enough to own private gas lamps. The early gaslight era was part of an industrial, social, and technological revolution in American society.

3

Discovering
Natural Gas

WHILE THE MANUFACTURED gas industry expanded rapidly in America, natural gas was neither widely available nor utilized. In fact, it was manufactured gas, a synthetic fuel, that spawned the gas industry long before natural fuel became predominant. During colonial times, observers of gas and oil springs typically described them as either curiosities or sources of medicinal salve. In several cases, explorers and colonists observed ponds covered with oil in which gas sometimes bubbled through. There was also direct observation of gas escaping from crevices as early as the seventeenth century, but this ethereal gas could not be captured or otherwise used.

Joseph de la Roche Dallion, a Franciscan missionary, may have been the first European to record observations of a North American oil and gas spring. During 1627, after spending time with the Huron Indians of Ontario, he traveled south to visit an Iroquois tribe occupying land surrounding the Niagara River. He wrote to a friend that the Indians there "have squashes, beans, and other vegetables in abundance, and very good oil, which they call Atouronton."[1] While Dallion only mentioned oil, the site he observed was later identified as an oil and gas spring located near present-day Cuba, New York.

The French explorer Robert Cavelier, Sieur de La Salle, provided the first recorded observation of a North American "burning spring" in August 1669. It was located at present-day Bristol Center, New York, approximately 60 miles northeast of the Cuba oil and gas spring. La

Salle and his companion Galinee, a Sulpician missionary, and two Indians observed the "very extraordinary spring."

> The water is very clear but has a bad odor, like that of the mineral marshes of Paris. . . . I applied a torch and the water immediately took fire and burned like brandy, and was not extinguished until it rained. This flame is among the Indians a sign of abundance or sterility according as it exhibits the contrary qualities. . . . I can neither offer nor imagine any better explanation, than that it acquires this combustible property by passing over some aluminous land.[2]

Pehr Kalm, a Swedish naturalist and student of Carolus Linnaeus, recorded in his journal on November 1, 1749, that several members of his party observed an oil spring also located near Cuba. Kalm wrote that native American Indians visited a lake in the spring and set fire to leaves saturated in oil floating on the surface.[3] Seneca Indians described through legend the origins of this oil: A large woman one day observed a pool of water, approached too close, fell in, and drowned. Her body was never recovered. Ever since, oil with special curative powers rose from the spring. The local Senecas used the oil to soothe many pains and ailments.[4] The site remained a curiosity for over 200 years and is the present site of Oil Spring Indian Reservation.

Both George Washington and Thomas Jefferson observed natural gas springs. During the autumn of 1770, Washington participated in an expedition along the Ohio and Kanawha Rivers in West Virginia and Ohio. Near the present-day town of Pomeroy, Ohio, Washington described a location "wch. the Indians say is always a fire."[5] About perhaps the same site, Thomas Jefferson recorded his observations of "a hole in the earth . . . from which issues constantly a gaseous stream:

> On presenting a lighted candle or torch within 18 inches of the hole it flames up in a column of 18 inches diameter, and four or five feet height, which some times burns out within 20 minutes, and at other times has been known to continue three days, and then has been left still burning. . . . The circumjacent lands are the property of General Washington and General Lewis.[6]

Another group of visitors to these springs noted that hunters used the burning springs to cook food.[7]

During the early nineteenth century, the "burning springs" were little more than curiosities. People who had seen such springs knew that when lit, the springs produced both light and heat. There was no practical method of capturing the gas emanating from the springs and bottling it or redirecting its flow through pipes.

Fredonia, New York

Residents of Fredonia, New York, were the first Americans to use natural gas for lighting, but there are differing accounts of both its discovery and its initial utilization. Gas springs in the vicinity of Fredonia had been observed in the early 1800s, but popular lore dates the discovery of the Fredonia gas springs to 1821. One version has a traveler who, while taking a break on the shore of the Canadaway Creek, lit his pipe and ignited nearby escaping gas. Another version tells of driftwood burning in the creek, which aroused the suspicion of locals. The most widely quoted and detailed version involves a family cookout near the Main Street Bridge. After baking bread in an outdoor oven, a mother asked several young boys to extinguish the remains of burning embers in the oven. The boys began throwing the embers across the nearby Canadaway Creek. Every time one of the embers landed near a particular spot, a flame erupted from the ground. The parents investigated and noticed that gas was emerging from the earth at that spot. The father located the source of the gas and plunged an old piece of pipe into the hole. He then lit the gas coming out of the pipe.[8]

Sometime after the discovery, a gunsmith named William Aaron Hart organized an effort to utilize gas from the spring to light local homes and establishments. Hart provided gas service to some local stores and buildings, but the precise date of natural gas lighting in Fredonia is in question. It is controversial because an enduring legend of the U.S. natural gas industry involves Fredonia natural gas and the French military leader Marquis de Lafayette, who had fought with George Washington against the British in the American Revolution.

It is known that at the invitation of the U.S. Congress, Lafayette visited America during the years 1824–1825, and he traveled to New York in the summer of 1825. Lafayette was headed toward a steamboat rendezvous at Dunkirk on Lake Erie; the steamboat waited to transport him to Buffalo. On his way to Dunkirk, Lafayette's entourage passed through numerous villages, including Fredonia. In Fredonia, a large and enthusiastic crowd of men, women, and children welcomed him at 2 A.M. on June 4. While popular legend has it that Lafayette attended a banquet in his honor at the Abel House Inn and observed with both awe and trepidation the gaslights there, a careful examination of extant documents by industry historian Luke Scheer suggests that if Lafayette actually saw gaslights, he probably did not realize it.[9]

Upon hearing of Lafayette's impending visit, the town's citizens planned a grand celebration. With the lighting of a signal torch and 13-gun salute, many residents lit candles and bonfires as Lafayette and his entourage approached Fredonia. The General's private secretary, A. Levasseur, wrote that we "were immediately dazzled by the glare of a thousand lights, suspended to the houses and trees that surrounded us." At a stage that was "lighted by barrels of burning rosin," a speaker welcomed Lafayette.[10] The local newspaper featured a story on the same events and noted that "the platform erected in front of the house [Abell's Hotel], set round with green trees planted in the ground, overhung with lamps and chandeliers, with an arch in front . . . had an effect at that late hour of the night, and amid the illuminations of the village, bordering on enchantment."[11] In these accounts, however, there was no mention of gaslights at Fredonia. Earlier, in a Baltimore theater, Levasseur recorded observations of "gas blazing abundantly from numerous pipes, and throwing floods of dazzling light over the hall."[12] The French visitor clearly recognized gas lighting, but did not identify such lights at Fredonia.

Accounts of Lafayette's visit written several decades later state that he saw gaslights at Abel's Inn during the early morning hours of June 4. Contemporary articles published in the *Fredonia Censor* do not identify "gas lights" at Lafayette's early June visit. Instead, the paper carried a story in late August, nearly two months after the visit, noting that "there are now in this village 2 stores (one a grocery), 2 shops, and one mill that are every evening lighted up with as brilliant gas lights as are to be found in any city in this or any other country."[13] More than a year later, the same paper reported that "one shop, two stores and Abel's hotel have been added to the former number that are every evening lighted with natural gas."[14] Lafayette most likely did not see gaslights in Fredonia as popular lore suggests.

After Lafayette's visit, William Hart continued to develop his natural gas interests in Fredonia. During 1827, he also began work on a plan to supply natural gas to a lighthouse at Barcelona Harbor. After receiving a contract from the U.S. government for this service, he and his associates installed a primitive gasworks. They placed a fish barrel over a gas spring located at Westfield along Lake Erie. The barrel served as a gasometer, or gasholder. They sealed the gasometer and used hollowed out pine logs extending one-half mile as a pipeline to the lighthouse. Gas from the spring provided enough fuel to illuminate 144 burners and create a bright light.[15]

Gas and Oil at Titusville

Oil springs and seepages existed in eastern Pennsylvania and surrounding areas during the early nineteenth century. One person intrigued with oil was Samuel Kier, who in the late 1840s marketed "rock oil" as an all-purpose medicine. The name "rock oil" signified that the oil came from the earth rather than from whales or vegetables. Kier advertised and sold his oil nationally. By 1858, he claimed to have sold about 240,000 half-pint bottles for one dollar each.[16]

Others were interested in oil for more conventional purposes. George H. Bissell, a young New York lawyer, knew that Kier and others were promoting oil as a medicine. He suspected that rock oil might be very similar in chemical composition to coal oil, which was beginning to be used during the mid-1850s as a fuel for illumination. Dr. Abraham Gesner pioneered commercial coal oil utilization in the United States in 1854 when he established the New York Kerosene Oil Works. Gesner first used the term "kerosene" for coal oil, although oil-based kerosene would not be developed until petroleum was more widely available later in the nineteenth century.[17]

Bissell and a partner, J. G. Eveleth, found investors to help finance the purchase of oil properties in Titusville, Pennsylvania. The investors required that the partners personally visit the land and contract for a scientific report on the oil there. Benjamin Silliman Jr., a Yale University professor, and Luther Atwood, a chemist and pharmaceutic manufacturer, wrote the report and submitted it in April 1855. The report confirmed Bissell's belief that oil could be utilized as an illuminant. Satisfied, the investors, who lived in New Haven, Connecticut, stipulated that the new oil firm be incorporated in Connecticut. Bissell and Eveleth formed the Pennsylvania Rock Oil Company on September 18, 1855, and leased 1,200 acres of land. A variety of delays prevented any attempt to develop the property until 1857.

In that year, James M. Townsend, a New Haven banker who was president of the Pennsylvania Rock Oil Company, began seeking someone to drill on the company's property. Townsend hired Edwin L. Drake, who had been living with his daughter at the Tontine Hotel in New Haven. Drake, a 38-year-old former dry goods salesman and express agent for the Boston & Albany Railroad, was then a conductor for the New York, New Haven, and Hartford Railroad, but he was not an experienced oil man. Nevertheless, he was available and the fact that he had his own railroad pass meant that he didn't require travel funds. Drake moved to Titusville, and Townsend sent mail addressed to "Colonel" Drake to improve Drake's standing among Titusville's residents.[18] In early 1858, the Seneca Oil Company, controlled by the same New Haven investor group, acquired the Pennsylvania Rock Oil leases as well as those acquired by Drake.

Drake decided to drill for oil, rather than to dig a deep well. He hired "Uncle Billy" Smith, an experienced salt-well operator, to do the drilling. On August 28, 1859, they struck oil at 69 feet.[19] The Titusville oil discovery marked the beginning of the U.S. oil industry. Petroleum served as an industrial lubricant, and kerosene, a by-product of refining petroleum, served as a fuel for lighting. By 1865, John D. Rockefeller had devoted himself to the oil-refining business, and he quickly became wealthy from the sale of kerosene.[20] The kerosene lamp was the least expensive and most portable of all lighting sources. Joel Tarr noted that "by the 1870s and 1880s, most of the urban working class, as well as a substantial part of the middle class, used kerosene lamps for domestic illumination."[21]

While the petroleum boom provided kerosene for lighting, it also resulted in the discovery of massive amounts of associated natural gas. For many years natural gas was considered by oil well operators to be an unwanted by-product of oil production. Although natural gas is commonly found in association with oil, and natural gas provides the pressurization necessary for oil flow to the surface, gas was then commonly allowed to escape into the atmosphere while the oil was collected.

Origins of Commercial Natural Gas Utilization

By the mid-nineteenth century, only those factories or towns located near a natural gas well could utilize the fuel. The difficulty of containing a natural gas spring, storing the gas, and transporting it over long distances limited its use. Alternatively, manufactured gas plants could be built and operated anywhere as long as coal or the feedstock was readily available. Significant natural gas discoveries such as the high-volume well discovered by William Tomkins in 1841 near Washington's burning spring on the Canadaway Creek attracted some attention but little commercial interest.[22]

The earliest recorded use of gas for industrial purposes in the United States occurred in 1840, near Centerville, Pennsylvania. The gas was used to distill salt from brine water. Gradually, in the 1860s and 1870s, local deposits of natural gas were utilized for a variety of industrial heating applications.[23] In Fredonia, some residents had used natural gas for home or shop lighting after its discovery in about 1821, but a formal natural gas company was not organized there for many years. In 1858, a group of businessmen established the Fredonia Gas Light and Water Works Company to operate the original wells and others that were subsequently discovered and developed.

Natural gas would not be used on a large scale until the 1880s, and gas wells were most likely to be abandoned when oil was not concurrently discovered. An example of this occurred in 1865 when a 480-foot drilling effort struck a natural gas deposit near West Bloomfield, New York. The operators estimated the gas flow to be about 200 Mcf per day; they directed the gas into a large balloon and attempted to measure the flow by calculating the time required to fill the balloon. The investors were disappointed that oil was not discovered, and they abandoned the project.[24]

Not everyone was disappointed that this well contained only natural gas. Several businessmen formed the Rochester Natural Gas Light Company and purchased the gas well in 1870. They had named the new company after the nearest town interested in utilizing natural gas; Rochester was about 25 miles distant from the well. The company decided to construct a pipeline system to connect the well with the town. They built a pipeline out of Canadian white pine. The two- to eight-foot log segments were planed to a uniform 12.5-inch exterior diameter, and they were bored for an 8-inch interior diameter. Construction and maintenance of the wood pipeline system was particularly problematic, but the company began transporting natural gas during the winter of 1872.[25]

Consumers in Rochester discovered quickly that hotter burning natural gas was not easily interchangeable in their burners with manufactured gas. This situation resulted in lower-than-expected demand for natural gas. Continuing problems with rotting and leaking wood pipelines created other difficulties. Soon, the company ceased operation.

A more successful attempt to transport natural gas took place in 1872. New natural gas discoveries created a demand for specialized gas pipelines. In this case, a two-inch wrought-iron line was constructed and used to connect a gas well five and one-half miles distant. The line trans-

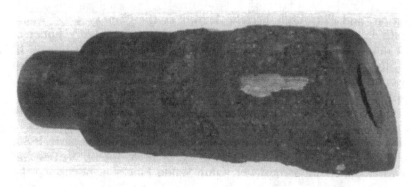

Wood gas pipeline segment from near Piqua, Ohio.

Photo courtesy of the Dayton Power and Light Company Archives.

ported "waste" gas from nearby oil fields to Titusville. This pipe reportedly transported 4 MMcf/d (million cubic feet per day) to 250 customers, both residential and industrial.[26]

The primary obstacle to the expansion of the natural gas industry was inadequate pipelines. Hollow log pipelines leaked and disintegrated, but cast- and wrought-iron lines also suffered from significant intrinsic defects. Wrought-iron lines in the period 1872–1890 were typically less than eight inches in diameter, and the pipe segments were attached with couplings tightened with screws. Gas leaks were common. Most of the gas transported in pipelines during this period flowed under the natural pressure of the well without the aid of additional compression.

The discovery of both oil and natural gas in Western Pennsylvania also emphasized the importance of the study of geology. Trained geologists were needed not only to help oil and gas companies determine the most likely places where oil and gas might be located, but to identify the types of geologic structures that precluded the existence of fossil fuels. In some respects, it was more important financially for drillers to know where not to drill. Beginning in 1874, John F. Carll led the efforts of the Pennsylvania survey to study the geology of Pennsylvania.[27]

Pittsburgh and Natural Gas

Pittsburgh became the first major U.S. city in which industry used large volumes of natural gas, and gas supply did displace some coal there. The abundance of coal deposits in the Pittsburgh area and the importation of iron ore from the Juanita region in central Pennsylvania and later from the Mesabi range facilitated development of a large iron industry fueled by coal. Extensive coal burning for industrial heat created significant air pollution, and Pittsburgh became known as the "Smoky City" where "hundreds of tall chimneys belched forth continually huge volumes of black sulphurous smoke, tinging every building with its sooty hue."[28] In 1884, the *New York Times* proclaimed that natural gas would henceforth be used in Pittsburgh's industries and reduce the unpleasant coal smoke pollution.

The earliest recorded use of natural gas in a Pittsburgh ironworks occurred at the Great Western Iron Company on the Allegheny River in 1870–1871. Widespread natural gas utilization began in the early 1880s after the development of nearby gas wells. In 1883, Joseph N. Pew and Edward O. Emerson, a cousin of Ralph Waldo Emerson, purchased the Haymaker gas well and formed the Pennsylvania Fuel Company. Penn Fuel transported gas from the well to buyers in nearby Pittsburgh. The

Haymaker had been discovered in late 1878 when two brothers, Michael and Obediah Haymaker, drilled to a depth of 1,400 feet in a search for oil. Instead, they drilled a 30 to 40 MMcf/d gas well in what became known as the Murrysville field. Penn Fuel built a 5 5/8-inch diameter line from the field to transport gas to Pittsburgh.[29]

The Fuel Gas Company of Allegheny County unsuccessfully attempted to purchase the Haymaker, but soon purchased other property that produced natural gas and also began distributing natural gas in Pittsburgh. Formed in 1874 to produce and distribute coal gas, the Fuel Gas Company claimed that under its charter it had an exclusive right to distribute natural gas as well as manufactured gas in the city. Despite this claim, the Pennsylvania Supreme Court ruled that natural gas was a different fuel than manufactured gas and was therefore not subject to manufactured gas company charters. Then, in 1885, the Pennsylvania legislature passed the Natural Gas Act, which allowed natural gas companies to compete for business.[30]

After this political victory, Pew and Emerson founded the Peoples Natural Gas Company on June 26, 1885, as the first natural gas company to be chartered under the new Natural Gas Act. The company soon developed gas fields in the Murrysville field and began selling gas in Pittsburgh, Wilkinsburg, and later in surrounding communities. In 1887, Peoples had an estimated 35,000 household customers.[31]

Entrepreneurs soon organized other regional gas firms. One group of Pittsburgh area manufacturers established the Chartiers Valley Gas Company in 1883 to transport natural gas from local gas fields to their glass and steel plants. The company's first line extended from the Hickory gas field to Pittsburgh. This wrought-iron line was the first "telescoping" pipeline, meaning that a smaller diameter pipe was installed at the well's origin leading to a larger diameter pipe in the city. The telescoping line system was useful for lowering the pressure in the line as gas flowed into the city. The first line segment diameter was 8 inches and it fed into a 10-inch pipe.[32] For pipe less than 12 inches in diameter, the typical connection was a screw coupling. Pipe segments were threaded on the outer edge of each length-end and turned into a screw coupling.

As of 1886, the Chartiers company also laid claim to operating the largest continuous pipe in the world. Fearing gas leaks in a long cast-iron line, the company instead used wrought iron. The company installed a 16-inch pipe extending from the Murrysville gas field to Pittsburgh. After eight miles, the 16-inch line was fed into a six-mile-long 20-inch pipe, and it in turn fed into a five-mile section of 24-inch cast-iron tubing, tested at 300 psi. (pounds per square inch). This line was constructed by the National Tube Works, controlled by J. P. Morgan.

The company soon decided to install another line to meet the rapidly expanding demand. In this case, the Chartiers company opted to use the Converse patent joint, which entailed the use of locking joints on the pipe ends and filling in the joints with lead. This line was successful, and the company later built a duplicate line that paralleled the original 16-inch line so that if one line ruptured a valve could immediately redirect flow into the other system.[33] With a total of four main lines feeding both Pittsburgh and Allegheny, the company could deliver as much as 200 MMcf/d.

As natural gas became available in Pennsylvania, local engineers addressed technological problems associated with its utilization. Solomon R. Dresser, an unsuccessful oil driller, decided to focus his attention on oil field–related drilling technology instead. In 1880, he formed S. R. Dresser & Company and conducted pioneering work in pipe coupling. In 1887, Dresser received a patent for using a rubber ring in pipe joints to create a leakproof coupling. While this method proved not entirely satisfactory, less than a year later he designed a second coupling that was more effective. For this coupling, he developed a two-part mechanical device that pulled the pipe segments together. Between the tightened sections, an internal rubber ring created a seal. Dresser proved the leakproof qualities of his coupling when he developed his own gas field near Malta, Ohio, and used his couplings in a line that transported gas to town. The Malta Natural Gas Line put Dresser in the natural gas business, and his couplings attracted widespread favor; gas companies located throughout the country ordered them. These couplings were widely used by as much as 90 percent of the gas pipeline industry into the 1920s.[34]

Improved couplings not only reduced leakage but also lessened the possibility of explosions. In Pittsburgh, gas lines were prohibited from operating at pressures higher than 13 psi.[35] This pressure limitation was intended to reduce leaks prevalent in lines more highly pressurized. Leaks, in turn, resulted in accumulations of gas in cellars and increased the possibility of explosions and fires. Within the city, regulating valves further reduced the gas pressure. To prevent leaking gas from ending up in residential cellars, the Chartiers company used its patented "broken stone escape system," which involved laying a pipe in a trench filled with dirt to the center of the pipeline. Workers placed about nine inches of broken stone on top of the line. A layer of tar paper was then placed over the stone; dirt covered the tar paper. The stone barrier was placed adjacent to every city lamppost so that escaping gas could vent through the stone. In addition, gas companies used "escape pipes," very small diameter lines leading from each pipe joint to a lamppost. Inspectors could check each escape pipe for possible leaks and identify the joint to which each escape line was connected.[36] A system of 4-inch pipes distributed gas to individual residences. In these pipes, gas pressure was limited to about 5 psi. As the gas entered homes, an additional regulator/shut-off valve lowered gas pressure again to about 5 ounces per square inch so that gas could be burned satisfactorily in gaslight fixtures. Some companies such as Chartier claimed that they distributed gas at this pressure so that residential customers would not need to purchase the in-house regulator. Cases of in-house regulator malfunction that allowed gas at the higher 5 psi into a residential piping system could result in disaster.[37]

George Westinghouse, inventor of the railroad air brake and a resident of Pittsburgh, also became interested in the burgeoning natural gas industry. He decided to explore for natural gas close to home; he began drilling in his own backyard located in a fashionable Pittsburgh neighborhood. He contracted a drilling firm to begin its work on December 29, 1883. In late February, a small volume of gas began flowing from the well. The workers continued drilling to a depth of about 1,560 feet. At three o'clock one morning, Westinghouse awoke to the sound of a tremendous explosion and the loud sound of hissing gas from the well.[38]

Westinghouse needed a company organization to proceed with his new plan of selling the newly discovered natural gas in Pittsburgh. His attorneys discovered the abandoned Philadelphia Company, which had received an omnibus charter in 1870 from the Pennsylvania legislature. Westinghouse purchased this company to produce and distribute natural gas in Pittsburgh. As president and director of the company, Westinghouse watched the Philadelphia Company become one of the largest gas companies in the Pittsburgh area. For additional supply, it leased substantial gas production acreage in western Pennsylvania. By 1887, the Philadelphia Company supplied approximately 5,000 residential and 470 industrial customers with gas produced from about 100 natural gas wells located on 54,000 acres. In that year, it charged $2.50 per month to heat a typical shop.[39]

Westinghouse's financial participation in the natural gas business brought his inventive mind in touch with some of the major problems of this new industry. Westinghouse quickly learned that gas lines broke and leaked frequently. When gas lines were shut down for repairs, gas users would not always turn off their gas appliances. After servicemen repaired the lines, gas began flowing into homes without the residents' knowledge that the nearly odorless and colorless fuel was accumulating in their homes or shops. The result could be tragic—asphyxiation or explosion.

Westinghouse put his mind to solving some of these problems. In the years 1884–1885, he applied for 28 gas industry patents, and during his lifetime he applied for a total of 38 for gas equipment. His previous experiences using compressed air in the development of the railroad car air brake provided him with valuable knowledge that he could apply to natural gas transportation and utilization technologies. Some of Westinghouse's most important inventions for natural gas included a system for enclosing a main gas line in residential areas with a conducting pipe to contain gas leaks. Westinghouse also developed a method for "stepping-down" the highly pressurized gas in main trunk lines to lower pressure in residential areas. To prevent accumulations of gas in homes and shops after gas service was shut down and then restarted, Westinghouse patented a pressure regulator and cutoff valve that automatically restricted gas flow when the pressure dropped below a particular point.[40]

Tragedies nonetheless occurred. On the morning of January 31, 1885, two major explosions at Thirty-fifth and Butler Streets in Pittsburgh nearly leveled an entire city block while killing 2 and injuring 25 others, some severely. The first explosion occurred at George Hermansdorfer's butcher shop after an accumulation of gas in his cellar; two or three persons were badly burned. People rushed to investigate the explosion, when a second, much more powerful eruption occurred at John Mueller's saloon. This and subsequent less horrific explosions caused substantial injury to life and property, damaging as many as 15 buildings. Local residents threatened a riot against the gas company, and a representative of the Fuel Gas Company made a stunning admission. The *New York Times* reported that he said that "the pipes where the explosion occurred were laid at night, and that they were never tested before the gas was turned on at high pressure."[41] Thus, the efforts of Westinghouse and others to develop gas regulators and emergency shutoff valves were absolutely required to ensure that this fuel could be utilized safely.

Regarding environmental issues, there was some hope that natural gas utilization might reduce the heavy air pollution caused by coal burning, but one newspaper reported that it was "doubtful whether the hopes of the inhabitants will be fully realized and Pittsburgh be relieved of all its smoke through the use of gas."[42] Increased use of natural gas meant fewer jobs for coal miners and was expected to reduce eastern Pennsylvania coal production by about 14 percent.[43]

The environmentally degrading effects of coal gas plants also received attention in the 1880s. Charles Munroe, a professor of chemistry at George Washington University, recalled that in 1882 the secretary of the navy requested that he investigate "the cause of corrosion of the copper sheathing of the newly fitted U.S.S. Juaniato and other vessels at the Brooklyn yard."[44] Munroe determined the cause to be coal tar deposited in the water by a nearby gasworks. Not only did coal tar runoff foul water and kill fish, it caused problems for ships. However, environmental awareness was based on specific instances and not on an overall concern for the environment.

By the late 1880s, Pittsburgh had become not only the center of the American steel and coal industry but also the center of the natural gas industry. Pittsburgh received its natural gas from the lines of six companies tied into 107 regional gas wells.[45] These companies drilled only 10 dry holes during the exploration that resulted in the 107 producing wells.[46] There were 500 miles of pipeline for transporting natural gas from wells to Pittsburgh, including 232 miles of line within the Pittsburgh city limits. According to the *American Manufacturer and Iron World,* in 1886 the Philadelphia Company had about two miles of 30-inch diameter pipe and more than 10 miles of 24-inch pipe installed.[47] Depending upon charges for right-of-way and line width, gas lines laid from 2 to 4 1/2 feet beneath the surface cost as much as $12,000 per mile.[48]

The unusual availability of locally produced natural gas in the Pittsburgh area gave rise to what one writer described as "some very extensive experiments in the use of this natural gas." Local industry utilized the fuel for the manufacture of iron, steel, glass, and chemical products. The potential for natural gas utilization in Pittsburgh attracted a great deal of money. Six million dollars was invested in land, labor, and equipment necessary for transporting natural gas to the city of Pittsburgh, and another $4 million for natural gas lines in surrounding towns and villages. By 1886, the maximum daily estimated consumption of natural gas in Philadelphia was 20 MMcf.[49]

"A year ago," one writer observed in 1886, "[natural gas] was insignificant; to-day it ranks in importance with the iron, steel, glass, and coal interests of Western Pennsylvania." Natural gas, with its high heating content and relative cleanliness, quickly attracted new industrial users. In 1886, there were 10 iron and steel mills using natural gas in their puddling furnaces with many more planning to convert to gas. Six glassmaking factories and reportedly every brewery in Pittsburgh was using natural gas instead of coal.[50] One novel and self-explained use of natural gas was advertised by the Sampson Natural Gas Crematory.[51]

Andrew Carnegie, Pittsburgh's foremost entrepreneur, was personally intrigued by natural gas. He became one of the first industrialists to use large volumes in his factories. Carnegie wrote, "In the manufacture of iron, and especially in that of steel, the quality is also improved by the pure new fuel. In our steel rail mills we have not used a pound of coal for more than a year, nor in our iron mills for nearly the same period." The iron and steel maker noted that natural gas burned much more cleanly than coal.[52]

A representative of Carnegie's Edgar Thompson Steel Works stated that "we have an 8-inch pipe through which we get the gas for making the steam for 40,000 horse-power every twenty-four hours and do heating for 600 tons of rails; in other words, the 8-inch pipe will represent 400 tons of coal every twenty-four hours."

Kurge Sorge, a German engineer and visitor to Pittsburgh in 1887, also singled out the Edgar Thompson Works for its use of natural gas. Sorge noted that the works, which produced 650 tons of steel rails daily, used no coal except for the coal used in the locomotives. The steel factory had its own gas wells and pipelines by 1887, but the firm had purchased natural gas in 1884 for $120,000. This price, agreed upon between the steel works and the gas supplier, was the price the works paid previously for an annual supply of coal. Natural gas utilization also led to reassignment or dismissal of 147 coal heavers and stokers.[53]

The German visitor also was dismayed at the volume of natural gas wasted in the Pittsburgh area. Noting that 7 1/2 cubic feet of gas was equivalent in heating value to 1 pound of coal, Sorge stated that 100 MMcf/d was lost in and around Pittsburgh, the equivalent wastage of approximately 6.7 tons of coal daily. At the time, coal cost approximately $1.25 per ton, so the equivalent daily loss of coal was $8,000.

Pennsylvania was the center of the nation's coal, steel, and lesser-known natural gas industry during the late nineteenth century; by February 5, 1885, 150 companies had been chartered to sell gas in Pennsylvania.[54] Gas discoveries in other Appalachian states, first in Ohio and then in West Virginia, made natural gas financially significant to the entire region. Industries located in cities such as Buffalo, Cleveland, Toledo, and Cincinnati all began using natural gas from nearby wells.

The future of natural gas was not certain, though, as gas fields tended to exhaust themselves within several years after discovery. Selwynn Taylor, a Pennsylvania mining engineer, stated that regional natural gas fields would soon be exhausted and the price of coal would rise to the levels existing prior to the widespread use of natural gas. His beliefs were typical of the time. Natural gas fields simply could not supply enough fuel to satisfy the demand, so natural gas was ultimately undependable. In addition, it was in limited supply. "It is not published," he noted, "but all the large gas fields are playing out. . . . In my judgment two years will see an end to natural gas as a fuel."[55]

Waste and poor planning did lead to many failed ventures. In one episode, the Indiana Natural Gas & Oil Company built the longest pipeline to date in 1891. The transmission system consisted of two parallel eight-inch lines extending from northern Indiana gas fields to Chicago, a distance of approximately 120 miles. These lines transported natural gas at 525 psi. The supply quickly declined and the lines were then removed from service. Episodes such as this but on a smaller scale were repeated throughout the region.

In Indiana during the late nineteenth century, an area of about 7,000 square miles included a large number of producing natural gas fields. Despite attempts to regulate the production and flow of natural gas, gas demand soared in the state. By 1907, many of Indiana's once productive natural gas fields had expended their valuable fuel. Natural gas customers had to return to manufactured gas utilization.[56] Gas discoveries in Oklahoma and in the eastern and southern Kansas gas fields suffered similar episodes of rapid development followed by depletion. Situations such as these characterized the natural gas industry, as opposed to manufactured gas, as fairly undependable.

By the turn of the century, the natural gas industry was most developed in the Appalachian region. Productive gas wells in West Virginia, Pennsylvania, New York, Kentucky, Tennessee, and Ohio led to the creation of regional gas companies that built pipelines to serve local markets in the Appalachian region. Natural gas was used primarily for industrial purposes, but where available, its higher heating content made it a superior cooking and heating fuel, although appliances for these purposes were still not widely available until later in the nineteenth and early twentieth century. Natural gas was a promising fuel, but its limited availability forced entrepreneurs to proceed cautiously with plans to develop fields and build pipelines.

The natural gas industry was distinct from that of manufactured gas in that the two fuels were produced through entirely different methods. While the production of synthetic fuels and products is commonly associated with technological progress, in the case of the gas industry the synthetic fuel established an industry that later depended upon the natural fuel. The urban gas distribution infrastructure developed by manufactured gasworks eventually transformed into a natural gas distribution system as drilling, transportation, distribution, and gas-burning technologies appropriate for natural gas were implemented. In the meantime, urban gasworks were typically coal based, while factories sought natural gas for its high heating content.

4

Competition and Consolidation

WILLIAM W. FOX, president of the New York Gas Light Company, acknowledged the value of public relations in 1859 when he became the first subscriber to the *American Gas-Light Journal.* How he became the "first" subscriber is incidental to the fact that the industry's first national trade journal recognized him as such. The gas industry was already stigmatized by the monopolistic charters granted to firms, and a new trade journal might help improve this young industry's public image. The journal reported Fox's subscription with the illuminating statement that "it was the more gratifying, because it had been intimated that that company especially, and perhaps the Manhattan, would look with disfavor upon any movement calculated to throw light on what has been considered a *dark* monopoly."[1] Charles Roome, president of the New York's competitor, the Manhattan Gas-Light Company, received mention as well for providing the journal unspecified favors.

In its first issue (July 1, 1859), the *American Gas-Light Journal* reported that there were at least 183 gaslight companies, representing an investment of $31,666,570, operating in the United States.[2] This number increased to about 971 by 1886, although the precise numbers are impossible to calculate. The dramatic rise in the number of gasworks reflected intense demand on the part of the American public for energy to light and heat homes and shops. These statistics also suggest the emergence of intense competition for the lighting market during these and later years. Marketers of manufactured gas, natural gas, kerosene, and electricity all sought to sell their product to the public. This competitive era in the gas industry spawned both technological and organizational innovation leading ultimately to industry consolidation.[3]

During the first 30 years of its development, the gas industry was regulated by state charters and local franchise agreements. For the most part, these charters and agreements stipulated service areas and maximum rates during a specific term. Otherwise, gas firms were essentially unregulated, and there was little cohesiveness among the large number of gasworks spread across the nation.

After kerosene lighting became more widely available and multiple gasworks in large urban areas began competing for sales, gaslight consumers became increasingly cognizant of disparities in their light bills. In one of the first regulatory efforts attempted to impose billing standards on the industry, the New York State senate and assembly in May 1859 enacted a law requiring that the state governor nominate, subject to consent of the senate, an inspector of gas meters for New York City. George H. Kitchen was the first such inspector, and the law required him to live in New York City but inspect meters throughout the state. His salary was $1,500 per year. While the state paid the inspector's salary, the cost of his salary was charged to the gaslight companies operating in New York. The gas inspector's term was five years.[4]

Accurate gas meters fostered indirect and in some cases direct competition among gasworks in large urban areas. By measuring the amount of gas actually consumed, these meters distinguished heavy gas users from small users and provided a method for gas companies to more accurately calculate their cost of service. With better accounting functions, gas companies could assess their own profitability and then chart a course to achieve better financial performance. As metering became more accurate and dependable, consumers could compare bills and deduce with more certainty the quality of service they were receiving from the local gas company.

Despite improved meters and the work of meter inspectors, residential gas consumers generally believed that gas meters were faulty and consistently gave inaccurately high readings. An enterprising New Yorker decided that the solution to this problem was to prevent meter readers from reading gas meters at all. This man bred what he called "gas dogs" with the sole purpose of biting any person attempting to read a gas meter. The gas dogs were sold and leased to gas consumers. Since meter readers came by only once a month, some people rented a gas dog for only a three-day period ($.50 per day). During a Philadelphia trial in which a homeowner sued a gas inspector for kicking his dog, it was disclosed that meter readers kept detailed lists of houses with dogs. The Philadelphia inspector said during the trial that "dogs are the torment of an inspector's life."[5]

A *New York Times* reporter investigated the gas dog business and reported these findings:

> Excellent results have been attained by the use of gas dogs. An amiable Christian lady residing in Thirty-fifth-street, in this city, has no less than forty-three samples of trousers collected by her gas dogs in the course of five years. . . . It need hardly be said that gas dogs are wonderfully soothing to the householder's mind. There are householders who make it a point to remain at home all day on the day when the gas inspector is expected merely in order to enjoy the yell of the inspector when the gas dog's teeth meet in his calf, or to listen to the inspector's language as a fresh hole is made in his trousers.[6]

General dissatisfaction with a local gas company's service also facilitated the entry of new gas firms into urban areas. Aggressive new firms with liberal charters and franchise agreements competed with older, conservative firms for gas business. In both New York and Chicago, several different gas firms competed vigorously for new business by seeking to extend service beyond their traditional service areas by cutting rates and sometimes engaging in cutthroat competition that threatened the financial viability of all the firms operating in the area.

Competition and Consolidation in New York

In New York City, the New York Gas Light Company and the Manhattan Gas Light Company operated for many years within well-defined service areas. This situation began to change when the Harlem Gas Company formed in 1855 to sell gas in a distinct territory well away from the established areas of the two existing firms. Harlem Gas began operating during 1857 in the area north of 79th Street. By the end of its first year in service, the company supplied gas to about 750 public lamps.[7]

At about the same time, another company emerged that further threatened the stability of the New York City gas business. James Bowen, former president of the Erie Railroad, organized a fourth New York City gas firm, the Metropolitan Gas Light Company. Bowen sought and received approval from the state legislature to operate this gas company in the city, and it was not explicitly restricted from competing with existing firms. On February 21, 1856, the Aldermanic Committee on Lamps and Gas met to consider the Metropolitan's request to install gas piping beneath the city's streets. At a previous meeting on the Metropolitan's application, the committee heard from a "retinue of lawyers." This time, the committee requested that only the presidents of the interested gas companies and several gas customers make statements. Those in favor of the Metropolitan's application uniformly stated that gas bills were currently too high. Another gas company could provide necessary competition and force rates to drop. One customer, Charles St. John, complained that his monthly gaslight bill of $19 for home lighting was exorbitant. Others gave similar testimony.

Strident opposition to the Metropolitan's application came from Charles Roome, president of the Manhattan Gas Company. Roome's opposition was expected, of course, and he argued in favor of the rights of a natural monopoly and against the duplication of gas service and gas facilities. He stated that he did not believe the Metropolitan was financially capable of building a gasworks and pipeline system. Even if it did, he said, competition would be marred by the problems of dual gas systems. Streets would lose their durability after being ripped up again for the placement of additional pipes. Then, gas companies would invariably have difficulty identifying their own mains for customer taps. Leaks would require that both pipes be shut down and inspected. Two pipes under the same street would result in more leaks, and more leaks would increase the likelihood of contaminated water supply, leakage of gas into open air, and explosions in people's houses. The end result, Roome stated firmly, would be more fires and tragedies. Thus, competition would not lower prices. Instead, much higher prices would result from the increased production and operating costs associated with competing systems and the increased cost of insuring both companies against losses and liability resulting from dual system competition.[8]

For the time being, Roome and his allies succeeded in preventing the Metropolitan from receiving permission from local authorities to operate a gasworks. But in 1858, the Metropolitan wrangled from the state legislature an amendment to its original charter. That amendment gave the Metropolitan the exclusive right to operate a gas distribution system between 14th and 79th Streets. Previously, the streets between 14th and 42nd were served exclusively by the Manhattan company. But the municipal government in June 1858 confirmed the state's decision and granted the Metropolitan a 30-year franchise to sell gas within that area. Although the mayor vetoed the city resolution granting such rights to the Metropolitan, the city council overrode the veto and approved the contract in December 1858.[9]

Roome countered with a successful legal challenge based on the factual contention that the Metropolitan's charter was null and void because it had not begun supplying gas on the deadline set in the original charter. Despite attempts by the Metropolitan to reorganize and begin building facilities, the company lost its charter in 1860. At that instant, the Manhattan quickly began installing pipelines and planning for a new gasworks to be located between 42nd and 79th Streets.

In the meantime, the Metropolitan's lead counsel, Waldo Hutchins, argued successfully at the New York Court of Appeals in Albany that the charter should be reinstated. The Metropolitan was back in business and began operations in June 1863. Its service area then included the portion of New York City bounded by 34th and 79th Streets; the Metropolitan purchased all of the Manhattan's gas properties beyond the 34th Street center line.[10] During the next two decades, several other gaslight firms in New York City organized and some successfully competed for the lighting business against established companies.

Water gas, a new type of manufactured gas, along with liberalized operating franchises, created new havoc in the New York City gas market. In 1863, William H. Gwynne founded the Anthracite Gas Lighting Company of New York, and he secured a transferable municipal franchise allowing his company to operate throughout New York City. Robert McCoskey Graham, who was a "human repository for moribund gas companies," ended up with the company and then sold Anthracite Gas to another new firm, the Knickerbocker Gas Light Company, in which he

Coal gas benches, Old North Beach Plant, San Francisco Gas Light Company.
Courtesy, Pacific Gas and Electric Company.

was also a principal. Another new company, the Municipal Gas Light Company of New York, which originally had formed under the name Municipal Oxygen Gas Company in 1874, had something in common with the Knickerbocker. Both of these firms planned to produce "water gas," composed primarily of hydrogen (47 percent) and carbon monoxide (37 percent), based on the first promising U.S. water gas patent (1867) issued to Marie Tessie du Motay and Charles Raphael Marechal.[11] Despite the lower heating content of water gas, gas distributors appreciated its lower production costs. Water gas could be mixed with existing coal gas production, thereby lowering the gas firm's overall production costs.

The standard water gas production method was a two-part process that required heating the coal or coke and then injecting steam. To produce water gas, anthracite coal or coke was put into a furnace, or generator. The carbon was heated to incandescence and steam was injected into a generator. The reaction of heated carbon with steam created a flammable gas composed primarily of hydrogen and carbon monoxide. This so-called water gas had a heating value of about 287 British thermal units (Btus) and was referred to as "blue gas" because it was not a satisfactory illuminant.

In 1873, Theodore Lowe received a patent for a modified water gas production method. Instead of using square- or rectangular-shaped furnaces to heat the carbon, he packed the coal in chimney-shaped furnaces and kept the coal heated by blowing hot air against the incandescent coal.[12] To increase the heating content of the gas, atomized oil was sprayed into the gas mixture to produce "carburetted water gas," which had a heating content of about 550 Btus and could be used for lighting and heating.

The advantages of water gas included lower production costs and lower costs for operating and maintaining production facilities. The superiority of water gas production methods over traditional coal gas quickly became evident. Reduced production and fuel storage costs for the water gas process made it easier for new firms to organize, distribute, and sell the fuel. By 1890, more than 350 newly operating water gas plants produced approximately 40 percent of all manufactured gas in the United States. In 1900, water gas accounted for 75 percent of all illuminating and heating gas produced in the country.[13]

Other problems confronted New York City's gasworks. In 1871, an explosion at the Metropolitan works' gas-purifying house on December 23, 1871, confirmed to local residents that something was wrong with this company's plant, which constantly emanated a strong odor. As many as 1,500 Metropolitan Gas customers subsequently and unsuccessfully petitioned the New York City Common Council to allow the NYGLC to build lines into the Metropolitan's service area so that they could buy gas from it instead.

With more gas companies operating in New York, new methods of producing gas, and a breakdown of the traditional service area system, a rate war ensued. The larger Manhattan and Metropolitan companies began losing significant amounts of revenue and customers to the new gas firms. While the Manhattan company was publicly disputing the superior lighting power of water gas, its engineers were planning to convert its production facilities to this fuel. Eventually, the tumultuous competitive situation led the companies to try to reach a truce that would stabilize the city's gas industry.

An agreement was reached on March 30, 1880. It was a pooling and price-fixing arrangement that stipulated rates and service areas. The agreement set a common rate of $2.25 per Mcf and prohibited laying gas mains outside of each firm's service area as established by the agreement. Each company also contributed $1.25 per Mcf sold into a general pool to be divided among the participating companies every three months in proportion to their total gas sales. Finally, the agreement was set for five years, "unless sooner terminated by consolidation."[14]

The growing labor movement in the United States affected the gas business as well as other industries from New York to San Francisco. A related problem for all the nation's gas companies and businesses was the growing eight-hour day movement, combined with the weakness in the national economy leading to the financial panic and subsequent strikes of 1873. Gas plant strikes were usually met with some form of compromise in pay, hours, or shift assignments.[15] The threat of labor action also resulted in stricter work rules for employees.

Gas versus Electricity

Competition in the gaslight business intensified in the 1880s as new gas firms and competing sources of energy emerged. The most potent competition for gas lighting was not water gas; it was electricity. In the late 1870s, Thomas Alva Edison (1847–1931) began experimenting with electricity at his lab in Menlo Park, New Jersey. Others had developed dynamos to generate electricity and brilliant arc lights, but Edison realized that electricity and a less cumbersome "subdivided" light could be used within homes to provide lighting. The Brush Illuminating Company demonstrated street lighting with arc lamps on Broadway in December 1880; this was the first time electricity had been used to light a street in the United States.[16]

RULES and REGULATIONS
POTRERO STATION,
San Francisco Gas Light Co.

1.

The Working Hours of those connected with the Retort House, Coke Cellar, and Coal Shed, are:

Day Watch, . . . 6 A. M. to 6. P. M.
Night Watch, . . 6 P. M. to 6 A. M.

2.

The Working Hours of the Shop, Yard and Purifying House men are: 7 A. M. to 12 M. 12:30 to 5:30 P. M.

3.

Employees on the Night Watch must bring their meals with them when coming to work.

4.

No Employee on the Day Watch allowed to leave the Works except for Meals, without permission from the Superintendent.

5.

No Employee on the Night Watch allowed to leave the Works between 6 P. M. and 5:30 A. M.

6.

No sleeping allowed during Working Hours.

7.

Any Employee known to be intoxicated during Working Hours, or to bring Liquor on the Premises, or to be absent from work by reason of Intoxication, will be punished according to Rule 8.

8.

For the First Violation of Rules 5, 6, and 7, Employees will be punished as the Superintendent may see fit; but for the Second offence, they will be discharged.

9.

The Watchman must report to the Superintendent any irregularities that occur during the Night Watch, such as leaving the Works, Intoxication, Neglect of Work, etc., under penalty of dismissal.

10.

Leave of absence must be obtained from the Superintendent by Employees if they desire to retain their position. In case of Sickness, notice must be given as soon as possible.

11.

Every Employee is required to be as economical in the use of time and material as possible. Employees must observe cleanliness with their work, otherwise they will not be retained.

JANUARY, 1878.   H. S. MURPHY, Superintendent.

"Rules and Regulations," San Francisco Gas Light Company, 1878.

Courtesy, Pacific Gas and Electric Company.

Edison was keenly aware of the gas industry, and he foresaw with clarity the gas industry's predicament in the new electric age; he "never tired of repeating the claim that the electric light would be clearly cheaper than gas."[17] Edison understood that the gas industry would have to begin marketing gas not for lighting but for heating and especially cooking, two uses for the fuel that gas businesses had heretofore ignored. By 1878, it is estimated that not more than 12 gas stoves were in operation in New York City and about 100 in the entire nation.[18]

Edison believed that electric lighting in particular was a practical solution to some of the most severe gas-lighting problems: bad odors, leaks, fires, and explosions. Edison unceremoniously described gas as a fuel transported underground through "sewer pipes" and representing the "dark ages." He noted that at the Madison Square Theater, special ventilator tubes were installed adjacent to every gaslight burner to carry away the foul gas odor. Studying the gas industry was important though, because Edison wanted electricity to supplant gas. In one notebook he wrote, "Object, Edison to effect exact imitation of all done by gas so as to replace lighting by gas [with] lighting by electricity."[19] The primary challenge for Edison was to devise a low-candlepower electric light and devise a method to distribute electricity to homes and businesses.[20]

Edison formed the Edison Electric Light Company on October 15, 1878, to control the patent rights of his electrical inventions. He announced a few days later that he would soon develop an electrical system made up of as many as 20 electrical generating stations in New York City. These stations would provide enough electricity to power urban street and residential lamps.[21]

Edison devised a detailed plan for electric lighting to replace gas lighting. He believed that the existing gas distribution system in any city could easily be converted for electricity; ironically, he had gas lighting installed in his office in August 1877 to permit him to work on his plans to extinguish gaslights. Edison had earlier considered a plan to convey telephonic communication through gas lines, and he now planned to use abandoned gas lines to carry insulated electrical conducting wires underground and into homes and businesses. Gaslight fixtures could easily be replaced with electric light fixtures.[22]

In both London and New York, the exciting news and other rumors about electricity and electric lighting created havoc with gas company stock values. The New York area light companies suffered substantial declines during the autumn of 1878. Manhattan Gas Light's stock fell precipitously from 187 1/2 to 147 1/2; Metropolitan's dropped from 132 1/2 to 106 1/2; and the Harlem Gas Light firm saw its stock value drop from 72 1/2 to 39. Not all the news about electricity and electric lights was coming from Edison or Menlo Park, but the gas companies understood by now as well as Edison did that it was only a matter of time before electric lighting would force gas companies to make radical adjustments in their business strategies if they were to survive.[23]

"The question of the substitution of the electric light for gas light," Henry A. Mott wrote to the *New York Times* in January 1880, "is now agitating the world, both this and the other side of the ocean."[24] A few months earlier, the British Museum in London demonstrated the effectiveness of electric lights during a period of heavy fog that prevented visitors at the reading room from seeing well enough to read. The new light provided "a magic ray of sunshine, to the great satisfaction of all present."[25]

Edison was not simply inventing and developing a new lighting system; he was consciously strategizing against gas. Edison later recalled that he had

> hired a man to start in every day about two o'clock and walk around through the district noting the number of gas lights burning in the various premises; then at three o'clock he went around again and made more notes, and at four o'clock and up to every other hour to two or three o'clock in the morning. In that way it was easy enough to figure out the gas consumption of every tenant and of the whole district.[26]

Edison continued his plans to build an electricity-generating station. Under the corporate name of the Edison Electric Illuminating Company of New York, he began constructing his station at 257 Pearl Street. He incorporated this firm under New York City's gas statutes in order to install wiring underneath streets.[27]

On September 4, 1882, the $480,000 generating station began producing electricity. Serving a one-square-mile area around the station, the Pearl station provided electricity for 1,284 lamps within one month. Electricity rapidly conquered the market for residential, commercial, and business lighting. The average Edison lamp had 16 candlepower (comparable to a gas light), burned for 40 hours, and cost one dollar each.[28] Even where electric lighting did not immediately replace gas lighting, new electrical devices were developed for lighting gas at the fixture. The Portable Electric Gas Igniter was particularly useful in theaters and places where careless use of matches might cause fires.[29]

Edison intentionally designed an electrical system that in many ways corresponded to the gas system. He wanted consumers to feel comfortable with electricity, and he wanted power customers to make an easy transition from electricity to gas. "Every effort," wrote Harold Passer, "was made to simulate the practices and terminology of the gas companies." Even monthly electric bills referred to "burners" instead of lamps.[30] He calculated that consumers paid $.01125 per 16-candlepower gaslight per hour, so he set a price of $.012 per hour of electricity supplied to a 16-candlepower electric lamp.[31] Edison also developed an accurate electric meter, although it could not be read by customers; it was a chemical device that had to be weighed back at the station to determine how much electricity the customer had used.

Edison was not content to compete with gas on technical terms; he also publicized electricity's better safety record. Bulletins of the Edison Electric Company and Edison Company for Isolated Lighting described how 14 people died in New York City during the last six months of 1883 due to various problems with water gas. Articles about fires, explosions, and deaths related to gas usage continued to remind readers of the dangers of gas. Not only was gas smelly, sooty, and dangerous, but one bulletin claimed that electric light cured nearsightedness (heat associated with gas lighting was considered responsible for nearsightedness).[32]

Complaints and problems with gas lighting made Edison's goal easier to attain. Gaslight was inefficient, particularly in poorly built streetlamp burners.[33] However, there were problems associated with electricity as well. Electrocutions and fires received widespread attention, but the most visible and for some most offensive manifestation of electrical energy were the poles and electric wires strung along streets. Some citizens objected strenuously to having poles and wires installed in front of their homes. Numerous accidents and fatalities soon forced electric companies to bury their electric lines. Edison had originally postulated the concept that electric wires could be strung through existing gas lines, but the gas companies continued to use their lines for gas distribution.[34]

Electricity quickly supplanted the gas industry's mainstay lighting market. Gas companies resolved to stay in business by marketing gas for heating and cooking purposes. The *New York Times* covered the August 1882 meeting of the British Association for the Advancement of Science, where Dr. C. W. Siemens became the organization's new president. In his address to the conference, "Electricity and Gas: The Probable Future of Each—Gas as a Heating Agent," Siemens stated that "gas may be used advantageously for domestic purposes with judicious management even under present conditions, and it is easy to conceive that its consumption for heating would soon increase ten-fold."[35]

In New York, the progress of electric lighting caused the gas companies to stop fighting among themselves and consider responding to the competitive threat with a unified response. A nine-month discussion among representatives from various firms resulted in an agreement dated November 10, 1884, between the New York, Manhattan, Metropolitan, Municipal, Knickerbocker, and Harlem gas companies. They agreed to merge into a single firm to be called the Consolidated Gas Company of New York.[36]

Competition and Consolidation in Chicago

A competitive situation developed in the Chicago gas market, which lasted much longer than that in New York. When the Illinois state legislature on February 7, 1865, passed legislation that removed landowning restrictions on Peoples Gas, the company began expanding operations. The incorporation of new competing gas firms, improved water gas production technology, and electricity brought to Chicago the same chaotic market conditions as occurred in New York, although the process leading to consolidation lasted substantially longer.

As in New York, new water gas technology hastened competition. In Chicago, Peoples Gas first produced water gas commercially in 1883, although it may have been manufactured there as early as 1879. After the introduction of water gas into the metropolitan market, a rate war ensued and gas rates plummeted 25 to 50 percent throughout the city. In 1883 Chicago Gas lowered its rates from $2.25 to $1.00.[37]

Competition increased over the next two decades when several other gas firms organized in the city. The Consumers Gas Fuel & Light Company (1881), Suburban Gas Company (1884), Equitable Gas Light & Fuel Company (1885), and others crowded the market. The Consumers Gas company received permission from the Chicago City Council to lay gas mains anywhere in Chicago, and in 1886 Chicago Gas invaded Peoples' service area. Generally, Chicago gas franchises prohibited consolidations but allowed firms in some cases to operate in each other's service areas. Just as new entrants to New York City's gas market in the same time period received franchises that did not respect traditional service areas, so did the new firms in Chicago.[38]

One solution to cutthroat competition was pooling agreements and mergers. The first attempt at consolidation occurred when local gas producers organized the Chicago Gas Trust Company in April 1887. Unlike the 1880 pooling arrangement among New York City's gas firms, the Chicago Gas Trust controlled in a holding company arrangement Chicago's four major gas companies including several subsidiaries. While a political battle over the Trust ensued, even more companies appeared in Chicago. The Trust was intended to maximize cooperation among the city's participating gas companies and stabilize prices, but the state charged the holding company with violating laws concerning corporate organization. Chicago Gas Trust changed its name in April 1890 by removing the word "trust," three months before the U.S. Congress passed the Sherman Antitrust Act. Although the new Chicago Gas Company was a holding company that did not control all the shares of each of the operating companies, it was forced to reorganize in order to continue doing business in Illinois. In April 1891, the Chicago Gas Company reorganized as an actual trust, and its trustees held the stock of the same companies previously organized under its holding company structure.[39] Complete operational consolidation was thwarted by political and legal initiatives. Legal challenges and populist beliefs about the inherent evil of big business muted popular support for consolidation, despite publicity promising that consolidation would provide efficiency and lower prices. Consolidation of the city's gas firms finally occurred on June 5, 1897, when Illinois governor John R. Tanner signed the "Gas Consolidation Act." This act allowed any gas company to sell or merge its properties and franchises with any other company operating in the same city. The Peoples Gas Light and Coke Company became the lead firm, as it acquired all the gas firms previously included in the Trust. These included the Chicago; Lake; Consumers; Equitable; Suburban; Illinois Light, Heat & Power; and the Chicago Economic Fuel companies. Two firms, the Universal Gas Company and the Ogden Gas Company, had charters that prohibited them from merging with another firm. Peoples eventually gained control of these firms as well.[40]

The gas company consolidations in New York and Chicago were mirrored on the west coast. In San Francisco, the Pacific Coast Gas Association formed in 1893. Its agenda was dominated with issues related to the competition between gas and electricity. In southern California, gas service did not even begin until 1867. The newly formed Los Angeles Gas Company, which had a 15-year exclusive franchise, obstinately refused to lower its high gas charges. This forced the city government to refuse to renew its street lighting contract with the gas firm in 1872, leaving the city's streets in darkness until the contract was renewed in 1876. Six years later, the city replaced its gas lamps with electric lamps to be served by the new Los Angeles Electric Company. The gas company then began marketing gas, and appliances, for heating and cooking.[41]

The movement toward gas company consolidation in major urban areas coincided with the widespread use of the gas mantle that temporarily instilled hope at gas companies that gaslights might effectively compete with electric lights. An Austrian chemist, Carl Auer von Welsbach, working in the German laboratory of Robert Wilhelm von Bunsen, developed the incandescent gas mantle in 1883, and it became commercially available in the mid-1890s. Welsbach, aware of other experiments with chemicals that glow when heated, developed a cotton meshed cylinder, or mantle, soaked with a mixture of thorium dioxide (99 percent) and cerium oxide (1 percent). Mantles were typically five inches long and two inches in diameter. The mantle, situated in a special gas burner that allowed a strong airflow through the fixture, produced a bright and stable flame. The cotton mesh burned off during the first burning, leaving the metal oxide mesh structure intact. These mantles reduced by nearly two-thirds the cost of gas lighting, made less heat, produced light measured at between 22 and 35 candlepower, and had a life of 800 to 2,000 hours.[42]

The United Gas Improvement Company of Philadelphia, which had incorporated in 1882 to produce Lowe water gas for which it held the patent, created a subsidiary, the Welsbach Incandescent Light Company, located in Gloucester, Massachusetts, to produce the new mantle. The mantle even allowed less expensive, low-Btu water gas to be used satisfactorily for lighting.

The success of the Welsbach mantle in staving off the end of gas lighting was short-lived. Despite advertisements claiming that Welsbach mantles had "All the advantages of Electric Light and none of its drawbacks," this was the last gasp for gas lighting.[43] Improvements in electric lighting, particularly in the development of the tungsten filament, had reduced the cost of purchasing electric power. By about 1910, gas lighting was nearly extinguished by electric lights. To ensure a future for the gas industry, gas companies had to target the cooking, space-heating, and water-heating markets.[44]

In the meantime, competition in urban areas where more than one gas firm conducted business, high prices in monopolized markets, and stock raids only exacerbated the shaky financial ground many gas firms occupied by the late nineteenth century. Industry instability prompted some gas company managers to call for government regulation. At a meeting of the American Gaslight Association in Philadelphia in 1886, the attendees voted in favor of the creation of state regulatory commissions modeled after the Massachusetts Board of Gas Commissioners, which had been established in 1885 to regulate gas lighting firms. Of course, gas firms did not want government intrusion so much as legally enforceable stability.[45]

New gas production and utilization methods prolonged the life of the manufactured gas industry into the mid-twentieth century, although gas was used less for lighting and more for cooking and heating. Electricity quickly dominated the lighting market and the combination of water gas and the Welsbach mantle only provided some encouragement for gaslight firms seeking other markets for their fuel. At the same time, new entrants into the gas market brought forth intense competition. Consolidation was the solution to reckless rate wars, the breakdown of geographical service areas, new water gas companies, and the advent of electric power. Consolidations and mergers within the gas industry, however, were only the first steps toward the creation of combined gas and electric power firms that would grow into large financially and politically powerful corporations in the early twentieth century.

PART 3

Emergence of a Gas Cartel, 1890–1938

5

Creating the Power Trust

A MERGER MOVEMENT took place among once competitive gaslight and electric power firms in large urban areas, particularly during the period 1880 to 1910. This episode coincided with a similar trend toward merger and consolidation throughout the U.S. economy.[1] It was the era of trusts, pools, and holding companies, all perceived by the public and politicians alike as close variations on the theme of big business. One or more large companies that dominated their industry often attracted the imprecise label of "trust." The sugar trust, the meatpacking trust, the tobacco trust, and the oil trust among others would be followed by the "power trust."

The power trust, like many of the other trusts, was the result of mergers following intense periods of competition. Consolidation offered economic stability and market control, and Alfred Chandler's contention that "the visible hand of management proved to be more efficient than the invisible hand of market forces in coordinating the flow of materials through the economy" proved true in the gas industry as well, at least until the late 1920s.[2]

The merger movement first among urban manufactured gas firms and then including electric power businesses paralleled a similar trend in natural gas. Standard Oil was at the forefront of consolidating natural gas production. Abundant natural gas in the Pittsburgh area specifically and the Appalachian region generally suggested that this fuel was worth utilizing, and not wasting, even when a driller's primary goal was extract-

69

ing oil. The largest new firms formed first in the Appalachian area and then in the South and Southwest. Oil and gas discoveries in California spawned large companies there as well.

Standard Oil Enters the Natural Gas Industry

One of the largest gas firms of the early twentieth century was a subsidiary of Standard Oil. While Standard focused on oil refining as opposed to oil production, it did engage in the gas production and transportation business. In the early 1880s, Daniel O'Day, a high-level manager of the Standard Oil Trust, kept John D. Rockefeller informed of developments in the natural gas business. After writing Rockefeller about these opportunities, the domineering oil man replied to O'Day: "I am desirous to have our National Transit Company pursue the gas business earnestly."[3] Subsequently, O'Day ordered work begun on a new gas pipeline to supply gas to Standard's oil-pumping stations.

The National Transit Company was a Standard subsidiary formed in 1881 to manage all of Standard's oil and gas pipeline interests; at this time National Transit "was the largest single unit among Standard's holdings."[4] National Transit quickly expanded its natural gas interests. This included moving more aggressively into pipeline operations as well as acquiring gas-producing properties.

Calvin N. Payne was the longtime manager of Standard's natural gas interests; his son Christy later took over management of Standard Oil (New Jersey) natural gas operations. Payne had grown up in the oil fields of eastern Pennsylvania, but he distinguished himself in managing the construction of the first natural gas line from McKean County, Pennsylvania, to Buffalo, New York. By 1883, he had become president of the Pennsylvania Gas Company. In 1885, Standard Oil offered him the position of manager of its natural gas interests. In 1889, he was appointed as general manager of National Transit.

In 1884, National Transit acquired United Pipelines, which had been formed by Captain Jacob Jay Vandergrift and his partners. Vandergrift was a pioneer in both oil and gas pipeline construction, and he had consolidated all of his pipeline interests into United Pipelines. Under Standard's control, these lines made up the beginnings of Standard's extensive natural gas pipeline network. By 1886, National Transit had spent $7 million in the acquisition of nine natural gas companies operating in New York, eastern Ohio, and Pennsylvania.[5] With extensive natural gas interests, National Transit transferred seven of its natural gas affiliates to the newly formed Natural Gas Trust in 1886.

Concern about the public's belief that Standard Oil sought to monopolize the gas business, as well as general apprehension about the Gas Trust's legal status, caused trustee Benjamin Brewster to recommend in 1888 that the Trust's certificates be transferred to Standard Oil. The disappearance of the Trust in no way ended Standard's continuing efforts to develop its natural gas business.

By the late 1890s, Standard began to consolidate its natural gas properties in Ohio and West Virginia. This was accomplished in 1898 when Standard established two new companies: the East Ohio Gas Company and the Hope Natural Gas Company. The Hope company consolidated Standard's West Virginia properties. It acquired at cost all natural gas wells drilled by the South Penn Oil Company as well as the operated and unoperated leases of the Carter Oil Company, Mountain State Gas Company, and the Reserve Gas Company. In addition, Hope had 40,000 acres under lease, and in 1902 Hope began its own extensive drilling program. The East Ohio Gas Company produced and delivered natural gas to industrial consumers in Ohio.[6]

Standard's involvement in the industry increased in 1902. National Transit incorporated the Connecting Gas Company to transport gas from its West Virginia properties to its Ohio distribution system, essentially connecting the newly formed Reserve Gas Company and the Hope company with the East Ohio Gas Company and the River Company also operating in Ohio. National Transit Company also entered the retail gas distribution business when it purchased Peoples Natural Gas in 1903 for $4,483,000. As the gas fields near Pittsburgh began to decline in 1906, National Transit financed the construction and installation of a compressor station in Brave to transport gas produced by Hope in West Virginia to Pittsburgh.[7]

Monopolization of the oil pipeline industry by Standard Oil compelled Congress to mandate common-carrier status for oil pipelines through the Hepburn Act (1906) in order to open access for smaller, independent oil producers who were otherwise in danger of being kept out of the market. During consideration of this bill, which gave the Interstate Commerce Commission (ICC) regulatory power over interstate oil pipelines, Congress considered imposing common-carrier status over natural gas pipelines even though there were few pipelines that actually transported gas across state lines in 1906.

Extended congressional debate over the Hepburn Act disclosed considerable concern about the natural gas industry. Some members of Congress agreed that the economic conditions that had permitted Standard Oil to dominate the oil fields was similar to those in the natural gas and manufactured gas industries. Senator Benjamin R. Tilman (South Carolina) argued that without common-carrier status imposed on natural gas lines, a monopoly situation would eventually arise similar to that for petroleum transportation.[8] Senator Foraker of Ohio objected to common-carrier status with a simple message: entrepreneurs would not build new pipelines to exploit gas fields for the growing demand if those pipelines automatically became common carriers. He described a pipeline venture under construction from the gas fields of West Virginia to Cincinnati, Ohio. Some gas from this line would be used for city lighting, but most of the supply was dedicated for industry. The pipeline promoters decided that if their line was to be a common carrier, they might lose the ability to make the industrial gas sales. With no effective control over their $5 million line, they would "terminate the enterprise."[9]

The final version of the Hepburn Act exempted both natural gas and water pipelines. While the interstate aspects of the gas industry escaped federal oversight at this time, Standard's oil operations continued to attract attention from antitrust policy makers. In the same year as the Hepburn Act, the U.S. Department of Justice filed suit under the Sherman Antitrust Act against Standard Oil. In 1911, the U.S. Supreme Court ruled against Standard and dissolved the oil giant in 1911. The ruling did not mandate dissolution of Standard's natural gas business, and Standard Oil (New Jersey) absorbed National Transit's natural gas properties.

After the dissolution, Standard's natural gas operations were controlled and operated primarily by the East Ohio Gas Company, Hope Natural Gas Company, and the Peoples Natural Gas Company. By 1918, Standard had seven natural gas affiliates that were producing and distributing more than 100 Bcf (billion cubic feet) annually. In 1927, Standard's gas producing affiliates were leasing about 2.7 million acres with 10,000 wells producing either gas or a combination of oil and gas.[10]

The Origins of Public Utility Holding Companies

As electric lighting began to overtake gas lighting, many gas and electric firms merged and offered both gas and electric service. The first serious discussion about creating a gas and electric company had occurred in Boston during 1887. At a meeting of the National Gas Association of New England, participants discussed at length the possibility that a gas company might operate an electrical generating plant in conjunction with its existing gas service. The meeting ended with an agreement that "a union of gas and electric light interests was highly desirable from the standpoint of both producer and consumer." The coke by-product from the gas manufacturing process could be used to make steam for running the electrical power generators. In addition, the existing executive and management staff of the gas firm could oversee the electric side of the business. These two features could result in "a saving of from 33 to 50 percent . . . in the production and service of both lights from a common center."[11]

Concerns that such a gas and electric company combination might result in a monopoly were dismissed as "the sheerest nonsense" by W. A. Stedman, general manager of the Newport (Rhode Island) Gas Works and treasurer of the American Electric Manufacturing Company; this was reportedly the first U.S. firm to both generate electricity and distribute gas. "It is the record of all the gas companies of the whole United States," he said, "that they have continually reduced the price and improved the quality as business has increased and the cost of production grown less."[12]

Excavation for gasholder, ca. 1890.

Courtesy, Pacific Gas and Electric Company.

In San Francisco, an "if you can't beat the enemy, embrace him" attitude geared gas and electric firms toward consolidation. As the gas company's street-lighting contracts neared expiration, the firm feared losing those contracts to the electric company. Accordingly, the gas company sent its president, Crockett East, to Europe with the express purpose of inspecting electricity generating plants there in preparation for the construction of electric facilities under the control of his San Francisco gas firm. Both San Francisco Gas and the Electric Company desired not to engage in destructive competition, so a merger was the solution. San Francisco Gas merged with the local Edison Light and Power Company in December 1896.[13] The new firm, San Francisco Gas and Electric Company, was not without further competition. In 1901, there were still eight other electric firms and three other gas firms competing for business in San Francisco.[14]

The continuation of cutthroat competition in San Francisco's gas and electric market led to further consolidation. In 1903, San Francisco Gas & Electric purchased four competitors, including the Equitable Gas Light Company and Pacific Gas Improvement. Two years later, the California Gas and Electric Corporation, which operated outside of San Francisco city limits and to the north, purchased the San Francisco firm. The new northern California utility giant was renamed and incorporated as the Pacific Gas and Electric Company (PG&E) in October 1905.[15]

Philip Gossler and the Columbia System

The Cincinnati Gas Light & Coke Company, which first sold manufactured gas for lighting in 1843, became a centerpiece for a public utility empire that was geographically similar to Standard Oil's natural gas interests, except that this business would include a substantial electric power division. In 1893, the General Assembly of Ohio approved legislation granting Cincinnati Gas the right to produce commercial electricity. This act allowed it to acquire the newly formed Cincinnati Electric Light Company and compete with the Cincinnati Edison Electric Illuminating Company. During 1901, Cincinnati Gas acquired the Cincinnati Edison and four other electric power firms and then changed its name to the Cincinnati Gas & Electric Company.

In 1905, the city of Norwood, completely enclosed by Cincinnati, signed a natural gas supply contract with the Ohio Fuel Supply Company. Through a series of corporate reorganizations, Ohio Fuel came under the control of Union Gas & Electric Company, which subsequently leased all of the facilities of Cincinnati Gas on September 1, 1906.

Executives from Union Gas then formed the Columbia Corporation on September 11, 1906, to build a natural gas line extending from West Virginia to Cincinnati. Columbia built a 20-inch line extending 183 miles from West Virginia and Kentucky gas fields. Within two months, this new business changed its name to Columbia Gas & Electric Company. Columbia Gas began an aggressive campaign to expand into natural gas production and distribution as well as electric power generation.[16]

Columbia's chief, Philip G. Gossler, guided the firm after his election as chairman of the board in 1912. Gossler had graduated from Pennsylvania State College in 1892, after which he found employment at the United Electric Light & Power Company. After a stint with the Royal Electric Company of Montreal and the Montreal Light, Heat & Power Company, he worked for J. G. White & Company, an electrical engineering firm, before taking charge at Columbia in 1912.

At Columbia, Gossler negotiated a deal with Standard Oil (New Jersey) in 1915 that resulted in the sale of Columbia's stock holdings in the East Ohio Gas Company. Columbia in turn acquired a controlling interest in United Fuel Gas Company, which owned leases on 800,000 acres of natural gas–producing property in West Virginia. Combined, United Fuel and Columbia controlled leases on 1.12 million acres of land in West Virginia and Kentucky. Columbia Gas would soon become one of the largest gas and electric companies in the nation.[17]

Henry L. Doherty and Cities Service Company

The early twentieth century gas industry's most successful promoter and salesman was Henry L. Doherty. He had first found work in the gas industry as an office boy at the Columbus Gas Company, where he rose to the position of chief engineer and manager's assistant by 1896. The Columbus company was one of several firms controlled by the New York banking firm of Emerson McMillan & Company. Another utility company owned by these bankers was Madison Gas & Electric, which was suffering from low gas sales. The bankers asked Doherty to go to Madison and investigate the problems.

Doherty learned that Madison had been unsuccessful in promoting gas as a fuel for cooking. The problem was with the gas cooking stoves. Working with the local appliance manufacturers, improvements were made in the design of the burners and other elements. In the meantime, Doherty hired salesmen to first canvass Madison to determine the interest in gas cooking and gas cooking appliances. With this statistical information, Doherty developed a quota system for the salesmen, who then began selling the appliances throughout the city. Doherty's ideas about promoting gas cooking were presented in a paper titled "How Can We Make the Use of Gas for Cooking More Universal?" to the American Gas Light Association in 1898.[18]

Doherty knew that he had to demonstrate the positive advantages of gas cooking. He hired a chef from Boston to demonstrate at a cooking school the advantages of cooking with gas. The "Housewife League" sponsored neighborhood cooking demonstrations to promote gas cooking and its appliances. To pay for the appliances, Doherty allowed customers to make partial payments along with each monthly gas bill. Finally, poorly installed or malfunctioning appliances received a prompt visit from a serviceman as well as follow-up correspondence. Doherty understood the value of marketing and customer service.[19]

Doherty's success in Madison made him Emerson McMillan's choice to tackle problems that were brewing in Denver. Two electric firms there, Lamcombe Electric Company and Denver Gas & Electric, had engaged in a destructive rate-cutting war. First, Doherty took over as president

Gas car, ca. 1910.
Courtesy, Public Service Company of Colorado.

and treasurer of Denver Gas & Electric in 1900. To deal with the rate war, he instituted a novel plan; he raised Denver Gas & Electric's rates. Low-volume electric customers discovered that Denver Gas actually encouraged them to switch to Lamcombe.

At Denver Gas & Electric, Doherty instituted a three-part rate system, which he had first described in an 1894 essay. The three-part rate consisted of a charge for actual fuel or power consumed, an equipment installation fee, and a readiness-to-serve charge. The rate war continued as Doherty attracted large-volume customers as well as the appreciation of politicians and the local elite. Doherty's rate system benefited large-volume users and translated into political advantage. Ultimately, Doherty outlasted Lamcombe, who sold out to Doherty and McMillan in 1902.[20]

Doherty's talents in gas and electric company organization and sales promotion outgrew his association with Emerson McMillan. In 1905, at the age of 35, he formed Henry L. Doherty & Company, which specialized in the reorganization, management, and financing of public utility companies. With headquarters at 60 Wall Street, Doherty planned to make enough money in five years to return to engineering, which most interested him. To begin the process of enriching himself, he began acquiring financial stakes in numerous gas and electric firms. Doherty attracted investor interest by paying out large dividends, to the dismay of his associates. "Monthly dividends allow a small investor to come in," Doherty said. "Monthly dividends remind him twelve times instead of four times a year of the merits of participating in the capitalistic system and that he should increase his investment."[21]

The Doherty firm grew rapidly, but its identity was diffuse. It was a gas and electric utility holding company, an investment firm, an engineering firm, and a consulting business. Doherty found it necessary to form a separate holding company that could manage all these business activities, so he formed the Cities Service Company in 1910 to manage most of his gas and electric assets. The name of his new firm reflected his goals: to serve cities across the nation with gas and electric power. Originally, it controlled Denver Gas & Electric (which Doherty had purchased from McMillan), Spokane Gas & Fuel, and Empire District Electric. By 1913, it controlled more than 50 separate utility firms in 14 states.[22]

Doherty not only controlled what became one of the nation's largest public utility holding companies, he also promoted conservation measures and held more than 150 patents. Doherty was a multifaceted individual who realized that technology, gas rates, and consumers were all important parts of a successful utility business. Perhaps his greatest contributions were those based on his understanding of residential energy consumers. Historian Mark H. Rose noted that Doherty and his employ-

ees "learned that focusing on several common concerns of the day—
cleanliness, comfort, and convenience, especially for women—made
sales."[23] Doherty was an engineer who understood the importance of
marketing.

Samuel Insull: Public Utility Captain

In Chicago, the consolidation of gas and electric power firms had particularly significant ramifications for the future public utility industry. On
July 1, 1892, Samuel Insull became chief executive officer of Chicago
Edison Company, and he later became the most visible public symbol of
the new "Power Trust."

As a young Englishman, Insull had worked for an American banker,
George E. Gouraud, representing Thomas Edison in London. Gouraud
later recommended Insull to Edison for employment. Insull subsequently traveled to New York and arrived during construction of the Pearl
Street station. Insull served as a private secretary to Edison and worked
at the plant in the evenings. Insull learned a great deal about constructing and managing electric generating stations, and he also learned from
Edison the importance of understanding the gas industry—so that they
could successfully compete with it. Insull continued to work for Edison
through the merger of Edison Electric and Thomson-Houston, which
created the General Electric company (GE). At GE, Insull was the third-
highest ranking executive, but he was ready for new adventures. In 1907,
he accepted the chief executive position at Chicago Edison.[24]

Insull managed Chicago Edison's operations while creating a public
utility empire. He became directly involved in the gas business when the
Peoples Gas Company (Chicago) offered him a $50,000 annual salary for
accepting the position of board chairman; management hoped Insull
could help reverse the company's recent financial decline. Initially, Insull
refused the offer. Peoples then got Insull's attention when it claimed that
it was entering the electric power generation business with a unique generator. Insull's interest perked, and he accepted the chairmanship in
1913.[25]

Insull oversaw revitalization of the gas company during a particularly difficult time. Manufactured gas plants in Chicago and elsewhere were
confronting economic challenges once again. Water gas plants, which
had supplanted coal gas plants in the 1880s and 1890s, were becoming
increasingly expensive to operate. This time it was the oil used in the
Lowe process that increased the costs. The emerging automobile indus-

try proffered a new use for refined oil, in the form of gasoline, as a fuel to power cars. The new demand for gasoline resulted in higher prices for oil.

Faced with certain bankruptcy, Insull became actively involved in Peoples' management. He resolved serious tax problems while working hard to restore employee confidence. To save money, he arranged for Peoples Gas to purchase "waste gas" from factories that used coal and coke in the process of making steel and other products. Buying this waste gas for resale at prices far less than the gas firm's production costs, Peoples was able to save nearly $3 million per year in fuel costs. Insull also arranged financing for a new $20 million gas-manufacturing plant. This modern coal gas plant was designed to capture for resale a wide variety of the by-products from the coal gasification process. These by-products included ammonium sulfate, benzol, coke, and tar. Historian Harold Platt noted that "Insull could sell the gas and by-products for three times the cost of his raw material—cheap bituminous coal."[26]

In 1912, Insull formed Middle West Utilities, a holding company under which he would acquire and control other gas and electric firms outside of the Chicago area. Middle West became one of the largest and most notorious utility holding companies in the United States. Insull's public utility empire reached huge proportions even though his personal wealth in 1926 was reportedly less than $10 million. Insull and his associates eventually gained control of Commonwealth Edison (electricity distribution in Chicago), Peoples Gas (gas distribution in Chicago), Public Service of Northern Illinois (gas and electricity distribution to 300 communities in the Chicago area), Middle West Utilities (hundreds of subsidiaries serving gas and electricity to 5,000 communities in 32 states), and Midland United Company (selling gas and electricity to 700 Indiana communities). In addition to these gas and electric companies, Insull had a direct interest in interurban electric railways operating in metropolitan Chicago, elevated railways in Chicago, and North American Light and Power Company (connecting Insull's properties with the North American Company's properties in and around St. Louis). By 1930, Insull's gas and electric empire accounted for $3 billion in utility properties, 4 million customers, 600,000 stockholders, and 500,000 bondholders, and it produced approximately one-eighth of the gas and electricity used in the United States.[27]

By the second decade of the twentieth century, natural gas was widely recognized as a superior fuel compared to manufactured gas. But access to natural gas still depended upon being located near gas fields, particularly the large fields of the Appalachian region. Even these fields, however, were experiencing diminishing volumes.

State Regulation and Self-Regulation

The rapid growth of gas and electric firms in the late nineteenth and early twentieth century spurred calls for industry cooperation and rate regulation. Competition among coal gas, water gas, and natural gas firms along with the breakdown of territorially based service areas in urban settings led to cutthroat competition and eventually consolidation in the gas industry. Industry-specific associations, civic groups, and state regulatory commissions sought to bring economic stability to an industry on which the public was becoming increasingly dependent.

State regulatory commissions were formed originally to oversee railroad rates and schedules. The first of these agencies was created in Rhode Island during 1839. The first state agency granted specific powers over the gas business was the Massachusetts Board of Gas Commissioners formed in 1885; it was restructured as the Board of Gas and Electric Light Commissioners in 1887. Historian of regulation Thomas McCraw noted that this agency "did not wield strong authority over rates but tried instead to regulate more gently, mediating a host of difficult issues."[28] Similar agencies formed in other states where there was substantial gaslight business.

By the early twentieth century, the business elite sought state regulation that would provide industry stability. The National Civic Federation (NCF) and the National Electric Light Association (NELA) in particular pushed for utility regulation. In 1907, Samuel Insull and Henry Doherty were members of the NELA's Committee on Public Policy, and Insull was also on the executive committee of the NCF (along with Louis Brandeis and John Mitchell). In 1907, both organizations issued reports supporting general state supervision of the gas and electric utility industry. The NCF asserted that "public utilities, whether in public or in private hands, are best conducted under a system of legalized and regulated monopoly."[29]

Industry's interest in state regulation was not a simple acknowledgment that regulation provided economic stability. Instead, state regulation was a preferable alternative to what utilities often perceived as the vagaries of local, or municipal, rate regulation. For example, during a meeting of the Pacific Gas Association, the organization's president argued against municipal regulation and declared that "local men are not capable of fixing rates for public service corporations without prejudice."[30]

Robert M. La Follette, the Progressive political leader, agreed that state regulation was the best choice. He proposed state oversight, arguing that the state government was more likely to provide a systematic supervision of utilities, and he believed that local governments were subject to corrupt influences. He encouraged Wisconsin to adapt the NCF's utility regulation framework into a state regulatory commission. The resulting Wisconsin Railroad Commission (1907) provided a model for the 27 state commissions created in the following six years.[31]

Industry trade associations also sought industry cohesiveness and stability. Numerous local and regional gas associations formed during the late nineteenth century, including the New England Association of Gas Engineers (1871), the Society of Gas Lighting (1874) for New York, the Ohio Gas Light Association (1884), and the Pacific Coast Gas Association (1893). In 1906, several of the larger regional gas associations merged into the American Gas Institute, a national group that dealt with technical issues in the gas business. Another organization, the National Commercial Gas Association, focused on sales and marketing issues and accepted into its membership gas appliance manufacturers. In June 1918, these two large associations merged to form the American Gas Association (AGA), which was one of many large trade associations formed during this era of the associative state.

During World War I, the War Industries Board encouraged the formation of national trade associations, which served as centralized information services for their industry and sometimes engaged in management, policy setting, and price setting. Trade associations represented a new spirit of cooperation and coordination of business activity apart from government controls.

One important issue involved setting standards for measuring the quality of delivered gas. Throughout the nineteenth century, when manufactured gasworks distributed gas for lighting, gas was measured in terms of "candle power." Many cities adopted standards requiring that gas firms supply gas with a candlepower of anywhere from 12 to 22, depending upon the type of gas used.

By the early twentieth century, gas lighting was rapidly disappearing, but gas cooking and heating were becoming increasingly popular. The candlepower standards made no sense for cooking or heating. A new measurement standard, the British thermal unit (Btu) was gradually adopted nationwide. Between 1908, when Wisconsin adopted the Btu, and 1922, when New York's gas utilities began using this measurement standard, the nation's gas firms converted, sometimes reluctantly, to the Btu.

The Btu measurements more clearly delineated the differences between water gas, carbureted water gas, coal gas, natural gas, and mixed gas (a mixture of natural and coal gas). The average high Btu content of carbureted water gas was 650, while natural gas was nearly twice that at 1050. Accurate heat measurements were essential as state and local gas company charters mandated minimum Btu standards for delivered gas, and these standards varied among states and provided ample fuel for disputes and controversies between gas firms and state regulators. As R. H. Fernald stated in 1914, "It is undoubtedly true that many companies are today manufacturing gas of a considerably lower heat value than they imagine."[32] Another technical issue was the pressure at which gas would be delivered to a home. Gas pressure effected both the strength of the flame and the overall safety of domestic gas systems. Debates on pressure levels continued as well.[33]

The Gas Industry during World War I

World War I provided the federal government for the first time temporary centralized control over segments of the gas industry. While emergency controls were not long lasting, they may have contributed to the continuing development of a more coherent industrial organization.

The outbreak of war in Europe and subsequent American involvement placed heavy demands on the east coast manufactured gas industry in particular. Cold weather and increased wartime demand for coal lead both to shortages and to significantly higher prices, particularly during 1916–1917. This caused shortage problems for gasworks and their customers dependent upon coal gas for heating and cooking.[34]

During the war, the United States Fuel Administration (USFA) oversaw the gas industry.[35] Some gas and oil drilling work was curtailed to release men and equipment for war-related tasks. In the Midwest and Appalachian region, the USFA placed restrictions on gas deliveries to industrial plants manufacturing non-war-related products. In the East, additional natural gas was required at Pittsburgh area steel factories, which were operating continuously in some cases. Energy historian John G. Clark observed that "natural gas was to be diverted from nonessential industries such as brick and tile and cement to more essential industries that used fuel oil or coal, particularly oil refineries and various manufacturing firms engaged in filling military contracts."[36]

Restrictions became more severe in 1918. Several industrial groups found that the USFA curtailed their gas consumption by as much as 50 percent. Since some natural gas producers and distributors were ignoring USFA rules, the USFA drafted a licensing agreement signed by Woodrow Wilson (September 25, 1918), which mandated that gas companies acquire a license proving compliance with USFA regulations before delivering gas. Ultimately, Clark stated, the USFA "favored . . . the gas industry over consumers" during the war.[37]

The U.S. government's Ordnance Department in preparing for war requested in October 1917 that gas companies begin producing toluol for the manufacture of explosives. In particular, toluol was an essential component of the explosive TNT (trinitrotoluene).[38] The Consolidated Gas Company (New York) took the lead in both manufacturing toluol and producing the charcoal necessary for gas masks. As deadly mustard gas was killing Allied soldiers, charcoal filters were essential for protecting their lives. Consolidated Gas began manufacturing charcoal from the two sources deemed best for the required filtering characteristics: coconut shells and peach pits. The gas company dedicated nearly 300 retorts at the Astoria and Fourteenth Street gasworks for producing carbon from the shells and pits to be used in the gas masks worn by American soldiers fighting in France.[39]

By the end of the second decade of the twentieth century, the many gas firms located across the nation were becoming part of a recognizable industry. A national trade association grew out of numerous local and regional associations, standards for gas service were being adopted, and state regulatory commissions imposed operating standards on gas firms. A few very large consolidations of gas and electric firms were more formally organized into public utility holding companies, which dominated the power business. Informally, these larger firms, particularly those operating in the Midwest, constituted a utility cartel referred to as the "power trust." These companies became increasingly powerful, financially and politically, during the 1920s. Yet, the gas industry in some respects had not yet evolved beyond locally organized gas distribution firms. Urban areas were growing, and the gas production and distribution capacity of gasworks was increasing, but the industry was essentially a large collection of manufactured gas plants connected by distribution lines to specific urban centers; many of these were also associated with electric utilities. Manufactured gasworks did not require interconnection as long as sufficient coal or other feedstock was available. But as pipeline technology improved, new long-distance pipelines were built, affording the opportunity to replace manufactured gas with natural gas.

6

Long-Distance
Natural Gas Pipelines

THE DISCOVERY OF massive Southwestern natural gas fields combined with technological advancements in long-distance pipeline construction dramatically altered the 1920s gas industry market structure. In 1918, drillers discovered huge natural gas fields leading to the identification of the Panhandle Field in North Texas. In 1922, a Kansas gas well became the first of the Hugoton field wells, located in the common Kansas, Oklahoma, and Texas border area (generally referred to as the mid-continent). The combined Panhandle/ Hugoton Field became the nation's largest gas-producing area comprising more than 1.6 million acres. It contained as much as 117 Tcf (trillion cubic feet) of natural gas and accounted for approximately 16 percent of total U.S. reserves in the twentieth century.[1]

As oil men had done earlier in Appalachia, they initially exploited the Panhandle Field for petroleum only while allowing an estimated 1 Bcf/d (billion cubic feet per day) of natural gas to escape into the atmosphere. As new gas markets appeared, the commercial value of Southwestern natural gas attracted entrepreneurial interest and bolstered the fortunes of existing firms. These discoveries led to the establishment of many new firms, including the Lone Star Gas Company, Arkansas Louisiana Gas Company, Kansas Natural Gas Company, United Gas Company, and others, some of which evolved into large natural gas companies.

Houston natural gas well, "Christmas Tree," 1925.

Courtesy, Enron Corporation.

The sheer volume of these fields emphasized the need for advancements in pipeline technology to transport this gas to distant urban markets. In particular, new welding technologies allowed pipeline builders in the 1920s to construct longer lines. In the early years of the decade, oxyacetylene torches were used for welding, and in 1923 electric arc welding was successfully used on thin-walled, high-tensile-strength, large-diameter pipelines necessary for long-distance compressed gas transmission. Improved welding techniques made pipe joints stronger than the pipe itself. Seamless pipe was also available for gas pipelines beginning in 1925. Along with enhancements in pipeline construction materials and techniques, gas compressor and ditching machine technology improved as well. Long-distance pipelines became a significant segment of the gas industry beginning in the 1920s.[2]

These new technologies made possible the transportation of Southwestern natural gas first to Midwestern markets; the Southwest then began to supplant Appalachia's position as the primary region for marketable gas production. Until the late 1920s, virtually all interstate natural gas transportation took place in the Northeast, and it was based upon Appalachian production. In 1921, natural gas produced in West

Virginia accounted for approximately 65 percent of interstate gas transportation, while only 2 percent of interstate gas originated in Texas. Most interstate gas flowed into western Pennsylvania and Ohio.[3] Appalachian fields experienced serious depletion in the 1920s, and various state legislators attempted to prohibit out-of-state gas exportation. The West Virginia legislature designed the Steptoe Act to halt out-of-state sales, and Oklahoma proposed similar legislation.[4] These attempts to corral natural gas for intrastate utilization were largely unsuccessful.

Between the mid-1920s and the mid-1930s, the combination of abundant and inexpensive Southwestern natural gas production, improved pipeline technology, and increasing nationwide natural gas demand created a new interstate gas pipeline industry. Metropolitan manufactured gas distribution companies, typically part of large holding companies, financed most of the pipelines built during this era. Despite the high cost of the long-distance lines, access to natural gas even for mixing with existing manufactured gas would raise the heating content of the gas; natural gas was so abundant that it was often substantially less costly than coal gas.

In 1927, Cities Service built the first long-distance line originating in the Panhandle field. This 250-mile 20-inch pipeline connected the Panhandle field with a Cities Service gas distributor in Wichita, Kansas. With compressor stations located at 60-mile intervals, this line had a delivery capacity of 70 MMcf/d. By 1928, Cities Service extended this line directly into Kansas City.[5]

Standard Oil (New Jersey) also participated in several significant pipeline ventures during these years, the first of which was Colorado Interstate Gas Company. Organized in 1927 by Standard, Cities Service, and Prairie Oil & Gas, this firm built a 350-mile 22-inch line originating at the Texas–New Mexico border and extending to Denver. It received its gas supply from another newly organized firm, Canadian River Fuel Corporation, a partnership of Cities Service and Prairie Oil & Gas.[6] Standard also participated in the establishment of the Interstate Natural Gas Company. Standard originally had a 37.5 percent interest in this pipeline, which extended from Baton Rouge, Louisiana, to Alton, Illinois. Standard Oil (New Jersey) also joined a group that built the Mississippi River Fuel Corporation's line, a 430-mile pipeline extending from the Munroe field in Louisiana to St. Louis.[7]

In California, natural gas from the Buena Vista field in the San Joaquin Valley was already being used in Los Angeles, and in 1929 PG&E constructed a 300-mile line from the Kettleman field north of Los Angeles to bring natural gas to San Francisco. This city was one of the first major urban areas to switch from manufactured to natural gas. In 1928, two manufactured gas plants produced a total of 8.5 Bcf for

Natural gas pipeline systems, 1940.

Federal Trade Commission, *U.S. Temporary National Economic Committee: Investigation of Concentration of Economic Power*, monograph no. 36, 76th Cong., 3rd sess., 1940.

183,000 consumers; altogether PG&E operated 21 gas plants. Since the same volume of natural gas had nearly twice the heating content as coal gas, burners and airflow valves in stoves and water heaters had to be adjusted to accept the natural fuel. With near military precision, PG&E divided San Francisco into 11 districts, which were successively converted to the natural fuel. Six hundred trained men divided into 35-member crews converted PG&E's service area within five months. The conversion of 1.75 million appliances cost $2 million, but natural gas was less costly for the utility to market than coal gas. The utility did maintain several gas plants for communities too far from existing gas lines and for possible emergency use during an unexpected shortage.[8]

Laying the Kettleman to San Francisco line, 1929.

Courtesy, Pacific Gas and Electric Company.

New long-distance gas lines and expensive conversion programs were necessary if gas utilities were going to meet consumer demand. The new holding companies marshaled tremendous amounts of capital to build pipelines, extend service, and promote gas utilization. They also became adept at advertising and marketing. Trained salesmen, company servicemen, and even co-opted plumbers touted gas. During the 1920s, utility companies offered for sale a wide variety of gas-powered appliances, including space-heating units, water heaters, irons, stoves, and even gas-powered refrigerators. By 1926, about 50,000 automatic water heaters had been installed in homes. But gas appliances were not inexpensive; as John Herbert has shown, the average cost of an installed gas water heater in 1929 was $144.43.[9]

Another use for natural gas beginning in the late nineteenth century was carbon black production. A soot produced by burning carbon-based substances—principally natural gas—carbon black was used for coloring in paint and inks. It was also used as a reinforcing agent in rubber and automobile tires. Natural gas produced in fields not connected by pipelines to urban markets was a prime candidate for carbon black production. Even by the late 1930s, about two-thirds of the marketable gas produced was either flared, vented, or used to make carbon black. But greater profits awaited entrepreneurs willing to finance pipelines connecting gas fields to urban and industrial gas markets.

Urban natural gas utilization also brought forth efforts to develop a standardized odorant. Unlike coal gas, which typically had a distinct smell, natural gas is odorless. Thus, a leak or inadvertently opened valve might allow odorless gas to accumulate in an enclosed space and asphyxiate people or cause an explosion. Although experiments with odorants date to at least 1885, the Bureau of Mines conducted experiments with mercaptan in 1930, and this chemical (of the thiol family) later became the standardized gas odorizer.

The First Long-Distance Pipelines

By the late 1920s, four public utility holding companies dominated the U.S. gas industry and sought to control interstate gas transportation as well (see table 6.1). Two of the largest holding companies, Columbia Gas and Standard Oil (New Jersey), distributed more than half of the gas sold in the entire Appalachian region. Henry Doherty's Cities Service dominated the lower Midwest. The largest public utility conglomerates were Middle West Utilities and Insull Utility Investments, both controlled by Samuel Insull and headquartered in Chicago.[10] By the late 1920s,

TABLE 6.1 Interstate Movement of Gas, 1930

Company	Manufactured Gas (MMcf)	Natural Gas (MMcf)	% of Total Interstate Natural Gas
Cities Service Co.	45	94,895	24.9
Columbia Gas & Electric	145	46,533	12.2
Standard Oil (N.J.)	—	37,954	10.0
Electric Bond & Share	341	60,913	16.0
Insull Group	2,268	490	0.1
Total			63.2

Source: FTC, Utility Corporations, pt. 57, 49–50.
Note: MMcf—million cubic feet.

Insull's empire included 248 gas, coal, and electric power firms serving 4,741 communities in 30 states.

These large utility holding companies operated as an informal and unstable, yet powerful cartel popularly referred to as the "Power Trust." Pennsylvania governor Gifford Pinchot told the Pennsylvania legislature that "nothing like this gigantic monopoly has ever appeared in the history of the world. . . . If uncontrolled, it will be a plague without previous example. If effectively controlled in the public interest, it can be made incomparably the greatest material blessing in human history."[11] Subsequent events proved Pinchot to be correct. Industry observers later described the competition for Midwestern gas markets as "an amazing story of high finance, suppression of competition, division of territory, and capture of control or forced receivership by established interests of independent enterprises which aspired to a share of the apparently large and profitable markets of the Middle West."[12] In order to sustain their dominance, these utility holding companies had to build long-distance pipelines to connect distant gas supply with their urban markets.

Planning for the first one-thousand-mile pipeline began in 1926, when Samuel Insull and associates discussed the possibility of building a natural gas pipeline connecting southern gas fields with Chicago area gas utilities. They sponsored engineering studies, considered a pipeline route, and examined potential gas acreage. In April 1930 they incorporated as the Continental Construction Corporation; a year later the company changed its name to the Natural Gas Pipeline Company of America (NGPL). NGPL's proposed 24-inch line would extend 980 miles from north Texas to Chicago. Commonly referred to as the "Chicago pipeline," this line would allow Insull to convert Peoples Gas Light & Coke Company's service area from dependence on manufactured coal gas to cleaner, hotter burning, and less expensive natural gas.

This pipeline venture was jointly planned, financed, and controlled by three utility holding companies and three other oil firms. The three holding companies were Samuel Insull's Insull & Sons, Henry Doherty's Cities Service, and Standard Oil of New Jersey, the gas division of which was managed by Christy Payne. These three originally had a 23 percent interest each in the line with the remaining 31 percent interest divided among the other participants, including the Texas Company (Texaco), Southwestern Development Company, and Columbian Carbon Company.

NGPL purchased its gas supply from gas fields controlled by the pipeline's owners. Standard Oil (New Jersey) agreed to furnish 25 percent of NGPL's requirements indirectly through the Canadian River Gas Company. Canadian River was a partnership of Cities Service and Prairie Oil & Gas, Standard's partners in the Colorado Interstate line. The Texoma Natural Gas Company supplied the remaining 75 percent of NGPL's gas requirements. Texoma was another joint venture of the same participants except Standard Oil, which was particularly cautious in Texas regarding sales of its natural gas production; the Texas Railroad Commission was poised to declare Standard a gas utility and therefore subject to more stringent regulation.[13] Texoma acquired gas-producing acreage and wells in the Amarillo, Texas, gas field and would deliver gas to Gray Junction, Oklahoma, where NGPL planned to receive it for transportation to Chicago.[14]

Henry L. Doherty & Company contracted to build the NGPL pipeline. Construction began in August 1930, and the main line was completed 12 months later. A total of 418 million pounds of steel pipe buried six feet underground transported gas at 600 psi. Construction costs for the main line, nine compressor stations, and telephone lines totaled $35 million. While NGPL's major market was Insull's Chicago area utilities, some gas was also sold to gas distributors in Kansas and other states. The first gas deliveries in Chicago commenced on October 16, 1931, and by January 1, 1932, the system was delivering 55 MMcf/d with an originally designed total capacity of 175 MMcf/d.

With access to abundant volumes of natural gas, Chicago became the largest U.S. city to convert its utility distribution system to "mixed gas," and later to straight natural gas. Mixed gas, a mixture of lower Btu coal gas and higher Btu natural gas, provided a hotter burning flame than coal gas alone for both cooking and heating. At the same time, Peoples began charging for gas based on a price per "therm" (1 therm = 100,000 Btus) rather than by volume; natural gas had nearly twice the Btu rating as an equal volume of manufactured gas.

Peoples Gas Light and Coke Company first began producing a mixed gas with an 800 Btu content.[15] At the same time, Peoples organized a massive campaign to merchandise gas house-heating equipment. Peoples placed full- and three-quarter-page advertisements in newspapers serving Chicago and 50 outlying communities; advertisements appeared on billboards, streetcars, and show windows. In addition, the utility hired 270 company-trained salesmen, 60 heating engineers, and 14 sales directors to promote gas consumption. Within the first 10 weeks of the promotion, Peoples installed about 10,000 conversion burners, and the company made 30,000 gas installations during the gas sales promotion.[16] Servicemen adjusted existing residential furnaces to accept the higher Btu mixed gas. In order to convert appliances, gas mains required cleaning to remove oil residue and other impurities from manufactured gas.[17]

While the Chicago Line was under construction, a consortium led by North American Light & Power Company, which owned gas and electric properties throughout the Midwest, purchased from Odie R. Seagraves and William L. Moody III (Moody-Seagraves Interests) the beginnings of the pipeline these two men had planned to build from Seagraves's Hugoton gas field properties to Omaha. North American Light & Power joined the Lone Star Gas Company and United Light & Power Company in a partnership to purchase the Moody-Seagraves project and rename it the Northern Natural Gas Company. North American financed the construction of Northern Natural, which was completed in 1931. The 1,110-mile 24- and 26-inch line transported gas to various cities along its path to Minneapolis via Omaha. This line did not directly compete with the Chicago Line; Samuel Insull reportedly had a 40 percent interest in North American.

Both Northern Natural and NGPL were products of the Power Trust in the sense that representatives of these gas companies participated directly in the financing and/or management of both lines. The sponsors of NGPL and Northern Natural recognized each other's "territory," just as the early gas distributors in both New York City and Chicago initially respected each other's market areas. This informal gas cartel could continue to control the Midwestern gas business only as long as internal competition, or new competitors, did not disrupt the cartel's authority.

An independent group of entrepreneurs, who also recognized the financial rewards possible in the gas business, did plan a third pipeline to connect Southwestern gas fields with Midwestern customers. They formed the Panhandle Eastern Pipe Line Company. The early history of this "maverick" gas line is instructive of both the cartel's inherent economic strengths and weaknesses. Breaking the cartel resulted from cut-

Gas pipeline for Northern Natural Gas Company transported by train, 1929.

Courtesy, Enron Corporation.

throat competition that only the government could control. The next section of this chapter will examine this episode in detail.

Disrupting the Power Trust

Panhandle Eastern's history began with the efforts of 34-year-old Frank Parish. In 1927, Parish worked as a salesman for the manufacturing firm of Clayton, Mark & Company, covering much of the central United States. One of Parish's customers was Cities Service Company, which was then the sole supplier of natural gas to Kansas City. Intrigued by the potential for profit in the gas business, Parish and two men, C. Stuart Shippey and Samuel J. Maddin, decided to form a partnership to produce gas locally and sell it to Cities Service.[18] Cities Service encouraged Parish's efforts by loaning the partnership $40,000 and helping to arrange a $250,000 line of credit for equipment and supplies from the National Supply Company of Toledo, a pipe distributor for U.S. Steel.

The partners soon installed a 48-mile 12-inch line from the Belton gas field to a connection with the American Pipe Line that fed into the Cities Service system.[19]

By this time, Shippey, Maddin, and Parish realized that there was a huge potential market for natural gas throughout the Midwest, but they needed capital. To raise money, they transferred their partnership interests to a new company, the Missouri-Kansas Pipe Line Company (Mo-Kan), in May 5, 1928.[20] Mo-Kan grew rapidly, and between 1928 and 1930, it created, purchased, or otherwise achieved control of 16 subsidiaries as its leaders sought to create a vertically integrated public utility holding company. They were no longer content to sell natural gas to Cities Service and to perform business activities approved by its largest customer. Cities Service and its powerful leader, Henry Doherty, now perceived Mo-Kan as a potential competitive threat, if not simply an uncontrollable nuisance, and made it difficult for Mo-Kan either to expand further or to raise the funds it needed to pay the interest due on its bonds and notes.

Without access to development funds from Cities Service, Parish formed a stock syndicate to raise money through the stock market.[21] He used the syndicate to inflate Mo-Kan's stock price and then persuaded the firm's creditors to exchange their bonds and notes for common stock. The syndicate was profitable, and Parish attracted the attention of Francis I. du Pont, a great-grandson of Eleuthere du Pont who had founded the family's Delaware-based gunpowder firm in the early nineteenth century.[22] Parish courted du Pont, and he hoped du Pont would play a constructive role in Mo-Kan's future.

Parish was one of many Americans seeking to profit from the 1920s stock market. Utility stocks were attractive picks on Wall Street during these years, as Samuel Insull knew. By 1930, more than one million persons owned stock in companies Insull controlled. Halsey, Stuart & Company, a Chicago investment banking firm, helped to promote sales in the Chicago utility's stock.[23] Natural gas men hoped that their industry would now attract the high level of investor interest enjoyed by electric utilities.[24]

Mo-Kan stock traded as high as $35 per share during August 1929, but it dropped to $8 per share following the Wall Street crash. During the next year, Parish & Company "pegged" Mo-Kan stock, keeping its value artificially high by repurchasing its stock offered for sale; self-price-supporting was common and not illegal. From August 1, 1929, through August 21, 1930, Parish & Company traded approximately 2.2 million shares of Mo-Kan on the New York Curb Exchange and the Chicago Stock Exchange, and Parish's brokerage firm purchased 1.2 million of those shares.[25]

Parish relentlessly promoted the stock to new investors. He offered a quarterly dividend "at the rate of 10 percent per annum" paid in stock. He also developed a public relations campaign featuring as its centerpiece a monthly newsletter, the *Mo-Kan Bulletin*. The premier issue appeared in August 1929, and the company claimed to distribute 100,000 copies per month. Meanwhile Parish publicized the company's balance sheet showing assets of $68 million. An Arthur Anderson & Company audit revealed actual total assets of $11,131,000, plus cash and working funds of $1.7 million.[26]

H. L. Doherty of Cities Service was well aware of Parish's activities, and Doherty believed that the ambitious Parish was simply "carrying on a stock selling proposition . . . [and] did not know anything about the gas business."[27] Doherty's observations aside, Mo-Kan's gas business was growing rapidly. Within a year, its staff grew from 12 to about 200 employees located in downtown Kansas City. During the same period, Mo-Kan began leasing substantial natural gas–producing acreage. In July 1930, Mo-Kan began delivering gas to customers in Owensboro, Kentucky, and also transferred its executive offices from Kansas City to Chicago.[28]

The ambitious Parish was learning from the Power Trust leaders' own actions how to best compete against them. Parish and his partners considered the possibility of purchasing gas leases in the Panhandle region, and they did. By late 1930 Mo-Kan acquired an estimated 1.5 Tcf of natural gas reserves in 150,000 acres in the Hugoton field. Altogether, the firm controlled leases covering 500,000 gas-producing acres in seven states.[29]

Mo-Kan then took the next step by publishing articles in its newsletter about the potential profitability of a long-distance pipeline. A line from the Texas Panhandle to any northern city "would pass through, or reach, through short branch lines, scores of cities and towns where [the] cost of manufactured gas for industrial use is prohibitive."[30] Parish believed the Minneapolis/St. Paul metropolitan area might be a good market for industrial gas sales, and Mo-Kan investor Francis du Pont attempted to negotiate gas sales contracts there. Du Pont's efforts failed because Insull and his partners were busy signing up customers for their new Northern Natural line.

Parish was committed to the Minnesota market, and he contracted the engineering firm of Brokaw, Dixon, Garner & McKee to map a pipeline route extending from Liberal, Kansas, to Minneapolis. The Mo-Kan directors incorporated the Interstate Pipe Line Company on December 23, 1929, and Parish arranged a $20 million line of credit from Continental Bank in Chicago. He remained unable to negotiate the gas contracts with utility and industrial customers in the Twin Cities area.

Parish then contacted William G. Maguire for help. President of St. Louis Gas and Coke Corporation until 1928 when he left to form William G. Maguire and Company, Maguire specialized in the acquisition and development of Midwestern utility companies. He knew Clement Studebaker Jr., a Chicago broker and son of the founder of the Studebaker automobile company, as well as Louis E. Fischer. Studebaker owned a substantial interest in North American Light & Power Company, and Fischer was the firm's vice president; North American was the lead firm in the Northern Natural pipeline project.[31]

Maguire met with Studebaker, who suggested that Parish change his proposed pipeline route. Maguire consulted with Louis E. Fischer, vice president of North American and soon to be named president of the proposed Northern Natural pipeline. Fischer also strongly recommended that Parish shift the route of the Mo-Kan line toward Indianapolis. In return for his cooperation, Fischer told Maguire, North American's subsidiaries in Missouri and Illinois would purchase Mo-Kan's gas.

Maguire soon discussed the offer with Parish. The North American company had marked the Twin Cities market as its own, but it agreed to help Parish by purchasing his gas if he rerouted his pipeline toward the east. Parish recalled, "we were glad to do [it]; and we had the firm of Brokaw, Dixon, Garner & McKee survey the markets in Illinois, Missouri, and in Indiana, up to Indianapolis."[32] Parish and his partners formed the Panhandle Eastern Pipe Line Company in April 1930 to reflect the pipeline's Panhandle origin and new eastward route.[33]

Parish and Maguire negotiated gas sales contracts with several of North American's utilities in Illinois and Missouri, but they encountered unexpected problems while trying to sign up customers in Indiana. Maguire decided to meet with Philip Gossler, the 60-year-old chairman of Columbia Gas & Electric Company, which had influence among Indiana's utilities. Gossler surprised Maguire by stating from the start that he opposed the Panhandle Eastern line. He told Maguire, "If I would take a map of the Central United States and a pencil and a ruler I could not draw a line to raise more hell than that one."[34] The pipeline's path, Gossler said, would take it near Kansas City, where Doherty's Cities Service controlled the gas and electric power business. It would threaten Insull's control of the southern Illinois gas markets, and it would pass near St. Louis, which already received gas from Standard Oil subsidiaries. Furthermore, it would cross into Indiana on a path to Michigan and Ohio, Columbia Gas's territory. Gossler told Maguire "that it should be stopped; that it would influence the price of gas securities, and be generally demoralizing" to him as well as Mr. Insull. Gossler told Maguire that Columbia would oppose any new line into Indiana that it did not own. The Panhandle Eastern line represented a "raid" against the cartel and its markets—including those that the large utility firms were not yet serving.

Maguire discounted Gossler's warnings because Panhandle had already signed Illinois and Missouri gas sales contracts with the North American Power & Light subsidiaries.[35] Mo-Kan soon ordered $25 million worth of pipe from the National Supply Company and began constructing the pipeline and compressor stations.

News of the Panhandle line attracted media attention. *Time* magazine reported in early June that "last week one young industry prospered and expanded. . . . For when Missouri-Kansas Pipe Line Company announced that it would build a 1,250-mi. natural gas pipe line from the Texas Panhandle to Indianapolis, it evidenced not only increasing activity in the natural gas field but also helped to stabilize a sagging steel production through huge orders for steel. . . . The new M-K line will outdistance the 700-mi. Insull-Doherty Amarillo line from Texas to Chicago."[36]

Within a week, optimism faded as Mo-Kan's stock price began falling. Frank P. Parish & Company bolstered the trading price, but it became clear that unknown parties were conducting a "bear" raid on the firm's securities selling Mo-Kan stock.[37] In the meantime, William Maguire learned from Louis Fischer that the "powers that be" had decided to oppose construction of the re-routed Panhandle Eastern line, which threatened NGPL's Illinois gas markets. Parish and Maguire met again with Fischer, who told the pair that Doherty, Insull, and Christy Payne were determined to stop the Mo-Kan pipeline project. Fischer warned that if they persisted in building the Panhandle line, pressure would be brought on the Illinois Public Service Commission to oppose Mo-Kan's application for a certificate of public convenience and necessity.[38] Fischer suggested that Parish sell Mo-Kan's Texas gas reserves to Standard Oil (New Jersey) and its pipeline facilities to Cities Service. In return, Mo-Kan stockholders would receive up to 35 percent interest in Northern Natural and 10 percent in NGPL.[39]

Parish refused. Fischer knew that the cartel was behind the recent stock raids on Mo-Kan. He let Parish know that another bear raid was planned for Monday, June 16. They agreed that Parish and Maguire should schedule a meeting for the morning of June 16 with Christy Payne, manager of Standard Oil's (New Jersey) natural gas operations, in an attempt to convince him to use his influence to halt the raid.

Parish and Maguire traveled from Chicago to New York by train on June 15. Their train was late, but they arrived at Payne's office the next morning just after the stock market had opened. Payne would not agree to meet with Panhandle's promoters until late in the afternoon, after the market had closed. During the day, Mo-Kan stock plummeted from a high of 36 1/8 to a low of 15. Payne and an associate, Reed Carr, greeted the visitors: "Well, Parish, how did you like it?" Payne asked if after such a financial setback, they still planned to continue their pipeline project beyond the 200 miles already constructed. The two men simply left without further discussion.[40]

That day, Parish & Company attempted to support Mo-Kan's stock price by signing purchase contracts for approximately $28 million worth of Mo-Kan stock, but this was $20 million more than the firm could actually buy.[41] The next day, a Chicago newspaper reported that

> In the case of the Missouri-Kansas Pipeline, it appeared that the price was an artificial one maintained for the express purpose of aiding distribution of the stock. . . . In a general advancing market, this might not have appeared for a long time, but in the bad markets which we have been experiencing recently, the time arrived sooner than some expected. According to reports on LaSalle Street, the sponsors attempted to postpone the inevitable day by delaying delivery of stock, but last week pressure was brought to bear and finally, late in the week, delivery was begun of the stock. It was then only a matter of hours before sufficient stock came upon the market to make the burden of support too great for anyone to carry.[42]

It appeared that Philip Gossler of Columbia Gas and Christy Payne had orchestrated the raid. Payne, who was soon elected to the Columbia Gas & Electric board of directors, later denied under oath that he had raided Mo-Kan's stock. Mo-Kan was near bankruptcy, and Gossler offered to help Mo-Kan finance the Panhandle Eastern line. Gossler actually intended to gain complete control of this pipeline, which could transport natural gas to his utilities. Gossler followed through on his offer to help Parish when the Columbia Oil & Gasoline Corporation, a subsidiary of Columbia Gas & Electric, purchased 50 percent of Mo-Kan's stock interest in Panhandle Eastern for $9.8 million, and National City Bank of New York provided a $20 million loan.[43]

At this point, the Power Trust began to suffer serious internal dissension. Doherty read about Panhandle's new financial arrangement in the *New York Times*, and he immediately wrote Charles Mitchell, National City's president. He stated his opposition to the deal and attempted to persuade Mitchell not to provide any loans for the venture. Doherty expressed his "great shock" that National City would finance "the Parish natural gas line." National City understood, Doherty wrote, that the line was "an assault on existing utilities." Columbia, he maintained, had a "previous understanding" with Cities Service regarding the threat created by the Panhandle line, but Gossler had gone forward "on grounds of fear that Parish would raid their territory."[44]

Mitchell responded that National City was simply "working out as constructive a solution as possible of a disturbed situation, rendered so by others before it was brought to us for consideration."[45] Doherty replied: "I am still compelled to emphatically object to the part your company has played in this matter and the way your company has played its part." The new line, Doherty complained, would greatly interfere with Cities Service markets in Kansas. "I think your young men have made a bad mistake," he warned. "I have tried to be temperate in this matter. . . . There are endless possibilities for trouble."[46]

Nevertheless, the project moved forward, and Gossler sought to acquire Mo-Kan's remaining 50 percent interest in the line. Maguire had other plans and did not want Gossler to gain complete control. Charles Meyer, treasurer of National Supply and a director of Mo-Kan, introduced Maguire to J. H. Hillman Jr., who presided over the Hillman Coal and Coke Company of Pittsburgh.[47] Hillman eventually agreed to finance Mo-Kan's obligations for Panhandle Eastern. For a second time, Gossler had been prevented from acquiring outright ownership of the line. "We can only construe this as an act of aggression," Gossler explained to Hillman, "on the part of your associates against the best interests of Columbia, which, if pursued, we should have to resist to the full extent of our resources and ingenuity."[48] Gossler was unable to block the deal with Hillman, who was a substantial industrialist himself.

Construction resumed on the remainder of the line, and the *New York Times* reported its completion on August 21, 1931: "Pipes link the East with gas in Texas."[49] After a brief period of testing, the 930-mile Panhandle Eastern system began delivering gas to customers in Kansas and Illinois. The initial capacity was only 175 MMcf/d, powered by three compressor stations with a total of 14,000 horsepower. During the early 1930s, the firm continued to extend the system slowly, consolidating markets in Kansas, Missouri, and Illinois. The main line, however, terminated in a cornfield 75 feet across the Indiana-Illinois border near Dana, Indiana.

Parish knew that Gossler wanted complete control of Panhandle Eastern, but he wasn't aware of the depth of Doherty's opposition to the entire project. During August 1930, six weeks after the debilitating stock raid on Mo-Kan, Doherty's associates planted a spy, Elsie V. Walker, at the Frank Parish & Company. For $200 a month and assistance in paying off a debt to Cities Service, she agreed to gain employment at the firm. Let go during a company-wide layoff at the end of September, Walker was rehired by Mo-Kan in December 1930. She remained at that job through May 1932, earning an additional $110 a month as a secretary.

She passed information to Thomas Shannon, an internal investigator at Doherty's Cities Service, who had told Walker that he was only

Ditching machine and workers preparing trench for Panhandle Eastern line, 1929.

Courtesy, Duke Energy.

interested in learning about wrongdoing at the Parish brokerage firm and at Mo-Kan. Walker passed important financial and operational information to Shannon. By early 1932, Mo-Kan was headed toward bankruptcy, and Shannon abruptly terminated the espionage. He explained to Walker that Parish was headed for the penitentiary. In May

Inspecting a pipeline rupture, 1929.

Courtesy, Duke Energy.

1932, Walker signed a document releasing Cities Service Company, its subsidiaries, Henry L. Doherty, Henry L. Doherty & Company, and Gas Service Company, from all obligations and claims to her in exchange for a final $500 payment.[50]

In the meantime, Columbia Gas had effectively strangled Mo-Kan financially.[51] Parish petitioned for the receivership of Mo-Kan on March 6, 1932, a maneuver that delayed Columbia's attempt to gain complete control over his pipeline firm.[52] On March 24, 1932, a federal grand jury in Chicago indicted Parish and several associates on 49 counts; the most serious charges related to mail fraud.[53]

Prior to the trial, Parish followed the example set by Samuel Insull several months earlier and fled the country to avoid trial.[54] Parish returned voluntarily in late 1933, and his trial commenced. Horace A. Hagen, special assistant U.S. attorney general, contended that Parish, the "boy wizard of finance," had engaged in "one of the greatest exploitations in American financial records." The company's history was " 'full of fraud'—a 'bubble' which burst with a loss of $35,000,000 to investors."[55] During the testimony, Parish told how Cities Service used various illegal tactics, including stock manipulation and espionage, to damage Mo-Kan. Parish's attorneys charged that Doherty "raided" Mo-

Kan stock, forcing the firm to seek an unfavorable alliance with Columbia Gas and resulting eventually in the 1932 receivership. The jury apparently agreed that Parish and his companies were victims of corrupt competition rather than their own financial manipulation gone awry. The jury found Frank Parish not guilty on April 30, 1935.[56]

Parish avoided federal prison, but he lost complete control of Panhandle Eastern. During Parish's troubles, however, Maguire increased his Mo-Kan stock holdings. With the help of a variety of court decisions in Mo-Kan's favor and against Columbia, Maguire soon wrested control of Panhandle, which during the 1930s built an affiliate, Michigan Gas Transmission, in order to sell gas to Detroit's gas distributor.

Basic market forces caused the dramatic expansion of the 1920s interstate utility industry. The industry's monopolistic nature, however, meant that competition, which normally resulted in the lowest possible prices and efficient service, was not operative. While market forces clearly supported creation of the Panhandle line, the monopolistic practices of an intransigent combine sought to crush the new project. It seemed clear to many Americans that market forces alone could not provide an efficient, productive American economy. In fact, energy demand stimulated development of the technology necessary to produce, transport, distribute, and utilize natural gas, but it seemed that only the financially powerful utility captains, like feudal barons, had the strength to finance and build the gas industry's infrastructure. Maverick entrepreneurs might well instigate a project, but the cartel most likely wouldn't permit them to finish it, much less control it.

The public utility industry, a loosely organized cartel of the largest holding companies, became a highly visible symbol of American big business in the 1920s and 1930s. The Power Trust represented some of the least appealing aspects of the American economy and thereby helped launch a determined search for political solutions to these problems. Indeed, the utility cartel of the 1920s and 1930s, reminiscent of the railroads of the 1870s and 1880s, evoked strong calls for federal initiatives to reign in the public utility industry, which by name was meant to serve the public.

7

Dividing and Conquering the Power Trust

THE GREAT DEPRESSION halted the dramatic expansion of the 1920s natural gas industry. Many utilities lost customers during these years, and few firms sponsored new projects. Other than the three long-distance interstate pipelines constructed from the Southwestern gas fields to Midwestern markets in the late 1920s and early 1930s, no new long-distance lines were built until the United States entered World War II. Between 1932 and 1936, only three major pipelines were constructed, none of which were longer than 300 miles. The financial stagnation of the 1930s prevented new long-distance pipeline construction and industry growth.[1]

During the depression, many pipelines operated at below 50 percent capacity. Some companies had built shorter lines during the booming 1920s and 1930s before securing gas markets, and others suffered from diminished gas demand. Political scientist Elizabeth Sanders noted that during the depression the natural gas industry was in chaos: "In the East, it was marked by monopoly, shortage, and increasing prices. In the Southwest, there was an enormous oversupply," a great deal of which was allowed to dissipate into the atmosphere.[2]

In the Midwest of the early 1930s, Chicago was receiving natural gas, as were Omaha and Minneapolis/St. Paul. But many other Midwestern cities, including Indianapolis and Detroit, were forced to rely on manufactured gas. On the West Coast, Pacific Gas & Electric had built a line in 1929 from southern California to San Francisco and began distributing natural gas to residents of both San Francisco and Oakland. But this left large supply areas in Texas, Oklahoma, Kansas, and Louisiana with enormous amounts of the fuel unconnected to markets. Northeastern gas markets remained almost entirely dependent upon manufactured gas for heating and cooking. Meanwhile, Texas oil drillers, concerned only about "black gold," continued to vent trillions of cubic feet of unmarketable "waste gas" into the atmosphere (see table 7.1).

The lack of a natural gas conservation program was mirrored by the seemingly out-of-control accounting and financial practices of the huge power companies. The holding company system provided a corporate structure in which the holding company could own up to several hun-

TABLE 7.1 Estimated Waste of Natural Gas in the United States (Bcf)

Year	Total U.S. NG Waste	Panhandle Texas NG Waste	Total U.S. NG Consumption
1919	213	n/a	256
1920	238	n/a	286
1921	193	n/a	248
1922	233	n/a	254
1923	416	n/a	277
1924	343	n/a	285
1925	324	n/a	272
1926	417	220	289
1927	444	405	296
1928	412	351	321
1929	589	294	360
1930	553	252	376

Source: Federal Trade Commission, Report to the Senate on Public Utility Corporations, Senate Document no. 92, 70th Congress, 1st Session, part 84-A, 1935, p. 93 & 95.

Notes: Waste means gas production that was flared or vented and otherwise not utilized.

Bcf = billion cubic feet.

dred gas and electric firms. The subsidiaries were typically organized in a pyramid-like financial structure. Through various forms of stock manipulation, the top holding company could control a vast empire of utility companies while simultaneously raising a substantial amount of money from essentially worthless stock issues based on the overvaluation of its subsidiaries' assets.

During good economic times, big business in America was a symbol of national strength and superiority, but in bad times big business seemed to represent greed and corruption.[3] The problems associated with the monopolistic practices of the utility combines were real, but the overall state of the economy exposed weaknesses in those holding company systems that might have otherwise been ignored. Natural gas consumption declined precipitously during the depression years, and the drop was correlated to declining personal income. Utilities redoubled their marketing efforts and sponsored gas cooking and appliance demonstrations. For example, the Rochester Gas & Electric Company conducted a personal interview survey of 1,000 customers to learn how to better serve its customers.[4]

The manufactured gas segment of the industry fared less well weathering the depression years. While this business activity still represented a massive investment in assets, utilities distributing manufactured gas knew from the experience of Peoples Gas in Chicago that conversion to natural gas was desirable if not inevitable. Natural gas, with its higher heating content, would produce greater profits for the company that distributed it. While there were few large-scale conversions from manufactured gas to natural gas during the depression years, utility managers were simply waiting for better economic conditions and the construction of new pipelines to bring them the natural fuel.

During the depression the gas industry also suffered its worst tragedy in the twentieth century. In New London, Texas, on March 18, 1937, at 3:05 P.M., a tremendous explosion virtually destroyed the Consolidated High School, 15 minutes before the end of the school day. Initial estimates of 500 dead were later revised to 294 actual deaths. Texas governor Allred appointed a military court of inquiry, which determined that an accumulation of odorless gas in the school's basement, possibly ignited by the spark of an electric light switch, created the explosion. Only recently, the school had changed its gas supply from United Gas Company to the Parade Oil Company. During the inquiry, a United Gas official stated that his company had mixed an odorant in the gas, but the school had switched to the unmarketed natural gas by-product from oil production only a few months earlier. This terrible tragedy was marked in irony. On top of the wreckage, a broken blackboard contained these words apparently written before the explosion:

Oil and natural gas are East Texas' greatest mineral blessings. Without them this school would not be here, and none of us would be here learning our lessons.[5]

The New London explosion prompted calls for standardized use of odorants in gas delivered to all end users. The gas industry of the 1920s and early 1930s was characterized by monopolization and rapid expansion. The collapse of the Insull empire, general economic stagnation, and even tragedies such as the New London explosion necessitated standardization and systematization of the industry for the social benefit. The control over millions of people's lighting, heating, and cooking needs by a small number of utility company entrepreneurs, who were in business to make a profit, seemed incongruous to some of the nation's politicians. If gas and electric power were truly "public utilities," then private individuals seeking personal financial rewards from these businesses would have to endure public scrutiny.

Federal Trade Commission Investigation

The underlying problems effecting the entire utility industry evoked strong congressional response even before the 1929 stock market crash. Well publicized struggles such as those involving Panhandle Eastern confirmed politicians' fears that a Power Trust in fact monopolized the public utility industry. Several senators, including George Norris of Nebraska and Thomas Walsh of Montana, had assisted in launching an intense campaign in favor of government-owned power facilities.[6] These senators and their supporters prompted the Federal Trade Commission (FTC) to launch an investigation of the operations of General Electric and its subsidiary, the Electric Bond & Share Company, which in 1924 produced about 11 percent of the nation's electric power generation. GE had divested its interest in Electric Bond & Share by the time the FTC completed its report in 1927, but the commission noted with concern the increasing power of Samuel Insull and other public utility chiefs. Norris and Walsh pushed for a much more vigorous investigation.[7]

Although the senators desired an investigation conducted by a Senate committee, the Senate apparently bowing to lobbying pressure from utility interests mandated the FTC to conduct another study.[8] On February 15, 1928, the Senate mandated the FTC to investigate and report on the condition of existing public utility holding companies.[9] The result was what historian Ellis Hawley characterized as "one of the most widely publicized and extensive investigations of all time."[10] The

FTC, which was later joined by the House Commerce Committee, produced a massive 96-volume report published in 1935. These volumes introduced readers to the "jungles of holding company accounting, [and] some of the weirdest and most disastrous financing the nation had ever known."[11] The FTC report assailed the common practice among public utility holding companies of pyramiding. Historian Ellis Hawley explained that pyramiding enabled "a minimum investment to control a maximum of operating facilities, and the result was a variety of abuses."[12] (See table 7.2.) In addition, utility companies inflated the book value of their assets to secure a larger rate base and mounted political and public relations campaigns that increased their influence over local government, schools, churches, and the media.[13]

The federal government's first major investigation of the natural gas industry identified 16 "evils," including the following four: (1) waste, (2) unregulated pipelines, (3) unregulated and monopolistic control of gas production, and (4) reckless financial manipulation.[14] The FTC report also revealed that Columbia Gas, Standard Oil (New Jersey), Cities Service, and Electric Bond & Share controlled directly and indirectly more than 60 percent of all natural gas produced in 1934 and 58 percent of the total pipeline mileage in the United States.[15] By 1934, nearly 40 percent of all natural gas crossed state lines, and the fuel was being used in 34 states by 7 million industrial, commercial, and residential customers. The FTC said these consumers needed an "adequate, dependable, and safe service at reasonable prices."[16]

TABLE 7.2 Largest Utility Holding Companies, 1927–1932

Holding Company	Number of Subsidiaries	Number of Corp. Levels
Associated Gas & Electric	205	10
Cities Service Co.	194	6
Columbia Gas & Electric	73	3
Middle West Utilities	262	6
National Power & Light*	127	7
North American Co.	91	4
Standard Gas & Electric	136	6

Source: House Committee on Interstate and Foreign Commerce, *Public Utility Holding Companies,* 74th Cong., 1st sess., 1935, pt. 1:355.
*Part of the Electric Bond and Share group.

The FTC investigation explained that the ability of individual state governments to regulate natural gas was "at best indirect, partial, and poorly founded because of their limited authority to ascertain facts and their lack of authority to regulate interstate commerce."[17] The report outlined the cartel's operations, noting the traditional "system of so-called 'ethics' which hold that it is unfair and unethical for a pipeline to invade any territory already being served or claimed by another line. Such invasions are classed by the industry as 'raids' and the fear of retaliation by powerful interests is usually sufficient to preclude them."[18] The Panhandle Eastern case served as a prime example of these practices.

The FTC proposed greater government oversight of the natural gas industry:

> A federal regulatory law should be enacted applicable to interstate natural gas pipe lines which transport gas for ultimate sale to and use by the public, regulating contracts for purchase of gas to be transported interstate, or regulating rates for carriage or city gate rates at the end of such transportation, or all of these.[19]

The commission made additional recommendations on the need for (1) conservation and the elimination of gas wastage; (2) federal authority to order reasonable extensions of service; (3) separation of the electric utility and natural gas businesses; and (4) a law to restrict banks from investing in, rather than managing, natural gas firms.[20] The massive amount of evidence collected in the FTC report, the antibusiness sentiment of the depression years, and the problems of the utility industries made it inevitable that a more formidable regulatory system would be created. This was especially true by the middle of the decade, after the National Recovery Administration (NRA) experiment with government-sponsored cartels collapsed.

The Cities Alliance, a group representing approximately 100 Midwestern city governments, joined the drive to impose federal regulation on the gas industry. Organized in the mid-1930s, this organization promoted federal natural gas industry regulation as a means to ensure an adequate gas supply to the nation's cities. In a booklet published in 1937 titled *The Natural Gas Monopoly*, the Alliance focused on the abuses that had occurred and were occurring in the Panhandle Eastern situation in regard to the gas cartel's manipulation of that pipeline system and its markets.

Public Utility Holding Company Act

Franklin Roosevelt was a particularly strong proponent of public power and regulation of the utility industry. His support of the Tennessee Valley

Authority and attempts to develop other public power initiatives are well documented. FDR's administration also supported congressional initiatives to impose new regulations on a number of industries, including banking, securities, airlines, trucking, and utilities.[21] During the 1932 presidential campaign, FDR attacked Samuel Insull by name as well as the "evil" powers of the electrical power industry. Previously, as governor of New York, Roosevelt had waged a campaign for cheap electric power.[22]

While utility stocks had initially weathered the stock market crash, a combination of factors, including the banking panic of 1931, led to a massive decline in the value of Insull's utility company shares. Auditors subsequently discovered numerous accounting techniques used by Insull's companies to disguise unsound financial practices. To many Americans already suspicious of big business Insull was a symbol of the evil inherent in the huge public utility empires.[23] As a result of these and other related abuses, FDR in his 1935 State of the Union address called for the abolition of utility holding companies. Congressman Sam Rayburn of Texas and Burton K. Wheeler of Montana led the legislative attack against the multitiered utilities.[24]

Congress soon enacted five major pieces of legislation that had a direct bearing on utilities. These included the Public Utility Holding Company Act of 1935 (PUHCA), the Federal Power Act of 1935 (FPA), the Natural Gas Act of 1938 (NGA), the Securities Act (1933), and the Securities Exchange Act (1934), which charged the Securities and Exchange Commission (SEC) with regulating the securities industry.[25]

Congressional deliberations on the Public Utility Holding Company Act were described as "the greatest congressional battle in history."[26] Rayburn introduced the PUHCA, which contained provisions for federal regulation of utility holding companies, electric power, and natural gas. Public utilities objected vociferously to the bill in telegrams, telephone calls, and threats of lawsuits on the legislators. Rayburn persisted, although the Natural Gas legislation was delayed for several years.[27]

After Roosevelt signed the PUHCA, Rayburn said, "That ended the hardest battle I have seen in my more than twenty years in Congress. It was a battle against the biggest and boldest, the richest and the most ruthless lobby Congress has every known."[28] The PUHCA mandated abolition of the massive pyramid-structured public utility holding companies, and Rayburn stated that PUHCA filled "a gap in the existing regulatory laws caused by the fact that for all practical as well as legal reasons the states have been unable to regulate the great holding companies which control local operating companies."[29] It restricted utility company organizations to single, locally managed, integrated systems; it also required utilities to separate their natural gas and their electric operations. The PUHCA also authorized the Securities & Exchange Commission to oversee utility holding company restructuring and divestitures.

At first, most utility holding companies did not register with the SEC as they waited for the outcome of legal challenges. Electric Bond and Share Company (EBASCO) had challenged the act, and this firm prepared a detailed report justifying the existence and operation of utility holding companies. The report was "widely read and used by a variety of large corporations outside of the power industry, which feared that future federal laws of similar intent might be aimed their way."[30] The U.S. Supreme Court ruled against EBASCO in March 1938 and upheld the act's registration requirements; holding companies then started to register. In August 1938, the SEC began requesting the holding companies' plans for corporate simplification as required under the act. Hearings for corporate simplification did not begin until 1940, and historian Ellis Hawley noted that "even after the latter date, the SEC proceeded slowly, usually on the basis of voluntary reorganization plans."[31] Cash-rich life insurance companies found gas pipelines in the post–New Deal years to be good investments. The newly independent and rapidly growing pipelines proved attractive to insurance companies interested in new investment opportunities.[32]

The Natural Gas Act

Although Congress did pass both the PUHCA and the FPA in 1935, Rayburn separated the natural gas portion of the original bill. Three years later, Congress passed the Natural Gas Act.[33] This act was based on the language used to draft the FPA; Rayburn had given a copy of the FPA to a House legislative draftsman to revise it so that it would be appropriate for natural gas applicable only to the interstate operation of the gas industry. The original natural gas legislation was redrafted and submitted to Congress in 1936. This gas bill originally failed congressional passage due to lack of interest, and it was subsequently submitted a third time. Senator Wheeler pushed for passage and stated in Congress that "the purpose of the bill is to help the state commissions and the people of the country find out what is the cost of transporting natural gas to the large cities."[34] After the addition of several amendments, it finally passed without dissent. Roosevelt signed it into law on June 21, 1938.[35]

There were numerous significant changes in drafts of the proposed gas bill between 1935 and 1937, which led to wider support for gas pipeline regulation. Gas firms objected adamantly to provisions in the original bill that required gas pipelines to apply for a certificate of public convenience and necessity to transport gas from a gas field. Instead, gas interests argued that certificates should be required for entering a new market, particularly one already served by a gas pipeline. If there were going to be new regulations, pipeline interests argued, then they should protect a pipeline from market invasion by another line. In addition, gas firms wanted direct sales to industrial firms exempted from interstate regulation.[36]

Another contentious issue regarded common-carrier status. Sam Rayburn spoke out against imposing common-carrier status on interstate gas lines, as did Clyde Reed, former governor of Kansas. Reed testified at the Hearings before the Committee on Interstate and Foreign Commerce, that "so far as my experience and knowledge goes a pipe line is built as an adjunct to distributing companies and for the sole purpose of supplying distributing companies a constant flow of gas."[37] Following this logic, Reed implied that pipelines should not be separated at the corporate level from distribution companies; he believed they should be affiliated.[38] Reed went on to say that common-carrier status would destroy "the assured efficiency of service" offered by affiliated merchant pipelines and distribution firms.[39]

According to energy historian John Clark, "of all the advocates of the Natural Gas Act of 1938," the coal industry "insisted upon the most rigid regulatory formula."[40] The coal industry supported regulation as a means to raise the price of natural gas and lessen its competitive effects. Since World War I, coal consumption had steadily declined due in large part to the increasing demand for natural gas. At the congressional hearings on natural gas held during 1936, John Battle, president of the National Association of Bituminous Coal Organizations, testified that "natural gas has displaced millions of tons of bituminous coal throughout the nation. . . . It is our opinion that natural gas is being sold for industrial purposes at prices that are unreasonably low. . . . We feel that the competition is unfair." Gas industry representatives suggested that coal and railroad interests along with their political supporters, which included the state of Pennsylvania, often refused to grant gas pipelines right-of-way into "coal territory."[41]

Congress empowered the Federal Power Commission (FPC) to regulate the gas industry. The FPC's new role seemed to be a natural fit. Congress originally created the Federal Power Commission under authority of the Water Power Act of 1920 to regulate the burgeoning water and hydroelectric power industries. In 1930, the FPC became an independent body with five full-time commissioners. The Federal Power Act had authorized the FPC to regulate the interstate electric power business, and the Natural Gas Act empowered the FPC to order natural gas companies to approve and/or set "just and reasonable rates," extend and abandon service, improve facilities, keep extensive documentation of operations and finances, ascertain costs for rate making, suspend rates, and otherwise dictate the operations of any interstate gas company.[42]

The FPC now had extensive power over interstate natural gas pipelines, as well as the interstate electric power business. In administering these powers, the FPC was required to conduct hearings on a case-by-case basis, using evidence to decide to grant, or not to grant, a certificate of public convenience and necessity. A natural gas company had to have this certificate before it could engage in interstate commerce. With the certificate, a pipeline company held a federally sanctioned franchise over a particular service area. The federal government had in effect replaced a market managed by cartels with a political cartel managed by regulators.

Federal certification, it was hoped, would solve numerous problems that had plagued the industry. To obtain a certificate a pipeline had to have under contract an adequate supply of natural gas (usually for 20 years). This provision reflected historical knowledge of the several Midwestern pipelines that quickly depleted gas fields and were subsequently abandoned. The line also had to have sound and proven financing and was allowed to charge only "just and reasonable" rates. In essence, the certificate became independent confirmation that the pipeline had excellent prospects, and a certificated pipeline firm was a relatively safe investment for banks and life insurance companies.[43]

Under FPC guidelines, pipelines set gas sales prices that reflected the line's operating costs and "rate base," or depreciated assets used in the transmission of gas, plus a 5.7 to 6.5 percent "rate of return" on gas sales.[44] The seemingly stable profit evoked the term "cash cow," which was applied to pipeline companies operating during times of abundant supply and demand. The FPC's powers also included dictating a pipeline's specific customers and gas sales allocation. The act did not grant eminent domain powers to natural gas pipelines because the railroad industry, which depended upon coal transportation for about one-fifth of its total revenues, generally opposed attempts by gas companies to lay lines underneath their tracks. Lack of significant right-of-way posed a problem to many pipeline companies attempting to extend service and would later present a major obstacle to the expansion of natural gas pipelines and their fuel into the Northeast.[45]

One feature of the certification process that caused significant problems for the FPC was Section 7 (c), which stated that

> No natural-gas company shall undertake the construction or extension of any facilities for the transportation of natural gas to a market in which nat-

ural gas is already being served by another natural-gas company . . . unless and until there shall first have been obtained from the Commission a certificate.[46]

This language, according to Congressman Clarence Lea of California, a strident supporter of the gas bill, meant that "before you can have competition in the same territory, a permit must be secured from the [FPC]."[47] It soon became clear, however, that the FPC was uncertain of its authority and jurisdiction to certify pipelines to serve areas in which natural gas was not already available.

The FPC's five commissioners responsible for regulating interstate natural gas commerce were Claude L. Draper, formerly of the ICC bar and staff of the National Association of Railroad and Utilities Commissioners; Basil Manley, past U.S. Senate staffer and official of the New York Power Authority; Clyde L. Seavey of the California Railroad Commission; and John W. Scott, a former U.S. Assistant Attorney General. Leland Olds, a New Deal utility economist with experience on Presidential Commissions and at the New York State Power Authority, was appointed in 1939 to fill a vacant seat. Once an inconsequential agency, the FPC now had the important responsibility of regulating the nation's interstate gas and electric business.

The FPC's most immediate task was asserting its authority over the industry. Chairman Clyde L. Seavey told his audience at an American Gas Association meeting that they should comply with FPC jurisdiction. Seavey reminded the company representatives that the FPC had recently mailed questionnaires to all persons and companies engaged in the gas business to determine which ones were subject to FPC jurisdiction. Many of the largest companies complied by the deadline, but numerous others did not. Seavey also stated that many companies now required to file rate schedules with the FPC had not yet done so, and he urged full cooperation with the FPC by the natural gas industry. In his closing remarks, he stated, "if the industry will fulfill its obligations under the Act in the same spirit, immeasurable benefits from the enactment of the Natural Gas Act will follow for the public and industry."[48] Clearly, Seavey presented the newborn FPC as an agency with the best interests of the natural gas industry at heart.

By the late 1930s, the structure of this industry was far different than it had been only 10 years before. Several long-distance pipelines traversed the Midwestern states, abundant volumes of Southwestern natural gas awaited a market, and federal regulators forecasted a cooperative future with industry. But the industry itself was in the process of being restructured by federal mandate, delayed only by futile legal challenges. Historian Richard Vietor noted that "the Securities and

Exchange Commission did not begin arranging divestitures of holding companies in any serious way until 1940. Company registrations, information gathering, and legal challenges accounted for much of the delay."[49] Ultimately, however, the SEC investigated 929 gas and electric firms (1940–1954) leading to the divestiture of 158 of the former (valued at $874 million) and 259 of the latter (worth $9 billion).[50]

One of the gas industry's largest players, Standard Oil (New Jersey), practically exited the natural gas business as a result of the PUHCA and NGA. The SEC ruled on February 5, 1942, that Standard had to divest its stock in its valuable natural gas properties. Standard's application for an exemption from PUHCA rules was denied. Standard created a new holding company, Consolidated Natural Gas Company, and then transferred to it the stock of the East Ohio, Hope, River Gas, Peoples Natural Gas, and New York State gas companies. All of this stock was then distributed to Standard's shareholders.

Standard was also sufficiently concerned about Department of Justice investigations into its gas pipeline holdings that it decided to exit the interstate gas pipeline business as well. The threat of federal legal action combined with the relatively low 6 percent return on gas pipeline operations caused Standard executives to decide to sell all its gas pipeline interests acquired during the 1920s. Beginning in late 1947, Standard began selling its stock interest in NGPL and Colorado Interstate. In 1948, it sold its interest in Mississippi River Fuel Company; it retained its majority interest in Interstate Natural Gas Company until 1953.[51]

As the old power trust disappeared, industry observers speculated about the largest potential natural gas market still untapped. When would natural gas be made available in Philadelphia and New York? *Fortune* magazine, which devoted its August 1940 cover story to the natural gas industry, noted that "as for markets, not only is the richest one in the country, the Atlantic seaboard from Philadelphia north, still virgin (as in the state of Wisconsin), but natural gas does not begin to envelop the territory it serves or through which it passes."[52] While the article noted that the undeveloped market areas promised future growth for the industry, "a portentous group of natural gas enemies" was likely to oppose the expansion of the industry.[53] These enemies included wastefulness, the coal industry, the railroads that transported coal, and the manufactured gas industry.

Contemporary estimates indicated that Northeastern markets could boost total U.S. natural gas sales by 25 percent, but no significant pipelines had been built into those areas. Columbia Gas & Electric owned a small line extending into Paterson, New Jersey, and Tappan,

New York, as well as into the Philadelphia area. It also owned the 20-inch Atlantic Seaboard pipeline, which extended from Kentucky and West Virginia into Virginia, Maryland, and on to a single customer at Coatesville, Pennsylvania, west of Philadelphia, and to Washington, D.C. But the Atlantic Seaboard line was not used to capacity. Natural gas interests accused coal and railroad companies of plotting to keep natural gas out of the Philadelphia area by suggesting that Appalachian area gas reserves were not sufficient to supply the region with natural gas.[54]

World War II ultimately overwhelmed domestic politics. The exigencies of war required much closer government scrutiny of industry and imposed a new set of rules on American business. Perhaps the forced wartime cooperation—through the effects of either patriotism or strict government control—lessened the impact of the new utility regulations placed on the industry. As the gas industry moved to support the war effort, many within it recognized a special opportunity to expand operations under emergency war conditions and then to be well positioned for continued growth and expansion after the war.

PART 4

The Regulated Gas Industry, 1938–1985

8

The Gas Industry in War

WORLD WAR II energy demands reinvigorated the U.S. gas industry as war emergency agencies sought to increase both gas production and deliverability. Unlike the pattern of industry growth during the 1920s, when entrepreneurs built gas pipelines connecting midcontinent production with Midwestern urban markets, the war initially facilitated construction of long-distance pipelines extending from Gulf Coast gas fields to deliver fuel to the Northeastern war industry. The federal government financed pipeline systems as well as war production plants while strictly managing the nation's energy supply.

During these years, industrial plants required record quantities of natural gas and its by-products for the manufacture of steel, aluminum, high-octane gasoline, synthetic rubber, chemicals, and explosives, and for industrial and domestic heat as well as power generation. Residential gas demand increased as well for heating the many newly constructed homes built to house the growing military and domestic war-related labor force. In response to wartime demand, natural gas production increased by 55 percent. By the end of the war, strong Northeastern gas demand stimulated the construction of additional gas pipelines to bring the fuel from the Southwest to urban and industrial markets.[1]

Appalachian Gas Supply and Federal War Planning

The Appalachian region was the center of American war production. The Pittsburgh, Youngstown, and Wheeling areas contained hundreds of steel mills and metallurgical factories, as well as rubber and chemical plants that required large volumes of natural gas.[2] Natural gas was a particularly important fuel because it burned at a constant specific temperature, providing high-quality product manufacture. Approximately 660 Appalachian area factories required an average of 24 Bcf of natural gas per year. As a region, Appalachia required 400 Bcf per year of gas, about half of which was accounted for by industrial consumption.[3] Wartime energy demands put further pressure on Appalachian gas reserves. Appalachian natural gas production had peaked in 1917 at 552 Bcf, or about 63 percent of total U.S. gas production; this percentage declined to approximately 16 percent by the late 1930s. The decline resulted from diminishing Appalachian gas reserves as well as a proportionate increase in gas produced in the Southwest. By 1943, Appalachian production became insufficient for meeting regional industrial, commercial, and residential demand.[4] (See table 8.1.)

The intense drain on Appalachian reserves stimulated private entrepreneurial efforts to increase production and build new pipelines. Industry executives were well aware that the wartime expansion was not a temporary development, as speeches at the American Gas Association's annual meetings made clear. At one meeting held during 1942, J. French Robinson, a prominent gas utility executive stated, "In the post-war sunshine of abundant materials for our use, we will be able to realize the potential values of natural gas to all this nation as never before."[5] Patriotic fervor aside, the business of war stimulated both industrial production and entrepreneurial ambition.

To direct the federal government's wartime energy policy, Roosevelt chose Harold I. Ickes, who was then secretary of the interior. On May 28, 1941, Ickes assumed his new position as the first Petroleum Coordinator for National Defense; this agency was later renamed the Petroleum Administration for War (PAW). In this role, the new "oil czar" exercised special emergency powers over much of both the oil and gas industries.[6] Despite initial industry fears, Ickes implemented a cooperative relationship with the energy industry during wartime.

For good reason, the PAW was more concerned about oil than natural gas. During the war, recalled J. R. Parten, director of transportation for the PAW, "natural gas didn't stand very high, didn't take much of Ickes' time . . . natural gas was not a hot spot. Production of crude oil

TABLE 8.1 Natural Gas Production by Region, 1912–1970

Year	Appalachia (%)	Southwest (%)	Other (%)	Total Marketed Production (Tcf)
1912	74	22	2	0.56
1920	55	34	11	0.80
1922	46	37	17	0.76
1924	31	45	24	1.14
1926	26	50	24	1.31
1928	21	57	22	1.57
1930	17	61	22	1.94
1935	16	65	19	1.92
1940	15	68	17	2.66
1945	10	73	17	3.91
1950	6	80	14	6.28
1960	3	87	10	12.80
1970	2	90	8	21.90

Source: U.S. Bureau of Mines, *Natural Gas Annuals* & *Minerals Yearbook*, (Washington, D.C.: GPO), various years, and Energy Information Administration, "Natural Gas Production and Consumption," *Energy Data Reports* DOE/EIA-0131, (Washington, D.C., GPO: 1978). Also see David Gilmer, "The History of Natural Gas Pipelines in the Southwest," *Texas Business Review* (May–June 1981):133.

was."[7] While natural gas was not a top priority, its value quickly became evident to government officials.

On December 4, 1941, only three days before Pearl Harbor, the PAW met to discuss natural gas supply and demand in Appalachia. Representatives from the War Department, Navy Department, and FPC, among others, attended. Less than a few months earlier, the Office of Production Management (later renamed the War Production Board) began receiving a slew of letters from Pittsburgh area industrial firms requesting natural gas supply. In one letter, the Aluminum Company of America (ALCOA) stated that it desperately needed natural gas. "You understand," the company official wrote, "we are engaged in the production of defense work 100 percent and it is very essential that we are furnished gas to carry on our production."[8] At this meeting, there was also discussion of the need for access to new natural gas supply that could be provided by a new pipeline.[9]

The PAW created a Natural Gas and Natural Gasoline Division to be responsible for the gas industry. E. Holley Poe, a former executive of the American Gas Association, headed the division. His charge was maintaining natural gas production and deliverability, particularly in the Appalachian region. Poe also attempted to marshal support for joint-industry cooperation while administering the wartime industry. The PAW's authority over natural gas was relatively modest compared to that of the Supply Priorities and Allocation Board (SPAB). The SPAB, which later merged into the War Production Board (WPB), had much broader powers over industry. Regarding natural gas, the agency dictated specific gas sales allocation orders to gas pipelines.

During late 1941, representatives of the natural gas industry, military, PAW, WPB, and the American Gas Association met several times in different cities to discuss recommendations for restricting some classes of natural gas consumption and maintaining production levels during the war.[10] J. A. Krug, chief of the WPB Power Branch, was particularly concerned about potential shortages in Appalachia, southern California, and the midcontinent areas. He proposed a special limitation order for conserving natural gas. The order had two major goals: (1) to increase production and (2) to curtail nonessential consumption.[11] Major General H. K. Rutherford wrote a letter of support and noted the critical situation faced by war industries dependent upon natural gas.[12]

In early February 1942 the WPB issued Order L-31. This action called for voluntary compliance with pooling arrangements "to achieve practicable maximum output in the area or areas in which a shortage exists or is imminent."[13] The order authorized the WPB to integrate natural gas systems, curtail gas sales when necessary, and reallocate existing gas sales. The WPB actively encouraged pipelines to transport gas at a 100 percent load factor, to use gas storage fields whenever possible to free up pipeline capacity for gas transmission, and to develop curtailment schedules. Six months later, the WPB issued L-174, which imposed the same restrictions on the manufactured gas industry.[14]

The PAW and WPB also addressed the Appalachian gas production problem. First, the PAW set guidelines for a new drilling program, M-68, for developing a nationwide oil and gas drilling program "consistent with the availability of material and equipment."[15] This program limited drilling of gas wells to not more than 1 every 640 acres. Industry leaders objected to M-68, believing that it would stymie efforts to maintain current production levels. In response, the PAW issued new spacing provisions that permitted drilling one well on each 160 acres for specified deep horizons and one to each 40 acres for shallow wells.

The importance of Appalachian natural gas supply to the war effort was reflected in the disproportionate number of wells drilled there. Between 1942 and 1945, approximately 70 percent of all gas wells drilled in the country were drilled in Appalachia, even though overall production levels did not rise significantly. Wartime demand simply sped up the depletion of Appalachian gas fields. Government drilling and consumption regulations could not reverse this trend.

Gas Pipelines and Appalachian Markets

The wartime shortage reinforced the belief held by some gas men that the time was right to build a pipeline extending from the Southwest to Appalachia. The Reserve Gas Company, in which Standard Oil retained an interest, planned a line from the Southwest to New York in the early 1940s, but abandoned its efforts after meeting opposition from Northeastern manufactured gas interests. Curtis B. Dall led another group in a significant attempt to build such a line, and Dall's efforts are instructive of both the economic and political forces affecting the gas industry of the 1940s.

Dall was a former Wall Street broker with Lehman Brothers, and he was the ex-husband of Franklin Roosevelt's daughter, Anna.[16] Dall saw opportunity in the Appalachian gas situation. He and several others planned to build a gas pipeline to deliver gas to war industries. They formed the Tennessee Gas and Transmission Company on April 1, 1940.[17] Working out of his Manhattan office and the Willard Hotel in Washington, Curtis Dall actively promoted the pipeline plan, the estimated cost of which rose rapidly from $12 to $20 million.[18]

Apparently unaware that this project clearly qualified as an interstate pipeline under FPC jurisdiction, Tennessee Gas first approached the Tennessee Railroad and Public Utilities Commission (PUC) for a certificate of public convenience and necessity. In its application, Tennessee Gas proposed a 20-inch pipeline extending from Acadia Parish, Louisiana, where gathering lines would connect with four proposed southeastern Louisiana suppliers and ten gas fields, to a point near Brace, Tennessee. From there, two 12-inch extensions—one to Lebanon, Tennessee, and the other to Knoxville, Tennessee—would supply gas to numerous communities along the way. The new company feared that United Gas Corporation, the dominant gas distributor in the Louisiana area, might feel threatened by its plans. "We do not wish to get in a wrangle with United Gas on the southern portion of our line," reported one company official; Tennessee Gas did not target southern markets.[19] Substantial markets existed to the north.

Tennessee's directors soon learned that they needed a certificate from the FPC, not the state PUC. The company applied for an FPC certificate; despite rapidly increasing Appalachian demand for new sources of natural gas, Tennessee's initial application did not meet with FPC approval. "With all the demand for fuel, especially gas," one employee wrote to Dall, "I don't see how we can fail."[20] But this gas demand could not be met without a commitment for gas supply and financing, and Dall had trouble arranging both.

The FPC claimed that it did not have jurisdiction to grant a certificate to Tennessee Gas and dismissed the application in July 1941. The agency claimed that Section 7(c) of the Natural Gas Act prevented it from granting a certificate to Tennessee Gas. The commission ruled that its "jurisdiction to issue certificates . . . exists only when [a company proposes] to construct such facilities for the transportation of natural gas to a market in which natural gas is already being served by another natural gas company." Tennessee could not show that its potential market area constituted one already being served by another natural gas company precisely because the fuel had not previously been available there.[21]

Section 7(c), a poorly conceived part of the Natural Gas Act, was a legislative obstacle to natural gas industry expansion, even during the early phase of the war emergency. The provision actually protected the coal and manufactured gas industries by prohibiting the introduction of natural gas into "new markets." In 1941, Congress slightly modified the provision by allowing temporary war emergency expansions, but railroad and coal interests opposed any attempts by gas companies to use the emergency provision to expand service permanently.[22] Section 7(c) had to be modified before the FPC could certify pipelines to sell natural gas in areas not already served by natural gas.[23]

Demand for natural gas continued to grow, as an electricity shortage plagued some southern states due to the power demands of defense product manufacturers. The aluminum industry's demand for electrical power also benefited Tennessee's application to deliver gas to the region in which large aluminum plants at Alcoa, Tennessee, and Badin, North Carolina, were located.[24] Aluminum production increased dramatically after the outbreak of war in Europe in 1939. In 1939, United States aluminum production was 325 million pounds. The Office of Production Management (OPM) forecasted that U.S. wartime aluminum requirements would reach 1.4 billion pounds by 1942.

Dall realized that the wartime energy demand had created an opportunity for him to gain federal priority to build the line. To this end, he negotiated with the federal government to have his pipeline designated as a National Defense Project. Such a designation would facilitate WPB steel priorities. In the meantime, perhaps owing in part to Dall's intensive lobbying, Congress amended Section 7(c) of the Natural Gas Act. The amendment deleted the reference to markets already served with natural gas.[25] In fact, the FPC noted that the original 7(c) provision "proved unsatisfactory to all concerned."[26] Ironically, coal and railroad representatives led the fight for the amendatory legislation because they were particularly concerned about their ability to intervene in gas pipeline certificate hearings.[27] The new amendment did grant coal and railroad companies the right to intervene in all pipeline certificate applications, except in the case of limited expansions permitted within the line's existing market area. With this amendment, coal and railroad interests became the major primary intervenors in gas pipeline certificate hearings.[28]

The section 7(c) amendment provided Tennessee Gas a second chance to acquire a federal certificate. On February 9, only two days after the modification, the pipeline firm filed a second application with the FPC. Immediately after filing for the new certificate, Dall both met with and wrote to J. A. Krug, chief of the Power Branch of the WPB, to push for the requisite steel priorities. Krug responded to Dall: "As I told you . . . approval or disapproval of this project will depend upon the facts as to the increase in war production made possible from the increased availability of natural gas compared with the diversion of steel and other scarce materials required for construction of the pipeline."[29] During the interim, Dall took a leave of absence from Tennessee Gas without surrendering his financial interest and joined the Air Force, thereby removing himself from a direct role in the company's immediate plans although remaining in regular contact with company management.

After the amendment, other companies joined the fray and proposed new interstate pipeline projects. Before the amendment only 16 applications for certificates were pending under section 7(c), and the FPC approved only four of these. The remaining applications were dismissed by the FPC or withdrawn by the companies. After the amendment, natural gas companies submitted 140 applications under a "grandfather" clause of section 7(c); 100 were approved. The rush for applications under the grandfather clause related to the provision in the original section 7(c) allowing unauthorized expansion of systems within their market area. The 140 applicants included most of the interstate natural gas companies in existence. Furthermore, companies filed 319 certificate applications between February 7, 1942, and October 15, 1946. Of the 319 applications, the FPC granted certificates to 196 companies, accounting for 8,244 miles of pipeline and 449,695 compressor station horsepower.[30]

FPC chairman Leland Olds later discussed the natural gas situation after the amendment of 7(c). He stated that "as a result of the lifting of those limitations practically every natural gas company in the country of any proportion is coming into this commission and stating that the house heating load is growing so rapidly, the space heating load is growing so rapidly, and unless we handle certificate applications promptly, it is going to mean that people throughout these regions served with natural gas today are going to be unable to meet the requirements of heating in the coming winter season."[31] The FPC was so overloaded with certificate applications that it automatically allowed minor additions and expansions as long as the provision for the determination of service areas was followed.

Competition for Appalachian Markets

Early in 1942, the FPC staff conducted a survey of the Appalachian energy situation at the request of the War Production Board, which had authority to ensure that war production facilities had the necessary fuel to operate.[32] The resulting report described the increasing demand for natural gas in the Appalachian area and the ongoing curtailments of natural gas deliveries due to the lack of supply. The FPC report indicated that curtailments would continue. In response, the WPB requested that the FPC compel a pipeline company to connect the existing Panhandle Eastern Pipe Line system to the Ohio Fuel Gas Company, which served a part of the Appalachian region suffering from a gas shortage. The WPB finally agreed to provide the necessary steel allocation for the construction of a connecting pipeline as approved by the FPC. Ultimately, the FPC chose Panhandle Eastern to build and operate the connecting pipeline system.[33]

Tennessee Gas recognized now that success hinged on its ability to abide by the WPB's war fuel plans, and Dall continued to lobby for a national defense project designation. Buoyed by increasing private and governmental interest, Tennessee Gas amended its certificate application and proposed to deliver gas only to war industries.[34] The FPC conducted hearings on the Tennessee Gas application during the summer of 1943. Appalachian area distribution company executives presented data supporting the claim that their region was truly running out of gas reserves. The president of Hope Natural Gas Company, the large natural gas production subsidiary of Standard Oil Company (New Jersey), and the vice president and general manager of the Columbia Gas & Electric Corporation testified that by the conclusion of the war, neither company would be capable of meeting normal gas sales requirements. Thus, according to representatives of the two largest Appalachian gas distribution companies, which furnished 60 percent of the region's natural gas requirements, gas shortages would prevent them from meeting current and projected demand. The witnesses agreed that the shortages had begun before the war but were now being accentuated and accelerated by it. Their statements in theory supported Tennessee Gas's application to transport Southwestern gas to Appalachia.[35]

Hope Natural Gas's management, however, decided to build its own pipeline. Hope applied for a certificate to build a long-distance line extending from the Southwest to its Northeastern distribution system. Immediately, Hope became Tennessee Gas's most formidable competitor, rather than a supporting witness and potential customer.

The War Production Board was becoming increasingly anxious to raise the level of natural gas deliveries into Appalachia. The FPC made a correspondingly important statement confirming Appalachia's need for gas: the Appalachian region "embraces one of the most highly industrialized areas in the United States . . . [and] the use of natural gas, both for domestic and industrial purposes, has been substantial for many years."[36] The FPC estimated that during 1943 there would be a 15 Bcf shortage in the Appalachian region and peak day deficiency of 300 MMcf, figures that reflected a potentially serious shortage. "It is crystal clear," the FPC stated, "that additional natural gas is needed in the Appalachian region. It follows, therefore, that a realistic view of this situation definitely shows that the public convenience and necessity will be served by the construction and operation of the applicant's pipe line into the area if the additional showing hereinafter referred to is made."[37] Tennessee's application remained in peril because the company was unable to arrange either financing or gas supply. The FPC allowed Tennessee Gas 60 days to remedy these deficiencies.

Pressure on Tennessee Gas to resolve its difficulties increased when the WPB designated a project to bring Southwestern gas into Appalachia "as an essential part of the war program." The WPB agreed to issue the necessary steel priorities to whichever applicant received an FPC certificate authorizing construction and operation of the required line. The WPB stipulated that the pipeline be constructed and in operation for the winter of 1944–1945, and the agency required that the certified pipeline place all orders for pipe no later than October 1, 1943.

The FPC quickly had to chose either Tennessee Gas or its new competitor, Hope Natural Gas, to build the line. The primary difference between the two proposals was that the Hope line would receive its supply from the proven Hugoton field in north Texas and Kansas. As an established natural gas company in the Appalachian region with financial support from Standard Oil (New Jersey), Hope seemed to have a greater chance of gaining the FPC certificate. The FPC announced that it would begin hearings on the Hope pipeline plan on September 21.

In the meantime, Tennessee Gas's promoters learned that the Chicago Corporation, a Chicago-based investment trust, owned substantial natural gas on the Texas Gulf Coast near Corpus Christi. The two companies quickly negotiated a contract, and Tennessee agreed to extend its line southward to Corpus Christi. The Chicago Corporation had finally found a way to market its natural gas. For their part, the Northeastern utilities "didn't want to have their playhouse disturbed," recalled one of Tennessee Gas's founders, "and they had those artificial gas plants and they were making money and they had been making money for a hundred years and they didn't want anybody coming around there and changing their set-up and they wouldn't even talk about it for a long time."[38]

Tennessee Gas presented its new plan to the FPC. Once again the coal and railroad industries and their unions opposed the application. They agreed that "the use of natural gas for industrial and space-heating purposes constitutes a dissipation of the natural-gas resources, and threatens the coal industry with ruinous competition."[39] Although the commission recognized the ability of natural gas to compete favorably with coal, it stated that it did not have the authority to "regulate rates for natural gas sold directly to industrial consumers, which class of gas sales furnishes the keenest competition to the coal industry. Nor does our power to suspend rates extend to indirect sales of natural gas for industrial purposes."[40] The FPC would not referee interfuel competition.

In order to obtain the Chicago Corporation's Gulf Coast gas, Tennessee planned a 1,156-mile 24-inch line, instead of a 20-inch line, extending from the gas fields near Corpus Christi. The company signed a gas purchase contract with the Chicago Corporation. Soon, the Chicago Corporation turned the tables on Tennessee Gas and purchased the pipeline project in order to save it from bankruptcy. Dall and the other original directors resigned and were replaced. Tennessee Gas's new president was Gardiner Symonds, a new breed of pipeliner with a Harvard MBA.

With secure gas supply and financing, the FPC granted Tennessee Gas an oral certificate in September 1943, the day before the FPC had scheduled hearings on the Hope Company's competing plan; Hope's application was now defunct. Tennessee Gas's oral certificate became an official one on September 24.[41]

The Chicago Corporation now sought the assistance of Paul Kayser in financing the pipeline and acquiring additional gas supply. Kayser, a Houston attorney, was president of both El Paso Natural Gas Company and Gulf States Oil Company. In addition, Kayser was an attorney for fellow Houstonian Jesse Jones, who was chairman of the Reconstruction Finance Corporation (RFC). Kayser's association with Tennessee Gas aroused some suspicion after Jones agreed that the RFC would finance a large part of Tennessee Gas's construction costs, up to $44 million for 10 years at 4 percent per annum.[42] It is not certain exactly what role Paul Kayser might have had in the acquisition of the loan, but his influence was "credited with once saving that imperiled undertaking [Tennessee Gas] by persuading his old friend Jesse Jones to grant it an RFC loan in the New Deal days." Tennessee Gas purchased gas from Kayser's Gulf State's Oil Corporation.[43]

Tennessee Gas began delivering fuel through the pipeline on October 31, 1944.[44] By the end of 1945, its first full year of operation, Tennessee had delivered 73.5 Bcf of gas into Appalachia. Its customers, consisting of gas distribution companies, served a total of 750 Appalachian area communities. Approximately 95 percent of Tennessee's early gas sales, though, went to the two large Appalachian distribution systems: United Fuel Gas Company, a subsidiary of Columbia Gas & Electric Corporation, and its former competitor, the Hope Natural Gas Company, now a subsidiary of Consolidated Natural Gas Company. Tennessee became the first pipeline to transport Gulf Coast natural gas reserves to Appalachia.[45]

Tennessee Gas's success, however, caused problems for its parent company. During December 1944, the FPC instituted an investigation to determine whether the Chicago Corporation, through its ownership of 81 percent of Tennessee Gas stock, qualified as an interstate natural gas company as defined by the Natural Gas Act of 1938. If so, the FPC could investigate whether any rates, charges, or classifications relating to any of the Chicago Corporation's natural gas operations were also subject to FPC jurisdiction. Not wanting to risk an unfavorable FPC ruling that might entail federal regulation of all its natural gas operations, the Chicago Corporation began divesting its Tennessee Gas stock.[46] Stone and Webster, the lead underwriter, became Tennessee Gas's controlling stockholder. By September 4, 1945, the Chicago Corporation had no financial stake in Tennessee Gas.

Tennessee Gas continued to function effectively and expanded its system capacity to meet the increasing Appalachian demand. The War Production Board requested that Tennessee Gas "give consideration to the feasibility of installing additional compressor stations, compressors, and auxiliary apparatus" on its natural gas pipeline system to alleviate ongoing shortages.[47] After the WPB's request, Tennessee filed an application with the FPC for a Certificate of Public Convenience and

Necessity to expand its system. The expansion program called for the lease of four additional compressor stations to be constructed and owned by the Defense Plant Corporation, additions to its current compressor stations, and construction of 95 miles of 16-inch outside-diameter pipe from the San Salvador gas field in Hidalgo County, Texas, northward to Tennessee Gas's pipeline in Nueces County, Texas. The added compressor stations boosted Tennessee Gas's delivery capacity by 60 MMcf/d.[48]

FPC commissioner Leland Olds, an outspoken critic of his own commission, opposed the pipeline firm's wartime expansion plans. He believed that the Appalachian shortage was not serious, and he argued in favor of the coal industry and against what he feared might lead to its ruination. He stated that "cross examination of company witnesses developed that the Commission was being asked to give its assent to what was in fact only a limited segment of a broader plan for post-war deliveries of Texas gas to northeastern markets in much larger quantities."[49] Olds feared that as the war emergency production requirements tapered off, the commission was being inundated with applications for natural gas facilities, which "taken singly, do not appear too significant but cumulatively might seriously dislocate the balanced utilization of the country's energy resources."[50] He warned his fellow commissioners to view Tennessee's application within the context of the gas industry's unprecedented growth, and Olds was particularly worried that proposed wartime natural gas projects would be used as a springboard into the Northeastern coal and manufactured gas market after the war. Olds railed: "Thus I do not find in the record any sufficient evidence of war need to warrant action on the present application without full investigation of the impact of all plans for sale of southwestern gas in the Northeast. We cannot deal with the situation piecemeal and at the same time conserve the public interest for which the Congress made us responsible in 1942 when it amended section 7 of the Natural Gas Act."[51]

Olds's regulatory policy evoked the ire of the gas industry. When President Truman renominated him as FPC commissioner, a Senate committee chaired by Lyndon B. Johnson of Texas held hearings on the nomination. Olds was roasted. His opponents linked his former work as a labor organizer, support of public power, and journalism with the current socialist "menace." They branded Olds as un-American, and his renomination did not receive Senate approval.[52]

During the war, the FPC and the WPB worked together to alleviate the Appalachian fuel shortage. They approved pipeline projects that provided stable sources of natural gas for war industries and sought to increase regional gas production in an orderly fashion. The FPC determined when, how, and at what price interstate gas systems would operate. During these years, the FPC effectively served as a governmental pipeline promotion and management agency, and the FPC continued to exercise strict entry and price controls over the interstate industry during the postwar years. After the end of the war, federal control of the industry gave way to a form of regulated competition mixed with market-driven entrepreneurship. As many of its leaders had hoped, the war spurred industry development and natural gas demand. Now, the gas industry was poised for a second dramatic period of growth.

9

Competition for Northeastern Gas Markets

WORLD WAR II energy demand was as a catalyst for natural gas industry expansion. As gas consumption increased in the Midwest and Northeast, it became evident that new pipelines were needed to transport gas from producing fields to consumers, particularly in the Northeast. Appalachian gas production declined, and gas entrepreneurs sought to build pipelines connecting Southwestern gas with beckoning gas markets. These developments were particularly dramatic in the Southwest to Northeast corridor, where several new gas pipeline firms organized to begin transporting and selling natural gas to the traditional manufactured gas markets. Large Northeastern cities such as Philadelphia, New York, and Boston had remained dependent upon manufactured gas for over 100 years, but that would change rapidly in the postwar years. On the West Coast, natural gas consumption increased as well, but California, with its own substantial gas production and large urban markets, developed insularly; gas demand for many years was met primarily with in-state production.

During the early 1940s, the Tennessee Gas line became the first one to connect Southwestern reserves with Appalachian markets, but this pipeline did not reach into the large Northeastern urban centers. By the end of World War II, two other pipelines did extend from the east Texas oil fields to Phoenixville, Pennsylvania, and Linden, New Jersey, but these were oil pipelines built during the war. These "war emergency pipelines" became instrumental in the postwar gas industry's development.

Formal plans for the construction of the federally financed war emergency pipelines began in 1942 after German U-boat attacks on oil tankers transporting petroleum from the Gulf Coast up the Atlantic seaboard. The submarine attacks, and the continuing threat of attack, disrupted U.S. oil trade to Northeastern refineries, which threatened not only an East Coast oil shortage but an Allied forces oil shortage as well. "We tried to keep that [shortage] a secret," recalled Bill Murray of the Texas Railroad Commission. "It was a necessary effort not to let the Germans know how much damage they were doing, but we just couldn't move the oil."[1] During 1942, oil tanker shipments from the Gulf Coast to the New York harbor area fell from an average of 1.5 million barrels per day to approximately 75,000 per day.[2]

Subsequently, the RFC agreed to finance two war emergency pipelines to alleviate the Northeastern oil shortage and ensure oil supply

Harold Ickes inspects final weld on the Big Inch, 1943.

Courtesy, Duke Energy.

for the war effort. Completed in 1943, the Big Inch (24-inch) and Little Big Inch (20-inch) delivered more than 350 million barrels of crude and refined products to the New York harbor area during the war. Oil historian Arthur Johnson later wrote that "it would be difficult to measure what the availability of this amount of petroleum and petroleum products meant to the war effort, both overseas and at home. But clearly it was a major contribution."[3]

The Inch Lines, Natural Gas, and Philadelphia

The postwar fate of the Inch Lines resulted in a "classic clash of interest groups."[4] Large oil companies lobbied against continued use of these lines as oil transporters, stating that ocean-going tankers could do the job in peacetime less expensively; smaller oil firms wanted the Inch Lines to remain in the oil service. The smaller firms generally believed that the Inch Lines could be successfully operated as oil lines, but the industry as a whole rejected this idea. The coal and railroad industries adamantly objected to the suggested possibility of converting the Inch Lines to natural gas transportation. They feared that the introduction of natural gas into the Northeast would displace both coal and manufactured gas and decrease revenues from coal transportation service.

Initially, several major oil companies actively supported the idea of converting the Inch Lines to natural gas as a way to keep them out of petroleum transportation. Sidney A. Swensrud, vice president of Standard Oil (Ohio), proposed this plan. Early in 1944, he presented a paper entitled "A Study of the Possibility of Converting the Large Diameter War Emergency Pipe Lines to Natural Gas Service after the War" in which he echoed the concerns of his industry: "the disposition and future use of these lines constitutes, in the minds of many people, one of the most important problems of post-war readjustment in the Oil Industry."[5] Swensrud concluded that the Inch Lines could successfully and economically transport natural gas from the area of the nation's greatest natural gas reserves in the Southwest to the densely populated Northeast without causing a serious disruption in the coal industry. While Swensrud and other oil firm representatives publicly argued for oil tanker transportation, they were concerned that a single owner of the Inch Lines might monopolize oil transportation. Surreptitiously, Swensrud and J. Howard Marshall, former chief counsel and assistant deputy administrator of the PAW and president of Ashland Refining Company, financed a public relations campaign supporting the conversion of the Inch Lines to natural gas.[6]

After the war, the federally owned Inch Lines became subject to the jurisdiction of the Surplus Property Act of 1944, which required the Surplus Property Administration (SPA) to determine the disposal policy for war surplus property. The RFC hired the engineering firm of Ford, Bacon & Davis to write a report recommending a postwar use for the lines. The report concluded that both Inch Lines should be converted to natural gas transmission, but it was not binding. The RFC soon thereafter sent telegrams to 135 users and potential users of the pipelines requesting general inquiries or informal bids for the purchase or lease of the lines.[7]

In Congress, Senator Joseph C. O'Mahoney of Wyoming held a series of hearings to consider the disposition of a vast array of war surplus property. The Inch Lines were the focus of one set of hearings, which lasted for three days, from November 15 to 17, 1945. Twenty-eight representatives of government agencies, railroads, oil, gas, and coal interests presented oral and written statements about the lines.[8]

The SPA reviewed information collected during the hearings as well as various reports and studies and prepared the official disposal policy for the Inch Lines. The SPA published the Symington Report (after SPA administrator W. Stuart Symington) in early January 1946.[9] The report concluded that the Inch Lines "would be vital in the event of another emergency" and a "careful consideration of all the factors involved leads to the conclusion that the Big Inch and Little Big Inch should be kept in petroleum service."[10] This report pleased the coal and railroad industries, disappointed natural gas interests, and angered the major oil companies.[11]

The newly created War Assets Administration (WAA) prepared to auction the Inch Lines under the Symington Report's guidelines. The WAA advertised the auction in 38 newspapers and 5 oil trade journals. The advertisements stated that "in accordance with the disposal policy indicated in the Surplus Property Administration Report, first preference will be given to continuing the Big and Little Big Inch in petroleum service, thereby assuring availability of the lines in the event of a national emergency."[12] The disposal policy indicated that "special attention will be paid to offers which would give the many small and independent petroleum operators the opportunity of participating in both the use and acquisition of this facility in whole or in part."[13]

Representative Francis E. Walter of Pennsylvania, who had lead the coal industry's opposition to converting the Inch Lines to natural gas, told a reporter that Brigadier General John J. O'Brien, WAA deputy administrator, promised him that if no petroleum bids were adequate, the WAA would not act on the natural gas bids until Congress was first consulted. This was a victory, Walter said. "I've won my fight. If bids from any of the oil companies are acceptable and the lines are continued in oil transportation, that's fine. Otherwise, we still have a chance to stop their conversion into natural gas."[14]

The WAA received 16 valid bids by July 30.[15] Seven proposed oil transportation, three were for gas, five offered some combination of oil and gas use, and one did not state a preference. The task of actually evaluating the bids proved onerous. Having no standards for the bid format made it difficult to compare them. Especially important were the bidders' proposals to pay for the lines with a combination of cash, loans, and payments based upon gas sold, or other arrangements. The highest cash offerings came from natural gas bidders, and the WAA decided to consider only the cash portion of the bid. This decision, of course, conflicted with the Symington Report's criteria in favor of oil bidders.

The bid for the Inch Lines had become an intensely political episode of postwar demobilization and reconversion. Most of the bidding companies included high-profile former, and sometimes even current, political figures. One bidder, Big Inch Gas Transmission Company, included as its lobbyist a former Ohio Senator, a former justice of the Supreme Court, and a former chairman of the Maritime Commission. Attorneys for this company were former Roosevelt aide Thomas Corcoran, a former general counsel for the FPC, and a former FPC commissioner. American Public Utilities included a distinguished pair of Washington lawyers: former trust-buster Thurman Arnold and Abe Fortas, one-time undersecretary of interior for Harold Ickes. American Public Utilities also included maverick oil man Glenn H. McCarthy. Harold Ickes himself, writing in a syndicated column, stated that Jesse Jones, chairman of the RFC (which held title to the Lines), and an in-law of Jones's were secretly associated with a bid submitted by E. Holley Poe, who had served in the PAW during the war. Jones apparently was not a member of this group, but Herman and George R. Brown of the Brown & Root construction firm and close friends of Lyndon B. Johnson became the principal backers of Poe's effort.[16]

Ickes was even more concerned about the wanton actions of the nation's major coal union. He wrote another column supporting natural gas transportation by the Inch Lines in order to "end John L. Lewis' stranglehold on the economy of the United States."[17] As president of the United Mine Workers, Lewis had ordered the nation's coal miners to strike during the war, and the strike had consequently aggravated energy shortages in Appalachia and the eastern seaboard. The specter of future disruptions of energy supply by prolonged and often violent coal miners' strikes was a powerful incentive for government officials to reconsider their policy of favoring oil over natural gas in the sale of the Inch Lines. Ickes suggested that a good dose of natural gas competition via the Inch

Lines would serve Lewis right, and he chastised the WAA for not selling the Inch Lines to the highest bidder. Anything else, he wrote, "is just plain politics."[18]

Apparently, Lewis himself was not concerned about inadvertently supporting a natural gas policy for the Inch Lines. On November 20, he threw out the contract between the government and his coal union of 400,000 members. The resulting strike proved short-lived. Lewis called off the strike on December 7 after the government fined both him and his union. In fact, Lewis was personally unaffected by the coal strike and coal shortage. "Lewis' house at Springfield won't be cold on account of the coal strike," the *Washington Post* reported. "The United Mine Workers chief had gas heating installed in June 1945."[19]

On November 19, the Select Committee of the House of Representatives to Investigate the Disposition of Surplus Property (the Slaughter Committee) met to determine the best disposition policy for the Inch Lines. On the opening day of the hearings, General Robert M. Littlejohn, chairman of the WAA, announced his decision to reject all previous bids for the Inch Lines and to begin preparing for a second auction.

In the meantime, several bidders, as well as Tennessee Gas, which had not bid originally for the lines, discussed with the WAA the possibility of temporarily leasing the Inch Lines to alleviate the Appalachian fuel shortage.[20] On November 29, the company proposed to lease the Inch Lines on a temporary basis and deliver gas to Appalachia—but not farther eastward. On December 2, the WAA accepted Tennessee's proposal. The lease began at 12:01 A.M. on December 3, 1946, and lasted until midnight on April 30, 1947. Harold Ickes appeared again to condemn the lease agreement. He accused Tennessee Gas of seeking to monopolize natural gas shipments to the Northeast and using political influence to prevent any other firm from operating the pipelines. Tennessee did interconnect its system with the Inch Lines near Many, Louisiana, and began pumping gas through them on December 5 and December 9, respectively. By December 11, gas was flowing to consumers in Ohio.[21]

With the successful use of the Inch Lines for natural gas transportation, WAA administrator Littlejohn devised a new disposal policy for the Inch Lines. He issued three new recommendations: (1) The Inch Lines should be disposed of for natural gas or oil; (2) all pumping and other oil equipment should be maintained by the purchaser so government could recapture the pipelines within 90 days of a national emergency; and (3) the sale should be made to the purchaser offering the greatest net return in dollars to the United States government.[22] All bids for the second auction were due Saturday, February 8, 1947.

Representative Walters continued to oppose selling the Inch Lines for natural gas despite a new report published by the FPC, which described the tremendous gas volumes, as much as 1 Bcf/d in Texas and 2 Bcf/d in the Southwest as a whole, flared or vented each day into the atmosphere; this gas could be marketed if there were pipelines available to transport it. Walters represented coal and railroad interests, and he discussed the potential impact of natural gas deliveries to the railroad industry. If converted to natural gas, he said, "the Inch Lines would transport an annual equivalent of about five to six million tons of coal . . . [and if] the densely populated Eastern Seaboard is afforded natural gas service for domestic, industrial and commercial purposes, the quantities necessary to meet the demands of that area will result in the displacement of enormous quantities of solid fuel."[23]

On February 10, WAA representatives opened the 10 Inch Line bids. The three highest received were all for natural gas use. Texas Eastern submitted the high bid of $143,127,000, which was approximately the same amount as the Inch Lines' original construction cost. Transcontinental Gas Pipe Line Company submitted the second-highest bid of $131 million. Tennessee Gas came in third.[24] Texas Eastern's winning bid received accolades for providing the government "the best war-surplus deal it had ever made."[25]

The Texas Eastern bid became controversial after the company finalized its purchase of the lines. In its registration statement to the SEC, the company publicly disclosed that the founders had purchased a combined total of 150,000 shares of stock originally priced at one dollar per share; each of these shares was subsequently "split" into seven shares, so the actual price was then $.14 per share. Less than a year later, after the company was created, Texas Eastern stock was sold publicly for $9.50 per share. Thus, the original $150,000 investment had quickly transformed into $9,975,000 before taxes. The founders' high profits gained in this deal became the subject of a debate in two *Harvard Business Review* articles.[26]

After the bid, another political obstacle confronted the fledgling gas company. Interstate natural gas pipelines did not have federal eminent domain powers, and the state of Pennsylvania as well as coal and railroad interests used this to prevent Texas Eastern from transporting gas into Pennsylvania. Opposition to the gas line seemed to diminish somewhat in February 1947, when Pennsylvania governor Duff told a reporter that Pennsylvania was virtually powerless to prohibit the transmission of natural gas through the state, but democratic senator Myers of Pennsylvania said that the FPC would "never permit the transmission of natural gas to the eastern seaboard."[27]

The charge against natural gas was led most vociferously by attorney Tom J. McGrath, who represented eight coal, railroad, and labor organizations, including the National Coal Association, Eastern Gas and Fuel Associates (a coal and manufactured gas company), the United Mine Workers of America, the Chesapeake & Ohio Railway, and several others. McGrath used every means possible to persuade the FPC not to grant Texas Eastern a certificate; the FPC did grant a temporary certificate to the gas line so that it could begin operating the pipelines on May 1, 1947. The anti–natural gas interests were not popular during the severe winter of 1947. During early February, Pittsburgh newspapers reported that diminishing natural gas supplies resulted in 50,000 temporary layoffs. On February 12, Tennessee Gas's pipeline suffered a break, further aggravating the shortage in the Pittsburgh area.[28]

The shortage conditions facilitated Texas Eastern's attempt to push an eminent domain bill for natural gas pipelines through Congress. Company officials worked with several politicians to prepare a bill. In early April, Senator E. H. Moore of Oklahoma, along with Senators Connally of Texas, O'Mahoney of Wyoming, and Stewart of Tennessee introduced S. 1028 to the Senate. In the House, Representative Schwabe of Oklahoma introduced a similar bill, H.R. 2956. Since there were other controversial proposed amendments to the Natural Gas Act that year, the eminent domain bill somehow slipped through unnoticed even by the anti–natural gas crowd.[29] Congress subsequently passed the eminent domain bill without the expected opposition.

The newly created Texas Eastern company, with its ready-made pipeline, prepared to sell gas to Northeastern markets. The pipeline's first major customers were the Appalachia area's largest and oldest distribution companies: Consolidated Natural Gas and Columbia Gas System, which purchased most of Texas Eastern's gas in the late 1940s. But Texas Eastern's management desired to quickly contract for gas sales to customers farther east, who were dependent upon manufactured gas. With the eminent domain bill in hand, Texas Eastern signed gas sales contracts with Philadelphia Electric and Philadelphia Gas Works. Sales to these companies began in September 1948, making Philadelphia the first major eastern city to begin receiving natural gas from the Southwest. With access to substantial quantities of natural gas, Philadelphia quickly converted from manufactured to mixed gas.

Philadelphia Electric had a growing need for gas for its rapidly increasing residential customer base. The rising price of coal made manufactured gas more expensive than the natural variety delivered from Texas gas fields located more than 1,000 miles distant. Demand for service strained the company's manufactured gas division's ability to respond. During the summer of 1946, the company received 9,000 orders for gas installations, but only 1,721 could be made due to the limited supply of manufactured gas. Despite determined attempts by the coal lobby to keep natural gas out Pennsylvania, the growing demand in Philadelphia and the proximity of the Inch Lines encouraged the utility to contract for natural gas purchases from Texas Eastern.

During September 1948, Texas Eastern began delivering natural gas to Philadelphia Electric's Tilghman Street Gas Plant; the new supplies were used for reforming and enriching the utility's current manufactured gas production. Philadelphia Electric's president, Horace P. Liversidge, had even larger plans for the future. He noted the rapid increase in customer applications for natural gas and said, "the supply of natural gas to Philadelphia Electric will permit it to increase its capacity and bring nearer the time when all applicants for gas services may be accepted and adequately supplied."[30]

Since mixed gas had a heating content of about 800 Btu, the utility had to adjust all residential appliances set for lower-Btu manufactured gas to accept the new fuel. Philadelphia Electric hired 400 servicemen to adjust each residential gas appliance. The conversion team adjusted 380,000 appliances for 170,000 customers. Adjustments were made to 220 various kinds of gas ranges, 160 styles of water heaters, and numerous kinds of house heaters, exclusive of commercial or industrial gas appliances. Within several years, the utility had a stable natural gas supply, and it switched to natural gas. By the late 1950s, the Philadelphia utilities entirely eliminated manufactured gas from their distribution operations, and the Philadelphia manufactured gas business disappeared.[31]

The Philadelphia conversion episode was repeated in many other cities during these years. The most significant urban market was New York City. Millions of manufactured gas consumers in and around that metropolis promised a huge and ready market for the natural gas pipeline company that arrived there first. While Texas Eastern's lines already extended to a point very near the city, the Philadelphia and Appalachian markets were purchasing all the natural gas it could deliver. Texas Eastern did sell relatively small volumes of natural gas to the New York and Richmond Gas Company, but it did not reach gas sales agreements with the largest New York City utilities.

Natural Gas in New York City

A new group of entrepreneurs won FPC approval to build a line from Texas to New York City. Texas attorney Claude A. Williams led the enterprise along with Rogers Lacy, owner of substantial Texas oil and gas reserves. Williams had submitted the highest cash bid in the initial government auction for the Inch Lines and the second highest at the second auction. Even before the WAA sold the Inch Lines, Williams had applied to the FPC for a certificate to construct a new pipeline from Texas to New Jersey. After a nine-month hearing, the FPC granted a certificate to Transcontinental, Williams's pipeline company, and construction began in 1949 for a 30-inch 1,000-mile line extending from the Rio Grande Valley to Manhattan.[32] In January 1951, the $233 million pipeline began to transport gas, as the company claimed, "from the region of the world's greatest natural gas reserves to the world's richest market."[33]

Transcontinental competed with Texas Eastern for gas sales to Philadelphia, but most of its gas was reserved for its New York customers. Transcontinental's primary customers were concentrated in the five major New York gas companies, Consolidated Edison (Con Edison), Brooklyn Borough Gas, Brooklyn Union Gas, Kings County Lighting Company, and Long Island Lighting Company, which all contracted for purchases of natural gas from Transcontinental under contracts dated July 25, 1950, superseding contracts signed by all the same parties during 1948.

These utilities agreed to take joint responsibility for accepting natural gas from Transcontinental's terminus at the east bank of the Hudson River at 134th Street. The five utilities cooperated in financing and constructing several underwater pipelines to transport gas from the receiving point to their own distribution systems. Con Edison was the largest purchaser in this group of five utilities, and it accounted for approximately 20 percent of Transcontinental's total gas sales volume.[34]

The five utilities agreed to construct those sections of the line that ran through their own franchise territory. Some portions of the line were used by two or more of the five companies; in those cases all costs were apportioned appropriately. The utilities estimated the total cost of the 262,830-foot line to reach $14 million. It contained sections of pipe measuring from 12 to 30 inches in diameter with a working pressure capacity of 350 psi. Because the high-pressure line would run under heavily traveled metropolitan streets in densely populated areas, the pipeline had to meet stringent safety standards. Due to its high cost and extensive safety precautions, gas industry observers dubbed the line the "Safest Inch" as well as the "Costliest Inch."[35]

Consolidated Edison and Brooklyn Union began receiving natural gas on January 16, 1951. These two utilities distributed natural gas to the majority of New York City residential gas customers. Their eventual conversion from manufactured gas to natural gas represented a substantial loss to the manufactured gas industry as a whole. Consolidated Edison sold gas to more than a million customers, most of whom were residential. Brooklyn Union served approximately 350,000 customers in the boroughs of Brooklyn and Queens.[36]

Con Edison planned to convert its gas distribution system entirely from manufactured gas to natural gas, but the decision to convert to natural gas was not without short-term costs.[37] Energy historian Joseph Pratt calculated that Con Edison then had a $250 million investment in obsolete and expensive gas-manufacturing plants. Natural gas offered a cost-competitive fuel that was much more efficient and clean-burning than manufactured gas. After World War II, according to a management study of Consolidated Edison's decision-making process, "natural gas [had] a clear and unmistakable cost advantage over the traditional manufactured product."[38]

Many technical problems delayed a full-scale conversion to natural gas. Con Edison first began enriching its water gas with natural gas to raise its heating value. This method saved Consolidated Edison money while beginning the overall process of converting the total system to natural gas. Assured of a long-term and stable supply of natural gas, the utility directed its System Engineering Department to prepare studies to guide the conversion to natural gas; the Gas Planning Division was responsible for the actual conversion process. The first priority was determining the order in which different parts of Con Edison's service area would be converted to natural gas. After evaluating the layout of gas distribution mains, patterns of demand for gas, and the availability of manufactured gas, the company's Commercial Operations Center and System Engineering Department stipulated that each of the utilities' local service areas be converted in the following order: Westchester County, Riverdale section of the Bronx, the Third Ward of Queens, the First Ward of Queens, the East Bronx, the West Bronx, and Manhattan. These areas comprised approximately 1.4 million gas customers, each of which operated an average of two gas appliances. Every gas-burning appliance required adjustments to burn natural gas.[39]

Con Edison began converting Westchester County to natural gas in April 1950 and finished in the summer of 1951. To convert the appliances of the county's approximately 207,000 gas customers, the utility hired North American Conversion Company. North American used 600 experienced workers to visit each customer and adjust each gas-burning appliance. Having learned the process of converting appliances from North American, Con Edison converted the remaining service areas itself. By taking over the conversion process, Con Edison was able to employ many of the workers at the manufactured gas plants that were being mothballed, and the conversion team grew to 1,100 employees during the final stage of its work, the conversion of Manhattan. By the summer of

1956, the utility had converted most of its Manhattan customers to natural gas. Con Edison accomplished the entire conversion at a cost of approximately $36 million. Although several of Con Edison's gas plants were kept in working order for backup, they were rarely used.[40]

Brooklyn Union also converted its service area from manufactured to natural gas after investigating the costs of expanding its own manufactured gas system. During the late 1940s, Brooklyn Union began a 3-year $25 million program to expand its manufactured gas production facilities by about 10 percent. Yet, the company could not keep pace with growing demands for gas in its service territory. Brooklyn Union struggled with the decision to mothball its manufactured gas plants in favor of natural gas.

Brooklyn Union first seriously considered contracting natural gas service during the Inch Line bidding. The utility knew that Peoples Gas Light & Coke Company of Chicago and the Michigan Consolidated Gas Company of Detroit had purchased large quantities of natural gas and benefited financially from the decision. Brooklyn Union also considered using natural gas to produce mixed gas rather than converting directly to natural gas. By producing mixed gas from its proposed 70 MMcf/d allotment of natural gas combined with its existing 213 MMcf/d manufactured gas production capacity, Brooklyn Union could raise its effective gas output to approximately 265 MMcf/d with a total investment of about $4 million. A similar increase provided solely by the addition of manufactured gas production facilities would cost the utility $10 million. This calculation, essentially the same one made by every major urban gas distributor, resulted in a decision to contract natural gas pipeline supply.[41]

These studies pointed toward a obvious problem. If Brooklyn Union converted its entire distribution system to mixed gas now, and then within a few years converted entirely to natural gas, then it would have to adjust its customers' appliances twice and make several costly modifications to its own system. Therefore, Brooklyn Union decided to convert its entire system to straight natural gas.[42]

Brooklyn Union's customers had more than 2 million appliances, including oven ranges, gas refrigerators, water heaters, various indoor heaters, and other gas appliances, each of which had to be converted from the low Btu manufactured gas to high Btu natural gas. The conversion process began on March 6, 1952. The company's residential customers were converted to natural gas within six months. Its 5,000 industrial customers underwent a similar conversion process to their furnaces. By the end of the year, Brooklyn Union's entire service area was using natural gas.[43]

TABLE 9.1 Gas Sales of Utilities, 1935–1959 (in millions of therms)

Year	Total United States			Total U.S. Residential		
	Natural Gas	Manuf. Gas	Mixed Gas	Natural Gas	Manuf. Gas	Mixed Gas
1935	10,635	1,611	678	2,773	1,194	477
1937	13,480	1,535	758	3,365	1,110	512
1939	13,576	1,580	770	3,646	1,118	525
1941	16,358	1,726	925	4,113	1,149	600
1943	20,325	1,967	1,123	5,022	1,261	718
1945	22,563	2,088	1,194	5,601	1,365	769
1947	26,022	2,319	1,481	7,514	1,558	977
1949	32,234	2,274	1,191	9,541	1,526	701
1951	44,718	1,763	1,652	14,009	1,108	1,030
1953	52,800	838	2,351	16,013	478	1,487
1955	63,008	457	3,039	20,086	235	2,011
1957	74,649	215	2,105	24,278	123	1,541
1959	85,518	143	2,196	28,027	79	1,592

Source: American Gas Association, Historical Statistics of the Gas Industry (Arlington: AGA, 1964), 213.
Note: 1 therm = 100,000 BTUs.

The conversion of the New York City area from manufactured gas to natural gas was an important era in domestic fuel conversion. Indeed, it marked the end of manufactured gas as a significant industry in the United States (see table 9.1). Utilities mounted a tremendous labor-intensive effort to convert their customers' appliances to accept natural gas, and new customers were quickly added to the system. Not only had natural gas displaced an existing fuel, it had, by breaking into the largest manufactured gas market in the country, expanded into one of the most important energy-consuming regions in the United States.

Competing for New England

New England and Boston in particular were the last major Northeastern markets still without natural gas. Two pipeline companies, Texas Eastern and Tennessee Gas, planned to compete for gas sales there. Texas Eastern's first attempt to organize a New England pipeline ended in failure. The proposed Minute Man Gas Company, one journal reported, "got a freeze-out which is memorable even in New England, where the fiscal climate has long been adverse to outsiders who propose to make money New Englanders might be making themselves."[44]

A second effort was more successful when Texas Eastern's president Reginald Hargrove negotiated with Eastern Gas & Fuel Associates, New England Gas and Electric Association, and Providence Gas Company to form Algonquin Gas Transmission in 1949. The next year, Algonquin applied to the FPC for a certificate to construct and operate a pipeline connecting with Texas Eastern facilities in New Jersey and extending north to Boston; Texas Eastern would be Algonquin's major supplier.[45]

Tennessee Gas wanted the New England market as well, and the business press depicted the ensuing competition between Tennessee Gas and Texas Eastern as a virtual man-to-man duel between Reginald Hargrove of Texas Eastern and Gardiner Symonds of Tennessee Gas. Even before Algonquin's incorporation, Tennessee Gas organized the Northeastern Gas Transmission Company, a wholly owned subsidiary, to serve the New England market. Northeastern Gas would extend from Tennessee Gas's terminals at Buffalo, New York, to New England. These two major companies made competing applications to the FPC to supply natural gas to Boston and the remainder of New England.[46]

The FPC hearings on these two applications lasted for more than two years. Each side sought political allies and bitterly opposed the other's application. Disputes over initial FPC decisions ended up in the U.S. Supreme Court. Gradually, support for a dual supply suggested that both pipelines might be allowed to sell gas in New England. But how would the market be divided?

On July 1, 1953, all parties involved agreed to a dual supply for New England based largely on the FPC's earlier decision. Algonquin would serve Connecticut, Rhode Island, and eastern Massachusetts, including the Boston area. The FPC certified Tennessee Gas to sell gas in western Massachusetts and upstate New York and also allowed it to serve two local distribution companies that Texas Eastern previously served in Louisville and Pittsburgh, as well as several small Tennessee towns.[47] Symonds tied his company's final acceptance to FPC approval of an export license to sell gas in Canada. *Time* magazine then reported that Symonds was in "no mood to carry out the original agreement [the Algonquin-Northeastern settlement] until his Canadian market is guaranteed."[48] However, the FPC granted Tennessee's export permit within a few weeks, and Symonds supported the New England settlement.[49] The settlement led to an agreement between Tennessee and Algonquin in

1954 to interconnect their lines at Southington, Connecticut. The FPC acknowledged the oligopolistic nature of the pipeline industry by certificating two separate firms to serve the region rather than a single regulated monopoly.[50] The New England episode was the last in a series of highly politicized gas pipeline expansions into the postwar Northeast. It marked the demise of the U.S. manufactured gas industry, as similar events were occurring on the West Coast as well. The intense political battles between entrepreneurial firms seeking to sell their product in new markets received much attention in the popular press, and one reporter aptly characterized these episodes as proof that this was a "brawling, bawling industry."[51]

The delivery of natural gas to the Northeast occurred at the expense of manufactured gas. By 1953, with natural gas flowing into New England, leaders in the regional manufactured gas industry knew that their 100-year plus domination of the Northeastern gas market had ended. Natural gas did not simply take the traditional markets for manufactured gas; as more natural gas became available, it created entirely new markets for itself, becoming the fastest growing fuel in the postwar period.

10

Industry Growth in the American Era

DURING THE TWO decades following World War II, the gas industry continued to expand (see table 10.1). The most significant developments related to pipeline construction and public policy. New pipeline projects included major long-distance lines emanating from the Southwest toward Western, Midwestern, and Northeastern markets. Rapid industry growth evoked new calls for even more stringent regulatory controls, but in this era of plenty the gas industry grew despite imposition of new regulations.

Technological factors also contributed to industry growth during these years. Pipe manufacturers were able to produce seamless tubing with higher tensile strength than earlier pipes. The development of pressure gas welding, protective pipeline wrapping, and high-pressure centrifugal gas compressors enabled the construction and operation of larger and stronger lines that could transport more natural gas more quickly from supply area to demand. Stable regulated prices ensured that consumers would buy gas.[1]

Regulating Gas Production

Just as events in the Midwestern gas business of the 1920s attracted the FTC's attention, high-stakes competition in the same region during the

TABLE 10.1   Natural Gas Prices and Demand, 1945–1972

Year	Marketed Production (Tcf)	Average Wellhead Price (cents per Mcf)
1945	4	4.9
1950	6	6.5
1955	9	10.4
1960	13	14.0
1965	16	15.6
1970	22	17.1

Source: American Gas Association, *Gas Facts,* 1974. Adapted from U.S. Bureau of Mines.
Notes: Tcf = trillion cubic feet.
Mcf = thousand cubic feet.

The Flame Room, ca. 1950.
Courtesy, Enron Corporation.

1940s and 1950s prompted the implementation of new federal controls on the natural gas industry. Once again, the maverick Panhandle Eastern found itself in the middle of a competitive situation that federal authorities viewed with keen interest and that led to implementation of new industry rules and regulations.

In the early 1940s, Panhandle Eastern's management negotiated to sell gas directly to Detroit Edison for electric-generating purposes. The significance of this deal was that Panhandle Eastern wanted to bypass the local distribution company (LDC). Although gas sales did not actually occur, the proposed contract was a powerful challenge to the LDC, Michigan Consolidated (MichCon), which viewed direct sales as a "raid" on its own gas service territory. During the war, Panhandle had sold gas directly to two industrial firms: Michigan Seamless Tube Company of South Lyons and Albion Malleable Iron Company. Both signed contracts after the War Production Board requested the hookups for defense-related production. Since the federal government ordered these direct sales, and the volumes were minimal, MichCon did not object. It did, however, oppose Panhandle's repeated efforts to make direct delivery of natural gas to Detroit's industrial firms. For its part, Panhandle Eastern had opposed MichCon's efforts to acquire its own natural gas supply from a source other than Panhandle Eastern, even during World War II, while simultaneously seeking to bypass the utility by signing contracts with local industrial firms.

Panhandle Eastern's relationship with MichCon did not include cordial relations among the companies' leaders. In the past, utilities typically owned their own gas supply lines, but after imposition of the New Deal–era regulatory system, the gas industry had become more clearly segmented between production, transportation, and distribution. Corporate segmentation aside, MichCon believed that it was literally being held hostage by its gas supplier. Yet, the Detroit situation represented well the market tensions between the newly independent gas pipelines and the distribution companies they served. Not everyone clearly understood that the world in this regard had changed. As Michigan congressman Lesinski said,

> For approximately 15 years the Michigan Consolidated Gas Co. at Detroit, and its predecessor, Detroit City Gas Co., has been conducting a ruthless form of guerrilla war against every threat of competition for the great gas market which it dominates, a deliberate campaign in which it has had the assistance of the powerful Columbia Gas & Electric Corporation, and, more recently, of others whose activities merit attention.[2]

The dispute between pipeline and distributor contributed to the development of a new fuel crisis during the winter of 1947. Several manufacturing plants temporarily closed, and by February 1948, 95 industrial plants shut down wholly or partially because of the gas shortage. MichCon, the Detroit Common Council, and the Detroit media accused Panhandle of creating the shortage. Panhandle Eastern blamed MichCon. William E. Dowling, a city attorney, agreed with Panhandle and asserted that the "present shortage of gas is of artificial creation." The "onus," he said, was "upon the local company [Michigan Consolidated]."[3] Still, the bad publicity placed Panhandle's efforts to sell gas directly to area utilities in an unfavorable light.

The U.S. Supreme Court considered Panhandle's aggressive attempts to sell gas directly to industrial customers. The Court ruled that Panhandle Eastern must receive a state certificate of public convenience and necessity for making direct industrial sales. "It does not follow," wrote Justice Minton, "that because appellant is engaged in interstate commerce it is free from state regulation or to manage essentially local aspects of its business as it pleases."[4] The Michigan Public Service Commission expectedly sided with the Michigan gas distributor and refused to grant Panhandle the permission it needed for the sale.

MichCon had succeeded in stopping Panhandle Eastern's direct sales to industry. Now, it planned to build its own gas pipeline extending to the Southwestern gas fields. After building the line, MichCon expected to stop buying gas from Panhandle. In February 1945 American Light & Traction (MichCon's parent firm) filed with the FPC an application for a certificate of public convenience and necessity to construct the Michigan-Wisconsin (Mich-Wisc) pipeline from the Hugoton field near Guymon, Oklahoma, to points near Toledo, Ohio, and Detroit. From Detroit, the proposed line would continue to the Austin underground storage field near Big Rapids, Michigan. MichCon was developing this depleted gas field as a storage facility from which it could draw natural gas when necessary, particularly during the cold winter months. An underground storage facility, typically an abandoned gas well or salt mine, offered gas companies a place to deposit gas for later use.

In April 1945 the Mich-Wisc application was amended to include service to communities in Missouri, Iowa, and Wisconsin, and this change held significant future ramifications for the gas industry. At that time, no interstate pipeline sold gas to Wisconsin customers. Asked during SEC hearings why Wisconsin had no natural gas, Woolfolk explained somewhat slyly, "If the majority of the Board were coke oven inclined people, until they died, of course natural gas influence could not be successful."[5] Woolfolk also reiterated strongly that MichCon had no intention of renewing its contract with Panhandle Eastern.

Panhandle fought the new pipeline proposal. It contended that the FPC had no authority to grant a certificate.[6] Despite Panhandle's opposition to the plan, Mich-Wisc management signed a contract to supply MichCon's total gas requirements beginning December 31, 1951. Panhandle's management realized that MichCon might shortly achieve its goal of pushing Panhandle from the Detroit market.[7] Panhandle's attorneys filed a formal motion for dismissal. The company based its motion on three propositions: (1) that the FPC could not disregard Panhandle's "grandfather" rights to the Detroit market, (2) that Panhandle was able and willing to perform the service proposed, and (3) that Michigan-Wisconsin was not able to perform the service included in its application. Fearing competition from a new major interstate pipeline, the two other Midwestern long-distance pipelines, Natural Gas Pipeline Company and Northern Natural filed similar motions.[8]

On November 20, 1946, the FPC decided against Panhandle's monopolistic position when it granted a certificate to the Mich-Wisc line. FPC commissioners Olds and Draper dissented, but the three other commissioners approved the Mich-Wisc line.[9] American Light & Traction won another regulatory victory when on December 30, 1947, the SEC reversed an earlier ruling and approved American Light & Traction's plan to continue operating the Milwaukee Gas Light Company along with MichCon and Mich-Wisc. This decision was surprising to Panhandle's management, if not others, because it allowed the existence of a gas and electric holding company, albeit one that planned to operate regionally.[10]

With MichCon clearly in control of its market, it was Panhandle Eastern's turn to call for a truce. Panhandle attempted to exploit the situation by offering to sell gas to MichCon at $.185 per Mcf (compared to Mich-Wisc's price of $.21 to its own affiliate). There was no immediate response, but MichCon announced in 1949 that it wanted to continue Panhandle's gas deliveries after the completion of the Mich-Wisc line.[11] Dramatic increases in demand suggested that one line could no longer guarantee a long-term gas supply for Detroit. The FPC also ruled that Panhandle Eastern must continue delivering gas to MichCon under the terms of its original contract. At the contract's conclusion, Panhandle should, the commission ruled, continue participating in the growth of the Detroit and Ann Arbor markets.[12]

The Mich-Wisc line had contracted with the Phillips Petroleum Company for its entire gas supply, and the oil producer dedicated 633,460 acres of reserves to Mich-Wisc.[13] Coincidentally, Phillips also owned 25 percent of Panhandle Eastern's outstanding stock, but the company's executives decided to divest these securities after entering into a new competitive relationship with Panhandle. Phillips had also been concerned that its substantial financial interest in Panhandle might cause the FPC to exercise regulatory authority over all its natural gas business. Under the Natural Gas Act, gas producers, even those that sold gas to interstate gas pipelines for resale, were not subject to federal regulation.

City attorney Dowling was unimpressed with MichCon's new gas supply venture. "The whole plan," he stated, "is one of absolute monopoly, controlling the life of the local utility from the source of supply through the pipe line to the local utility and the ratepayer's burner tips."[14] In reality, Panhandle Eastern had enjoyed a monopoly over natural gas deliveries to Detroit since 1936. MichCon sought to re-create the cartel structure that had formally controlled Midwestern gas supplies, and this action evoked these new charges of monopoly. Since Phillips's gas sales to Mich-Wisc were unregulated, Phillips was effectually in control of MichCon's gas prices to Detroit's residential, commercial, and industrial customers. The council members were not at all pleased that Phillips had this price-setting power.

The dangers of monopolistic control in the utility industry became clearer when Phillips flexed its muscles. Since construction of the Mich-Wisc line had proceeded slowly, the project fell behind schedule. Mich-Wisc had to renegotiate its gas purchase contract with Phillips, and Phillips agreed to a six-month delay only in exchange for a 70 percent increase in its gas sales price. Phillips's position provided it all the leverage it needed to impose this new contract on Mich-Wisc and Detroit's gas consumers.[15]

The Detroit Common Council was outraged and filed a motion with the FPC demanding that Phillips be declared a natural gas company subject to FPC rate regulation. Wisconsin officials were also concerned, and the FPC agreed to study the situation. In the fall of 1948, the agency ordered an investigation of Phillips's rates and operations.[16] This was an important development, because Phillips was one of the largest gas producers in the United States. In 1950, it sold 60 percent of its natural gas to five pipelines, Mich-Wisc, Panhandle, Independent Natural Gas Company, El Paso Natural Gas Company, and Cities Service Gas Company. These sales accounted for about 15 percent of all U.S. natural gas transported in interstate commerce.[17]

The highly political nature of this conflict was reflected in the list of lobbyists lined up on each side. The *Detroit Free Press* reported that many prominent political figures were said to be on the payrolls of either MichCon or Panhandle Eastern. The list for MichCon included Prentis Brown, a former U.S. senator from Michigan; Murray D. Van Wagoner, former governor of Michigan; William J. McBreasty, former chairman of the Michigan Public Service Commission; and Donald Richberg, former director of the National Recovery Administration, among others. Panhandle Eastern's list included William E. Dowling, former Wayne County prosecutor and Detroit Corporation Counsel; John S. L. Yost, who had worked for the antitrust division of the Department of Justice; Leslie T. Fournier, an economist who had worked for the SEC on utility policies; Robert Patterson, former secretary of war; and Robert Morgenthau, son of FDR's secretary of the treasury.[18]

The FPC conducted an investigation of the situation, but the results were disappointing to those who opposed the MichCon-Phillips contract. After a long series of hearings, the FPC decided in 1951 that Phillips was not a natural gas company as defined by the Natural Gas Act. The agency terminated the investigation, but it also suggested that intervenors dissatisfied with the decision seek a new interpretation of the Natural Gas Act.[19]

The state of Wisconsin took these words seriously. Wisconsin attorney general Vernon W. Thomson led the charge. He wrote Wisconsin Senator Wiley:

> It looks to me as though a gross deception has been practiced upon the people of Wisconsin by the Michigan-Wisconsin Pipe Line interests. . . . Essentially, the fact as I see it is that Wisconsin is being deprived of its right to natural gas at a fair price, not only because of the tight pipe line monopoly here, or because of a seeming lack of arm's length dealing for natural gas from the Phillips interests, but principally because they [MichCon interests] are using the gas consumers of Wisconsin as mere tools or weapons in their fight to stand off competition by another pipe line for their Michigan market, especially at Detroit.

Thomson demanded that Phillips be subjected to federal rate regulation. He explained to the mayor of Cleveland, "An investigation by this office of Wisconsin's natural gas shortage is revealing a need for an amendment to the Natural Gas Act for the purpose of eliminating monopolistic practices in the production and transmission of gas." He filed suit against the FPC demanding that Phillips be subjected to gas price regulation.[20]

Wisconsin won the initial court battles, which affirmed that Phillips was a natural gas company subject to price regulation. On January 18, 1954, the Supreme Court agreed to review the contested matter. Six months later, the Supreme Court affirmed the lower court's decision.[21] This landmark case, which became known as the "Phillips decision," empowered the FPC to set the price of natural gas sold by producers for resale by interstate pipelines. Regulation of gas production dedicated for interstate markets seemed to be a logical and strangely missing element of the original act. Without control over production, the FPC's power to set "just and reasonable rates" for end users was limited since the agency didn't have jurisdiction over the wellhead price. While the Phillips decision would later be assailed for its unintended consequences, it was a reasonable decision at the time. Although the decision is commonly viewed as a price-control matter, its origins are rooted in a specific situation where a major gas producer attempted to exploit its monopolistic powers.

Gas companies expressed concern that the Phillips decision would have additional ramifications. One industry executive noted that "this development may seriously curtail the supply of natural gas that will be made available to interstate pipe lines."[22] Many gas firms, producers as well as pipelines owning production, urged Congress to pass legislation specifically exempting producers from regulation. They pointed out that the FPC currently had jurisdiction over 157 interstate gas companies prior to the Phillips decision, but there were 4,365 independent producers that sold natural gas to interstate pipelines; all of these producers would have to be regulated as well. New regulatory powers transformed the FPC into a much larger bureaucratic agency (see table 10.2).

While the Supreme Court deliberated the Phillips case, the FPC considered a separate case that might have limited the adverse effects that many gas companies believed the Phillips decision would have on interstate gas supply.[23] Panhandle Eastern had sued the FPC for permission to use the "fair field" price for company-produced gas; the Natural Gas Act had given the FPC power to regulate the price of gas produced for interstate markets by pipeline companies. The FPC agreed with

TABLE 10.2 Federal Power Commission Staffing, 1930–1958

Year	No. of Employees
1930	48
1932	57
1934	153
1936	338
1938	495
1940	709
1942	727
1944	661
1954	653
1958	750

Source: Federal Power Commission, Annual Reports (various years).

Panhandle and adopted as its formula (April 15, 1954) "a price reflecting the weighted average arm's-length payments for identical natural gas in the fields (and sometimes from the very same wells) where it is produced."[24] The fair field price would have allowed pipeline firms owning their own gas production to price it at rates comparable to gas that they purchased from other producers at the same fields.

Gas firms amplified their warnings about impending gas shortages, perhaps to encourage more public support against producer price regulation. As early as 1952, one company reported to stockholders that there existed "a growing scarcity of natural gas relative to the increased demands. Your company grows more reluctant to spend the large sums of money required to acquire new reserves in view of the Commission's persistent limitation of the Company's return on investment in production to a small fixed per cent."[25] The "fair field" ruling gave pipeline firms that produced a portion of their own gas supply financial incentive to increase their gas production. But the "fair field" price resulted in higher gas costs for consumers, and lawsuits once again followed. In Congress, democratic senator Lee Metcalf from Montana said, "The fair field price is the highest monopoly price the traffic will bear." He went on to lambaste the entire regulatory process: "Far better we should discontinue the pretense that the FPC is regulating natural gas rates. The consumer then would not be suffering the delusion that he is being protected against exploitation at the hands of natural gas companies."[26] The City of Detroit filed suit against the FPC for allowing this higher cost gas.

On December 15, 1955, the U.S. Court of Appeals, D.C. Circuit, overturned the fair field price decision. The court ruled that "the allowance of a field price should not lift the rates above the "just and reasonable" standards of the Natural Gas Act."[27] Regulatory historian Richard Vietor explained that "had this decision to allow a fair field price withstood judicial review, it would have meant that FPC regulation of independent producers under the Phillips doctrine could have proceeded with little disruption."[28] But that was not to be the case; appeals were unsuccessful.[29] The fair field doctrine was thrown out, and the FPC acquired full jurisdiction over interstate natural gas prices, including those of the producer selling gas to interstate pipelines, as well as the pipelines' gas sales price.

In a final industry-sponsored effort to release independent producers from regulation, Democratic senator J. William Fulbright of Arkansas and Democractic representative Oren Harris of Arkansas introduced the Fulbright-Harris bill. The bill proposed replacing the "cost-based" method of determining prices with the "fair field price," which the FPC had earlier approved. But on the very day the Senate voted, Republican senator Francis Case of North Dakota informed his colleagues that an oil industry lobbyist had attempted to bribe him. From President Dwight Eisenhower's perspective, these charges stained the bill. The Republican administration favored the measure, but after both the House and Senate passed it, Eisenhower exercised his veto power. He would not, he said, sign a bill that possibly was tainted with bribe money.[30] Eisenhower did note that such legislation was "needed because the type of regulation of producers of natural gas which is required under present law will discourage individual initiative and incentive to explore for and develop new sources of supply."[31] But subsequent efforts to pass the necessary legislation were unsuccessful.

The FPC later reopened the Panhandle rate case issue in order to learn whether the commodity value formula for gas price setting would save customers money and to encourage the development of additional gas supplies. "Reopening will not only give Panhandle an opportunity to introduce this additional evidence," the commission said. "It will also provide us an opportunity to consider the augmented record in this case at the same time we are considering the landmark Phillips Petroleum Co. independent producer rate case, Docket No. G-1148, et al., which is also before us now for decision."[32]

On September 28, 1960, the FPC issued its decision on the latter case by establishing five geographic area prices instead of using the cost-of-service method. In the decision, the commissioners noted that "rigid adherence to the rate base method will, in many cases, price the producers' gas completely out of the market."[33] In addition, the FPC asserted that "the better method would be to establish fair prices for the gas itself and not for each individual producer." The commissioners indicated that this decision would be considered "not lawful" by some, and if area-based rate making was ruled unlawful, "adequate regulation of producers appears to be impossible under existing law."[34] Nevertheless, the U.S. Court of Appeals, District of Columbia, affirmed this pricing scheme and was supported by the Supreme Court.

The new policy was difficult to implement for administrative and technical reasons. The FPC issued its first area price in 1965 for the Texas Permian basin, but the agency was being overwhelmed by the industry's complexities. For example, the Permian area price set one price for gas produced within the entire area despite widely varying costs of producing gas in different geographic settings within the area. It was not at all certain that area prices were actually fairer to both producers and consumers. By the end of the decade, the FPC had set area prices only for the Permian and Southern Louisiana areas. Area pricing policy did not last much longer.

Gulf Coast Supply and Trunkline Gas Company

While policy makers and gas companies sparred over rate making, new pipeline ventures promised to pump more natural gas into the national market. Indeed, the abundance of natural gas supply and demand from the 1940s through most of the 1960s mitigated any immediate affects of stringent gas pricing regulations on supply. Voluminous natural gas fields were located along the Texas Gulf Coast and Texas Eastern, Transcontinental, and Tennessee Gas all tapped supply located there. New pipeline projects soon developed as well. One of these involved a small group of independent businessmen led by Ralph Davies, the former deputy administrator of the PAW and vice president of Standard Oil of California (SOCAL). Davies, along with Lewis MacNaughton and Everett DeGolyer of the Dallas-based oil and gas consulting firm of DeGolyer and MacNaughton, P. McDonald Biddison, a leading pipeline engineer, and Carl I. Wheat, a Washington-based oil and gas attorney, had purchased substantial south Texas gas reserves.

Pipe lay barge lowering pipe into the water.

Courtesy, Duke Energy.

The men incorporated the Trunkline Gas Supply Company on March 12, 1947, and elected Davies as president. They filed an application for a certificate of public convenience and necessity with the FPC, but the project stagnated.[35] During the fall of 1949, Panhandle Eastern, which was then exploring the possibility of building its own line to the Gulf Coast, agreed to take over the project and purchase its stock. Panhandle acquired 96 percent of the stock and SOCAL retained the remaining 4 percent. The FPC now issued a certificate for Trunkline that extended to a compressor station in Tuscola, Illinois. Trunkline was a 740-mile 20- to 26-inch system that cost approximately $85 million. A group of insurance companies headed by Metropolitan Life Insurance subscribed to $61 million in Trunkline's first mortgage bonds. Gas began flowing on October 1, 1951.[36]

Texas Gas for California

While the most dramatic activity in the natural gas business centered around transporting Southwestern-produced natural gas to Midwestern and Northeastern markets, some Southwestern natural gas was also being delivered to the West Coast. California itself was a large producer of natural gas, but it also required natural gas imports to supply its rapidly growing post–World War II population and industrial base. Natural gas captured approximately 99 percent of the California home heating market in 1961. And as the state's electric utilities attempted to keep pace with increasing electricity demand, utilities such as Southern California Edison realized that fuel oil used as a boiler fuel exacerbated the growing southern California air pollution problem. Cleaner-burning natural gas could also be used to fuel steam-powered electric power generators, but additional supply beyond California's own production was required if natural gas was going to be more widely used.

El Paso Natural Gas had been the first out-of-state pipeline to respond to California's growing gas demand. Soon after World War II, El Paso extended its pipeline system with a 1,200-mile line connecting the massive gas fields of the Permian Basin in west Texas to the southern California border.[37] At the border, the El Paso system fed a line from Southern California Gas Company, which transported the gas to southern California utilities. In 1950, El Paso and PG&E constructed additional facilities to bring gas from northwestern New Mexico and Colorado into the San Francisco metropolitan area. California's gas market was unique in the sense that the California Public Utility Commission (CPUC) prevented "foreign" interstate pipeline companies from entering the state. The commission required El Paso's pipeline to stop at the

California border, where California-owned pipelines picked up the gas. Any pipeline company seeking to sell gas to California's utilities would have to abide by the same rules.

In the postwar era, southern California was one of the most promising markets for natural gas in the nation. By 1961, California's consumption of natural gas sold by utilities had surpassed that of Texas; the volume sold in California made it the largest natural gas–consuming state in the nation.[38] The state's own reserves were not sufficient to supply its needs. El Paso had single-handedly supplied "foreign" gas to California in the postwar era, but new supply lines were necessary. It was estimated that approximately 80 percent of the state's requirements would now have to be met with gas produced elsewhere.

A competitive situation similar in some respects to earlier ones in the Midwest and Northeast now developed in California. El Paso's monopoly on out-of-state gas sales was being challenged by new certificate applications at the FPC. One emerging competitor was Transwestern Pipeline Company. It had been organized in March 1957 by Warren Petroleum Corporation, a subsidiary of Gulf Oil, J. R. Butler and Associates (Houston), and Monterey Oil Company (Los Angeles).

The FPC granted a certificate to Transwestern in August 1959. W. K. Warren, chairman of the board and CEO of Warren Petroleum, was also chairman of the board of Transwestern. For Warren, Transwestern offered a convenient way to market the large, west Texas natural gas reserves owned by Warren and Gulf. Transwestern's gas deliveries to the southern California market began on August 9, 1960; its 1,300-mile 24- to 30-inch line terminated at the California border at Topock, Arizona.

At about this same time, PG&E sought to extend its gas pipeline outside of California to tap additional natural gas supplies. The Pacific Gas Transmission Company operated a 1,400-mile pipeline owned by Pacific Gas & Electric Company to transport natural gas from the Alberta "foothills" belt in Canada to PG&E's distribution system in the San Francisco Bay Area.

Market surveys suggested continued long-term growth in California gas demand, but competition was intense among the new supply lines. Transwestern could only fill its pipeline to 60 percent capacity during its first years of operation in the early 1960s, while El Paso Natural continued to be the state's major supplier, providing 75 percent of southern California's imported natural gas. Like Transwestern, El Paso delivered gas to Pacific Lighting Corporation (the largest distributor in the nation), which sold to various customers, including the Los Angeles Department of Water and Power and Southern California Edison.[39]

In an effort to force more natural gas from the earth and into its pipeline system, El Paso investigated the effects of detonating a nuclear device in a gas-producing area; the Atomic Energy Commission and Bureau of Mines participated. The venture was called Project Gasbuggy. On December 10, 1967, El Paso exploded the bomb, equivalent in power to 26,000 tons of TNT, 4,240 feet beneath the Carson National Forest in the San Juan Basin. Five months after the explosion, which did not leak radiation into the atmosphere, tests commenced to measure gas flow. In a 17-month period, El Paso produced 285 MMcf from the hole, more than three times the amount produced from a nearby well using conventional methods over a 10-year period. Thus, the company claimed that "nuclear fracturing" was a success, but the project was not repeated.[40]

Tennessee Gas decided to enter the competition for the California market as well. Pacific Lighting Corporation's control of distribution to southern California utilities and its gas purchase ties to El Paso Natural and Transwestern seemed to preclude entry of a new line. Ignoring these potential obstacles, Tennessee Gas announced in December 1960 that it planned to build a new pipeline from Texas through Mexico to the southern California border in order to serve Southern California Edison. Tennessee hoped that this project, known informally within the industry as the "Enchilada Inch line" or formally as the "Pemex Plan," could avoid FPC regulation since the line would not pass directly from one state to another. In Mexico, Petroleos Mexicanos (Pemex) would own and operate that portion of the line and supply some gas to it as well.[41] Both Southern California Edison and the Los Angeles Department of Water and Power expressed interest in the natural gas that might become available through this project. The FPC was understandably not enthusiastic about a major new U.S. pipeline detouring through Mexico to avoid its jurisdiction. This proposed line faced precarious political obstacles.[42]

El Paso proposed to increase the capacity of its gas delivery system by developing a new venture of its own, known as the Rock Springs project, which involved building a pipeline from the Rocky Mountains into southern California. Tennessee Gas management knew that El Paso's project would decrease the need for additional gas supply in California, so it intervened in the Rock Springs hearings at the FPC and stated its opposition. The competition between El Paso and Tennessee Gas for the California gas market resembled in many respects the competition between Texas Eastern and Tennessee for the New England market.

This industrial competition included a modern variant of the industrial espionage conducted against Panhandle Eastern 30 years earlier. Suspicions of spying emerged after November 14, 1961, when a Tennessee Gas attorney revealed that he had possession of a letter written less than three weeks earlier by James Moulton, PG&E vice president, to Howard Boyd, president of El Paso. In the letter, Moulton indicated that PG&E would not purchase a 200 MMcf/d block of gas from El Paso. Tennessee Gas disclosed this information in an attempt to weaken the Rock Springs application, as it suggested that California gas demand was less than previously believed. El Paso executives were miffed, and they were especially concerned about how their rival had obtained a copy of confidential correspondence.[43]

Five months later, a group of El Paso officials met in a Washington hotel suite. During the meeting, they inadvertently discovered a bugging device. Although several people were subsequently arrested, investigators were unable to conclusively identify the persons behind the bugging. Nor could El Paso complain too vehemently, because the investigation also revealed that El Paso's leader, Paul Kayser, had hired a private investigator to spy on Tennessee Gas. For months, stories of bribes and secret lobbying poisoned the atmosphere of the FPC hearings.[44] Finally, in July 1963, the FPC rejected the Rocks Springs project based on the grounds that additional gas supply was unnecessary.

Tennessee Gas's proposal, technically not under the jurisdiction of the FPC, was considered by the CPUC. As it turned out, Mexican officials were as unenthusiastic as the CPUC about the proposal. Mexican nationalists feared that the project might lead to the loss of Mexican control of northern Mexican gas supplies. In California, opposition pointed out Mexico's previous history of expropriating American energy companies. Economically, the project faltered simply because its proposed delivered gas price was higher than that for existing supplies. Tennessee Gas abandoned the plan in November 1962.

Not content to entirely abandon the California market, Tennessee proposed constructing a new line from Texas to the California border. For this plan, Tennessee signed contracts with Southern California Edison and the Los Angeles Department of Water and Power for deliveries of 865 MMcf/d of gas for boiler fuel. This Gulf Pacific project elicited competitive action from both El Paso and Transwestern, which proposed increases to their own system capacity. El Paso stated that for an additional $50 million investment, it could increase deliveries by 250 MMcf/d (or build a new pipeline for $134 million). Transwestern stated that by spending $46 million it could increase its sales volume to 640 MMcf/d. Taken together, the proposed expansions of the two systems would exceed the capacity of Tennessee's proposed line to the West. This left to the FPC the job of sorting out these various complex approaches and defining "the public interest."

The FPC consolidated all three proposals and began hearings. Tennessee asserted that Gulf Pacific would remove the potential of monopoly power by Pacific Lighting. It also argued that year-round supplies of natural gas to Southern California Edison would lessen air pollution by eliminating that utility's need to burn fuel oil during the winter months. The possibility of reduced air pollution gave Tennessee's proposal a unique advantage. Subsequently, in December 1965, the FPC's presiding examiner, Alvin Kurtz, unexpectedly and abruptly recommended approval of the Gulf Pacific line. His recommendation was subject to review, and the hearings continued. On July 26, 1966, the FPC formally denied the Gulf Pacific proposal. The FPC decided that the Gulf Pacific project would lead to higher gas prices and not significantly alleviate southern California's air pollution problems. Instead, the FPC endorsed the proposals of both Transwestern and El Paso to expand their existing systems. This decision guaranteed both Transwestern and El Paso a large stake in the current and future California market.[45]

Transwestern's position as a major gas supplier to the California market was assured, but the long and drawn-out FPC hearings and investigations worried some of its owners. The largest stockholder among many was Warren Petroleum Corporation, a Gulf Oil subsidiary, which owned about 32 percent of the outstanding stock, and the second largest shareholder was Northern Natural, which owned about 16 percent of the total. Gulf, which had the controlling interest, was concerned that the FPC might seek to regulate its operations due to its control of a regulated natural gas pipeline. Gulf sought a buyer and found one in Texas Eastern, which bought out the other investors as well.

The two large geographical regions that remained without natural gas supply were Florida and the Pacific Northwest. The Northwest Pipeline Company, completed in 1956, transported natural gas from the San Juan Basin in the Colorado and New Mexico border area to Seattle, Portland, and Spokane. In 1959, the newly constructed Florida Gas Transmission Company transported gas 1,500 miles from the Texas Gulf Coast to Florida. Texas Eastern later purchased Florida Gas and for a time was the only energy company with a "coast-to-coast" pipeline system.

During the postwar years, the natural gas industry expanded into the beginnings of a nationwide network, or grid, of pipelines that connected gas reserves with most of the nation's major urban areas. Natural gas availability led to the demise of the century-old manufactured gas industry and resulted in declining demand for coal as well. This era of expansion occurred under the FPC's regulatory management. While stringent if not ever-changing federal regulation did not prevent the gas industry from expanding in this era of abundant supply and demand, the economic costs of inflexible regulations would soon buffet the industry.

11

Shortage

GAS INDUSTRY GROWTH and prosperity slowed in the late 1960s. Ample supply and demand had stimulated development through most of the 1960s, but the days of wide open new markets and seemingly limitless supply were over. The Phillips decision had resulted in an unintentionally engineered shortage. Economists Stephen Breyer and Paul Macavoy noted that the failure to develop new reserves in the 1950s and 1960s created an emerging gas shortage at the end of the 1960s.[1] Quite simply, wellhead price controls had discouraged exploration and production for the regulated interstate commerce and thereby reduced the gas supply available for interstate sale.

In 1968, annual gas production for the first time exceeded the discovery of new reserves, and this trend continued (see table 11.1). Between 1968 and 1975, new discoveries yielded only 45 percent of total domestic consumption.[2] By the early 1970s, there was an emerging natural gas shortage as some pipelines curtailed gas deliveries to industrial customers. FPC chairman Joseph C. Swidler said in 1971 that the nation was in the midst of a critical shortage, despite the fact that only a few years earlier he had predicted natural gas abundance through the year 2,000.[3] The shortage had direct and indirect social ramifications. By 1970, electric utilities in three southern states used 832 Bcf of natural gas annually to produce electricity; this was approximately the same amount of gas used by all the residential customers in New York, Pennsylvania, and New Jersey. Thus, the shortage affected electric power production as well as natural gas consumers. The 1973 Arab oil embargo placed even higher demands on natural gas supply as some electric utilities initially sought to switch from fuel oil to natural gas for electric power generation, and this move only compounded the shortage conditions (see table 11.2).

Even before the embargo, shortage conditions forced interstate pipelines during 1970–1971 to curtail deliveries by as much as 1 Tcf of contracted gas supply. In 1972, for example, Long Island Lighting

TABLE 11.1 Annual Estimates of U.S. Proved Natural Gas Reserves (Tcf)

Year	Total New Discoveries*	Production	Est. Proved NG Reserves at Year End	Change over Previous Year
1962	19	14	272	6
1964	20	15	281	5
1966	20	17	289	3
1968	14	19	287	(5)
1970	37†	22	291	16
1972	10	23	266	(13)
1974	9	21	237	(13)
1976	8	20	216	(12)
1978	11	19	200	(9)
1980	14	19	199	(2)
1982	14	18	202	(.2)
1984	14	17	197	(3)
1986	9	16	192	(2)
1988	10	17	168	(19)‡
1990	12	17	169	2
1992	7	17	165	(2)
1994	12	18	164	1
1996	12	19	166	1

Source: American Gas Association, Gas Facts (Arlington: AGA, 1997), 4.

Note: Tcf = trillion cubic feet.

*Includes all discoveries, revisions, and extensions.

†Includes estimates of proved reserves in the Prudhoe Bay discovered in 1968 and not previously included.

‡Large revision decrease due to lack of NG transportation of North Slope gas to potential markets.

TABLE 11.2 Natural Gas Consumption by Sector in the United States
(percentages)

Year	Total Natural Gas Consumed*	Natural Gas Consumed as % of Total Energy	Residential and Commercial Energy Consumption	Natural Gas Used for Electricity Generation	Industrial Natural Gas Consumption
1972	22,698	32	35	18	44
1974	21,732	30	35	16	46
1976	20,345	27	40	15	41
1978	20,000	26	38	16	43
1980	20,394	27	37	19	41
1982	18,505	26	40	18	38
1984	18,507	25	39	17	40
1986	16,708	22	41	16	40
1988	18,552	23	40	15	41
1990	19,296	24	37	15	44
1992	20,125	25	38	14	45
1994	21,286	25	38	14	45

Source: American Gas Association, *Gas Facts* (Arlington: AGA, various years).
*Trillions of Btu

Company turned off the gas flow to 250 of its largest customers from November 1 through January 1973 so that the utility would have enough gas for its residential heating consumers. Curtailments increased to 3.8 Tcf by 1976–1977 (see table 11.3). In 1977, the curtailments evoked strong calls to deregulate gas production and let producers charge a market clearing price for their gas production. Some opponents of deregulation believed that the shortage was contrived, but consumers who had no heat in the winter cared less about the intricacies of policy making and more about simply getting gas.[4] Policy makers began to adjust and then readjust regulations to reinvigorate the gas industry.[5]

During the unusually cold and long winter of 1976–1977, the existing shortage conditions only intensified, particularly in the Northeast. Several interstate pipelines could deliver only 75 percent of their firm contract demand; other pipelines were in worse shape. In Northeastern

TABLE 11.3 Curtailments by U.S. Interstate Pipelines

Year	Curtailed Deliveries (Bcf)
1970	17
1971	286
1972	649
1972–73	1,031
1973–74	1,191
1974–75	2,418
1975–76	2,975
1976–77	3,790

Source: Federal Power Commission, *Natural Gas Survey* (Washington, D.C., 1975), Vol. 1, 105; FPC *Annual Report* (1976), 16.

and Midwestern gas-consuming states, the shortage forced the shutdown of more than 4,000 manufacturing plants and hundreds of schools, and it resulted in the layoff of more than 1 million workers.[6] In New York, Governor Carey declared a state of emergency on January 27, 1977, due to the winter gas shortages. There was simply too little natural gas available in the interstate system to fuel the nation through that cold winter.

Regulators encouraged renewed exploration and production for interstate commerce as the federal government subsidized development of alternative energy sources. At the same time, the environmental movement emerged as another politically powerful interest group that influenced energy policy and corporate decision making in the 1970s.

The Search for New Gas Supply

As the gas industry began to experience the first signs of a shortage in the late 1960s, changes at the FPC seemed to promise policy making more favorable to gas producers.[7] But FPC chairman John Nassikas, a Nixon appointee, ultimately was more concerned about protecting the public from unreasonable price increases than encouraging gas production. The FPC in 1970 did begin reexamining the area rate case hearing for the Permian Basin and southern Louisiana to determine whether higher wellhead prices might stimulate increased interstate supplies. The

FPC allowed an increase of 30 to 50 percent on the southern Louisiana price ceiling for new gas sold under new contracts, and it permitted producers to sell spot gas during emergency situations to interstate pipelines at prices considerably higher than the FPC-established area rates.[8] In 1969, the FPC abandoned its cost-of-service rate schedule for new gas produced by gas pipeline companies. The formula had essentially discriminated against pipeline firms that also produced gas. Now, a pipeline firm could purchase affiliated gas production at the same area rate as it purchased independent production.[9]

The oil embargo led by the Arab members of OPEC (Organization of Petroleum Exporting Countries) in response to the 1973 war between Egypt and Israel had exacerbated the domestic natural gas shortage.[10] As oil supplies declined, the demand for natural gas increased. The FPC responded with a 180-day emergency sales program which lifted price controls, but the D.C. District Court struck down this rule in a case brought by a consumer coalition. Consumer advocates and regulators reacted to current prices; they did not view the industry from the perspective of a disinterested economist who might favor a market driven industry that would theoretically result in increased production, thereby increasing output and lowering prices.[11]

The FPC also created a limited "self-help" program that allowed gas distribution companies to contract directly with producers. The distributors paid producers higher prices for natural gas than federal regulators allowed them to pay to their interstate pipeline suppliers.[12] Beginning in 1975, the FPC allowed industrial gas consumers to contract directly with producers under this program. Pipeline firms objected, as they realized that direct contracts between large customers and producers would begin the process of chipping away the pipelines' merchant status.

The advance payment program was another means of stimulating gas production for interstate commerce. Advance payments were essentially five-year interest-free loans, made by pipeline companies to producers for financing exploration efforts; the loan value became part of the pipeline's rate base. The loans were due in five years whether or not the drilling was successful, and the pipeline that loaned funds had the option to purchase any gas produced at regulated prices.[13] Many interstate transmission companies participated in the advance payment program in 1972. Commitments that year accounted for more than $1.6 billion. The Natural Gas Pipe Line Company advanced more than $260 million to producers between 1971 and 1974. During the period 1970–1976, Panhandle Eastern advanced about $320 million to nonaffiliated producers.[14]

The advance payment program stimulated some additional gas production, but it was short-lived. Alfred Kahn's New York Public Service

Commission challenged the practice in a lawsuit, objecting to pipeline firms loaning gas sales revenues in the form of interest-free loans to producers, many of which were major oil companies. The federal court remanded the program to the FPC for review, and the FPC responded by terminating the program in 1975. The same year, the courts ruled against the emergency purchase plan that allowed pipelines and producers to sell gas to other pipelines for up to 60 days without federal oversight.

Meanwhile, the FPC once again devised a new gas price-setting formula, this time to stimulate renewed exploration. In 1974, the FPC replaced its area price formula with a single national price that was not cost-based. The initial nationwide price for new gas was $.42 per Mcf, although this national interstate rate was as much as 50 percent less than many Southwestern gas producers were charging for intrastate gas.[15] The FPC subsequently created a three-tiered pricing formula allowing higher prices for recently produced gas: it established a price of $1.42 per Mcf for gas produced during 1975–1976; $1.01 per Mcf for gas produced in 1973–1974; and $.52 per Mcf for gas produced before 1973.[16] The new pricing formula simplified the FPC's price-setting responsibilities, but it did not simulate market forces.

While the FPC experimented with pricing formulas to stimulate gas production, pipeline firms began investigating new sources of the fuel. Several major pipeline firms invested in large-scale supplemental gas projects in an attempt to develop nontraditional sources of gas for traditional markets. Since pipelines were merchants, buying and selling gas, they essentially controlled the industry. Thus, in this era, pipelines had the responsibility for accumulating and allocating gas supply for resale, albeit in a regulated environment.

The Synthetic Gas Experiment

One of the "new" sources of gas was actually a modern version of manufactured coal gas. The modern technology for producing synthetic coal gas differed substantially from the earlier process, largely as a result of advances made in Europe and South Africa, and could produce nearly pure methane, the principal ingredient of natural gas. The obvious advantage of synthetic gas was that coal was abundant in America. By the 1970s, coal made up 90 percent of U.S. energy reserves, and the U.S. Geological Survey assessed the amount of recoverable U.S. coal reserves at 150 to 438 billion tons. One estimate states that approximately 27 percent of the world's total coal reserves are in U.S. territory.[17]

Since World War II, coal use had declined substantially, due in large part to the increase in natural gas utilization. After the Arab oil embargo and political support for reducing U.S. dependence on foreign oil, the country's coal reserves were literally rediscovered. One writer described coal as "a somewhat frumpy middle-aged ballerina rushed out of semi-retirement to fill an unanticipated gap in a show that must go on. Suddenly, the old girl is back in demand." The new industrial popularity of coal met determined resistance from environmental groups.[18]

Several pipeline firms sponsored synthetic gas projects, which for the most part absorbed a great deal of money but produced no gas. One of the first serious coal gasification projects was proposed by Texas Eastern in the early 1970s. Citing President Nixon's message to Congress on June 4, 1971, which noted the seriousness of the shortage and called for "an expanded program to convert coal into a clean gaseous fuel," company executives expected government support for synfuels. During late 1971, subsidiaries of Texas Eastern and Pacific Lighting Corporation organized the Western Gasification Company (Wesco). The partnership planned to build in northwestern New Mexico a $1.3 billion coal gasification plant capable of producing 250 standard MMcf/d.

The proposed plant site was approximately 30 miles southwest of Farmington, New Mexico, on land owned by the Navajo Tribe. Wesco chose this site because it was close to Utah International's coal reserves, which were also located on the Navajo Indian Reservation. The Wesco site was also near Texas Eastern's existing pipeline system, requiring only a 67-mile extension to connect with Transwestern's line. Utah International agreed to furnish the plant's coal and water requirements.

Wesco's certificated application to the FPC on February 7, 1973, was the first gasification project to receive full consideration by the commission.[19] Texas Eastern requested a cost-of-service rate for its gas production. Such a rate structure pleased investors and gave the venture a higher likelihood of success. The FPC granted Wesco a certificate of public convenience and necessity in 1975, but it did not authorize a full cost-of-service tariff. Instead, the FPC mandated an initial low price of $1.38 per Mcf. This decision increased the project's financial risk and made investment less attractive.

Texas Eastern's negotiations for coal supply also proved unsatisfactory. Since the coal was located on Navajo land, Wesco had to deal with both the Indian tribe and Utah International. The two sides could not agree on a mutually acceptable contract. Unable to get the two parties to settle their differences and unwilling to live with the FPC ruling, Texas Eastern dropped its first venture into synfuels. A similar venture proposed by El Paso Natural Gas suffered a similar fate.

In a joint-venture with Peabody Coal Company, Panhandle Eastern also planned a synthetic coal gas project called WyCoalGas in the early 1970s.[20] To be located in Wyoming, the plant was designed to produce 250 Mcf/d. One of the nation's largest coal producers, Peabody owned reserves totaling about 165 million tons in Illinois and 500 million tons in Wyoming. These extensive reserves were available for Panhandle Eastern's gasification project. WyCoalGas also negotiated for costly water rights and surface lands; in semiarid Wyoming, water was scarce and costly. M. W. Kellogg Company and American Lurgi served as consultants for the technological and ecological aspects of this project. The company also contracted with the South African Coal, Oil and Gas Corporation (SASOL) for design assistance and advice.[21]

SASOL had built its first synfuels plant in 1955, using technology initially developed in Germany during World War II. This plant used a modern version of the Lowe water gas process. Under extremely high pressure, steam and oxygen interacted with coal to produce carbon monoxide, carbon dioxide, hydrogen, and methane. Some of the gas was then liquefied to produce a synthetic oil similar to natural crude. South Africa's synfuels program attracted interest throughout the world, particularly after the 1973 oil embargo, and SASOL exported its technology to U.S. companies.[22]

WyCoalGas also confronted serious environmental considerations. The company had to complete an environmental impact statement and devise a wastewater recycling program. Solid wastes had to be disposed of in accordance with the requirements of the Resource Conservation Reclamation Act and the Water and Land Divisions of the Wyoming Department of Environmental Quality. In addition, airborne emissions would be monitored for compliance by the Air Quality Division of Wyoming. Environmental groups also opposed the WyCoal project for its plans to burn coal.[23]

Dealing with the environmental issues delayed plant construction and required WyCoalGas's full-time attention. The company stationed several employees in Wyoming to counter charges from environmental groups that gasification would damage Wyoming's air, water, and wildlife. To promote its project, the company produced and donated to the state a 30-minute Wyoming promotional film narrated by television personality Curt Gowdy, a Wyoming native. State legislators and environmental groups remained hostile.[24] Gradually, the WyCoalGas project shut down as the parent company, Panhandle Eastern, began writing off its project losses during 1976 and 1979.[25]

The only substantial synfuels project that produced and sold commercial synthetic gas was the Great Plains Gasification Association plant located in Beulah, North Dakota. This project was originally sponsored by American Natural Resources (ANR), which was the parent company of the Mich-Wisc pipeline. Failing to receive federal loan guarantees, ANR invited other partners to join in 1978, including Columbia Gas, Tenneco (Tennessee Gas's parent company), and Transcontinental Gas. The Great Plains project confronted numerous challenges. Complex issues regarding financing and tariffs were discussed extensively during numerous hearings and legal challenges. The plant was finally completed in 1984, but the original sponsors defaulted on their government-sponsored federal loans, fearing that they would never be able to sell gas at a price of $6.75 per MMBtu. Thus, the U.S. Department of Energy (DOE) acquired the plant in 1986 and then sold it to Dakota Gasification in 1988. The four pipelines originally obligated to buy the plant's gas (ANR, NGPL, Tennessee Gas, and Transco) agreed again to purchase the plant's gas.

These synfuel projects begged from the federal government an explanation of its current energy policy. While government officials and the FPC encouraged development of alternative fuel projects, gas companies found that the high economic and environmental costs associated with these projects could not be financed privately. Gas firms exploring alternative fuel projects argued for government subsidies. Synfuels not only provided additional gas during times of shortage but also represented an important step toward U.S. energy independence. While engineers improved the manufacturing processes for synfuels, Washington lobbyists sought to build a consensus for government subsidies ranging from loan guarantees to cost-of-source rates for the synfuels.

These issues confronted the Carter administration, which had declared "the moral equivalent of war" on the energy crisis. After the Iranian Revolution of 1979–1980 sparked a second energy shortage, Congress passed the Energy Security Act, which provided funding for the Synthetic Fuels Corporation (SFC) to subsidize commercial synfuels projects. The SFC was a controversial agency described as a "message to OPEC" by supporters and "just another boondoggle" by critics.[26] With a potential funding of $88 billion, the SFC promised substantial financial assistance for both ongoing and new synfuels projects. Congress granted the DOE authority to distribute up to $3 billion while the SFC was in the process of being organized. During July 1980, the Department of Energy distributed $200 million through its synthetic fuels commercialization program.[27]

After Congress approved the creation of the Synfuels Corporation, WyCoalGas attempted to restart its project. California's PG&E and Ruhrgas, a German utility, joined the venture. They quickly applied for funding from the DOE to continue design and development work. The project now confronted new hurdles. Inflation and high interest rates raised the projected costs to more than $3.5 billion, and the estimated price for its synthetic gas project reached $10 per Mcf, far above the price of natural gas.[28] Finally, the WyCoalGas project permanently ended in March 1982.

Texas Eastern's Wesco project also soon disbanded. Wesco had received a $3 million grant from the DOE's initial distribution of funds for research. But a study of the resulting project reached the gloomy conclusion that the "economics of the plant during its operating life are anticipated to be poor."[29] While technically feasible, that form of synfuel production was economically inefficient.

A new project, the Tri-State Synfuels Company (Tri-State), was a joint venture between Texas Gas Transmission and Texas Eastern, which received a $22.4 million grant from the DOE's synthetic fuels commercialization program. The funds were earmarked for construction of a coal liquefaction and gasification facility to be located in Geneva, Kentucky. In return for the grant, the Tri-State partnership agreed to contribute $20 million for this first phase. If Tri-State decided to go forward with the $4 billion plant, the DOE would continue to support the project. Once completed, the plant would produce synthetic gas, transportation fuel, and chemicals.[30]

The Tri-State project planned to use high-sulfur coal from Kentucky, and the state government agreed to pay for a test to ensure that this type of coal would work. Tri-State shipped 20,000 tons of high-sulfur coal to South Africa for tests, which proved favorable. Shortly, however, the Tri-State project began to encounter other technical difficulties. While SASOL technology allowed coal to be broken down into both gas and liquids, the process required substantial amounts of energy. The high costs associated with the project meant that Tri-State would have to charge a high price for its synthetic gas, a higher price than for existing natural gas. Otherwise, the Tri-State project could not be justified economically. In 1982, this project also began to dissolve. Regarding synfuels, a company official stated that "the technology is available today. Unfortunately, the world economy is not such that we can afford to do it."[31]

In the meantime, the Great Plains project enjoyed more success. It received substantial federal loan guarantees, which continued to increase annually. In 1981, President Reagan approved a $2.02 billion federal loan guarantee. The project received a fixed-price tariff of $6.75 per Mcf adjustable according to the price of fuel oil.[32] This plant became the only synfuels plant to become operational and sell synthetic natural gas.

Alaskan Natural Gas

The search for new sources of supply also led to Alaska. In 1967, a partnership of Atlantic Richfield and Humble Oil (a subsidiary of Standard [New Jersey]) discovered a huge natural gas field at Prudhoe Bay on the North Slope. This led to further discoveries of oil, making this the largest single discovery of crude oil and natural gas ever made on the North American continent. The estimates for those proved recoverable natural gas reserves ranged from 26 Tcf to 33 Tcf.[33]

During the next several years three groups of companies organized and presented competing proposals for bringing Alaskan gas to the continental United States.[34] Arctic Gas submitted the first proposal to the FPC in March 1974. This firm included 16 Canadian and U.S. firms, and it proposed a 2,500-mile 48-inch line originating at Prudhoe Bay. The line would extend along the coast of the Beaufort Sea into Canada, pass through the Mackenzie River Delta, and deliver gas to customers and pipeline connections in Alberta. Additional lines would transport the gas to customers in Illinois and California. The cost for this project was estimated to be $9.6 billion.[35]

Environmentalists attacked this proposal. They stated that the proposed route crossing the Arctic National Wildlife Range would damage, if not destroy, the coastline environment along its route. Arctic Gas executives disagreed, claiming that they would actually clean up trash along the route, particularly on the coastline.

El Paso Natural Gas proposed a second plan for bringing Alaskan Gas to the continental United States. Its planned 800-mile pipeline would follow the right-of-way of Trans-Alaska Pipeline System (TAPS), which transported oil from Prudhoe Bay to its terminus at Valdez on the Prince William Sound. There, El Paso would construct a gas liquefication plant and transport liquefied natural gas (LNG) to southern California using a fleet of 11 tankers. El Paso believed that its $7.9 billion project would receive regulatory approval since it did not involve Canadian jurisdiction.

The Northwest Energy Company submitted a third proposal to the FPC in July 1976. Northwest had been a participant in the Arctic Gas project, but Northwest offered its own proposal after environmental problems stalled the Arctic Gas project. Northwest proposed a 1,600-mile pipeline originating at Prudhoe Bay, following the TAPS right-of-way in Alaska, paralleling the Alcan Highway in Canada, and reentering the United States in Montana. Alcan's proposal had a $6.7 billion price tag, which was substantially lower than the competing proposals.

The prospect of transporting Alaskan natural gas to augment the existing gas supply received congressional support. Congress passed the Alaskan Natural Gas Transportation Act requiring the FPC to recommend one of the three systems to the president by May 1, 1977. Canadian and U.S. officials also signed a treaty, the "Transit Pipeline Agreement," providing for a U.S. gas line to cross through Canada.

After a prolonged period of debate and lobbying efforts among the three lines regarding the merits of their proposed routes, President Carter chose Alcan. This consortium reorganized as the Alaskan Northwest Pipeline Company. In 1977, the FPC issued a conditional certificate of public convenience and necessity for the project, which reorganized again as the Alaska Natural Gas Transportation System (ANGTS).

Financing problems plagued this project, and it was indefinitely postponed as of April 1982. Only the southern portions of the system were built to move southern Canadian production to U.S. markets. A partnership of U.S. firms—Columbia Gas, Mich-Wisc, Panhandle Eastern, NGPL, Texas Eastern, and Internorth (formerly Northern Natural)—formed the Northern Border Pipeline Company. Northern Border built a 42-inch 823-mile pipeline, which extended from the Canadian border in Saskatchewan to a connection with Northern Natural in Ventura, Iowa, which cost approximately $1.3 billion.[36]

Liquefied Natural Gas

The high demand for new natural gas supplies compelled several gas firms to seek natural gas from gas fields located on other continents. To transport gas across the ocean, it had to be liquefied. In 1914 Godfrey Cabot had developed a process to liquefy gas by lowering its temperature to –260°F, at which point its volume contracts 600 times. LNG was potentially volatile, but specially constructed ocean-going tankers could safely and economically transport the fuel.[37]

Serious accidents related to LNG had occurred in the United States. Initially, LNG technology was used to facilitate gas storage rather than transportation. In 1941 in Cleveland, the East Ohio Gas Company built the first commercial LNG plant operated in the United States. The plant exploded in 1944, killing 130 people and destroying a neighborhood. This disaster, wrote economist Arlon Tussing, "brought a halt to the domestic LNG storage business for almost twenty years."[38] LNG technology continued to improve, and by the late 1960s, LNG was being transported from gas-rich nations such as Algeria to England and France. Brunei, Libya, Indonesia, and Saudi Arabia later became LNG exporters.[39]

The first U.S. LNG plant was dedicated for gas exports. It was built at the Cook Inlet in Alaska and operated by Phillips Petroleum and Marathon Oil. They exported LNG to Japan beginning in 1969. In 1971, Distrigas Corporation began receiving relatively small volumes of Algerian LNG at its $10 million plant. This was a small venture designed only to provide extra gas (peak shaving) to customers during periods of high seasonal demand.

Much more substantial LNG projects were developed by Tenneco, Texas Eastern, El Paso, and Panhandle Eastern. These efforts clearly illustrated both the promise and risk in supplemental gas ventures. In the first project, Tenneco, Texas Eastern, and the Houston-based construction firm Brown & Root planned a $6.7 billion venture called North Star to import LNG from the USSR. Herbert Brownell, former attorney general of the Eisenhower administration, represented the consortium along with John B. Connally, former Texas governor and U.S. secretary of the treasury.[40] On July 2, 1973, the U.S. companies signed a "protocol of intent" with the Soviets "to discuss the development of a major natural gas export-import project."[41] One month earlier, the Occidental–El Paso consortium reached a similar agreement with Soviet authorities.

North Star planned to acquire its natural gas from the Urengoiske gas field in central Siberia. This field was the largest natural gas field in the world, containing estimated reserves of 141–280 Tcf. From the field, a 1,500-mile pipeline would transport the gas to an LNG plant 100 miles west of Murmansk. Converted to liquid, the LNG would be shipped by a fleet of 20 tankers 4,000 miles to Philadelphia, regasified, and sold to Northeastern customers through existing pipelines. Over a 25-year period, the venture expected to deliver a yearly average of 2 Bcf/d.

It appeared that by June 1974, the Soviet and American negotiators had agreed upon all substantive issues except price. The Trade Act of 1974 gave the Soviet Union most-favored-nation status so long as it did not unduly restrict emigration of its citizens, and this measure facilitated the negotiations. Thus by the summer of 1974, Texas Eastern and its partners seemed on the verge of completing an extraordinary agreement. A final meeting was to be held in Moscow, and during this meeting the American participants heard that the U.S. government had unexpectedly canceled the project (presumably for political reasons).[42]

El Paso Natural Gas organized the first substantial U.S. LNG project. In 1969, El Paso signed an agreement with Sonatrach, the state-owned Algerian oil and gas company. The 25-year agreement called for Sonatrach to build a $630 million gasification plant in Algeria. El Paso, which had no lines in the East, agreed to purchase a fleet of nine LNG tankers to transport the LNG across the Atlantic. El Paso contracted with three East Coast gas companies to receive the gas. Columbia Gas,

Consolidated Natural Gas, and Southern Natural Gas agreed to purchase 650 MMcf/d from El Paso for $.79 per Mcf.[43]

The FPC approved the project in 1972. Despite tremendous increases in the costs of the Algerian gasification plant, El Paso's tankers, and the price of delivered gas, El Paso began transporting Algerian LNG to the United States during the spring of 1978. East Coast utilities had agreed to pay $1.28 per Mcf for the gas.[44] Within one year, this ambitious LNG importation scheme was unraveling.

A combination of forces led to the demise of El Paso's LNG project. A change in Algeria's political leadership, the skyrocketing price of oil, and Sonatrach's own losses due to the project caused the Algerian firm to begin demanding higher prices. In 1979, Sonatrach asked for $1.75 per Mcf, and El Paso sought regulatory approval for this new rate. Before approval was granted, Algeria demanded increasingly higher prices, reaching $6.11 per Mcf, the equivalent of a $32 barrel of oil. The U.S. DOE entered negotiations on El Paso's behalf, but U.S. officials would not agree for El Paso to pay more than $4.00 per Mcf for the gas. During the spring of 1980, talks between the United States and Algeria collapsed. The following year, El Paso withdrew from the project and took a $365 million loss. The failed LNG venture combined with increased competition in the California market also led to a weakened corporate financial situation. Burlington Northern purchased El Paso in 1982.[45]

While El Paso was engaged in its Algerian LNG venture, Panhandle Eastern commenced negotiations with Sonatrach for a similar project. Panhandle organized Trunkline LNG Company to conduct negotiations with the Algerian firm, and they signed a contract on December 7, 1972. The agreement provided for delivery of 450 MMcf/d for a 20-year period beginning in 1979. Sonatrach agreed to finance and construct all production and liquefaction operations and supply half of the tankers needed for the project. Trunkline commenced construction of LNG regasification facilities at Lake Charles, Louisiana, which included a special dock for the tankers, unloading equipment, and three storage tanks each capable of holding 600,000 barrels of LNG.

The FPC quickly authorized the project; during the same year, the U.S. and Algerian governments also approved the plan. The FPC allowed Trunkline to sell the imported gas on a favorable "rolled-in pricing" basis, using a weighted average price based on the price of both LNG and domestic gas.[46]

As with the El Paso project, numerous financial and political problems soon emerged. Costs for the Lake Charles facility alone rose from $240 million to a final figure of $567 million.[47] Other costs increased as well. Panhandle's LNG contract contained an escalator clause based on the price of No. 2 and No. 6 fuel oil at New York. Before deliveries even

LNG tanker at the Lake Charles, Louisiana, facility.

Courtesy, Duke Energy.

began, Sonatrach pressed to invoke the escalator clause and increase the LNG price. Panhandle responded that the agreement did not permit price changes prior to the beginning of regular LNG deliveries.[48] It was during this time, in the Spring of 1980, when Sonatrach suspended all LNG deliveries to El Paso. The Trunkline project faced an even greater financial loss if the project collapsed. Trunkline's current customers would have to pay for the increasingly expensive gas from the LNG deal, and they were not happy.

The firm's LNG deal attracted unwanted media attention. In an article titled "Panhandle Eastern: A Gas-Shortage Gamble Is Blowing Up in Its Face," *Business Week* reported that "the whole range of company projects that once seemed admirable—liquefied natural gas imports, synthetic fuels, and sponsorship of the Alaskan gas pipeline—is beginning to sour." Sonatrach's attempt to renegotiate its gas sales price to $5.25 per Mcf was meeting stiff resistance in the United States.

Then in August 1982 two of Panhandle's largest customers, MichCon and Consumers Power, protested the high-priced Algerian gas. MichCon announced that it would take "every legal action possible" to avoid purchasing the high-priced gas. "We do not want the Algerian supplies," the company president stated, "we cannot sell it."[49] Since utilities passed their gas costs on to consumers, consumer groups protested the LNG as well. Despite active opposition to the contract, the FPC recommended that Trunkline proceed with LNG importation. In September 1982 Panhandle received its first delivery of liquefied natural gas equivalent to 125,000 cubic meters of LNG.

Controversy increased after LNG deliveries commenced, and Trunkline watched as its gas sales quickly declined. Sales volumes dropped from 526 Bcf in 1982 to 300 Bcf in 1983, and management projected sales of only 250 Bcf in 1984. Trunkline's delivered gas price had jumped from $2.96 to $4.69 per MMBtu, making Trunkline the highest-priced pipeline among its 15 largest competitors. The Algerian LNG made up 26 percent of all gas supplied to Trunkline customers and 53 percent of the company's purchased gas costs.[50]

Panhandle was now surrounded by angry customers, disgruntled regulators, and Algerian officials who demanded that Panhandle abide by its contract. One representative of the customers was Donald E. Petersen, president of Ford Motor Company, who was then a Panhandle Eastern board member. Petersen resigned his board position in a statement to the pipeline that said, "There appears to be a fundamental incompatibility between Ford's desire to shift from natural gas to alternative fuels, and its efforts to encourage its utility suppliers to do likewise, and Panhandle Eastern's goal of forestalling any additional loss of natural gas sales to industrial users and, indeed, to recapture if not increase such sales."[51] Democratic senator Thomas Eagleton from Missouri voiced popular concern when he said of the LNG deal, "The benefit will go to the Algerians who will make off like bandits and to the pipelines who lined up this ridiculous deal."[52] Sonatrach did agree to reduce LNG deliveries to Trunkline, and Panhandle pressed for further relief without success. The federal government was becoming increasingly involved in the venture, and on November 21, 1983, President Reagan signed a bill requiring Secretary of State George Shultz and Energy Secretary Donald Hodel to report to Congress within 30 days on efforts to "promote lower prices and fair market conditions" for U.S. imports of Algerian LNG.[53]

By this time, Trunkline's parent firm, Panhandle Eastern, had only one realistic choice: Trunkline LNG indefinitely suspended LNG purchases as of December 12, 1983. Sonatrach sued the firm in international courts. Panhandle later reached a $600 million settlement with Sonatrach as part of a successful strategy to outmaneuver a hostile takeover attempt by Wagner & Brown during its weakened financial condition.

Neither the economic nor political environment on the early 1980s favored supplemental fuel projects, most of which failed. All of these efforts, from coal gasification to Alaskan gas and imported LNG, had tremendously high development costs. Not only that, but they produced gas that had a significantly higher price than domestic natural gas. Indeed, the failure of these efforts coincided with the disappearance of shortages; earlier, the shortages and resulting higher prices had facilitated the supplemental gas projects. In the early 1970s, in response to the shortages, energy companies had engaged in numerous supplemental gas ventures, often with direct support and subsidies from the federal government. President Jimmy Carter and the Congress also sought to stimulate domestic gas production by beginning to deregulate gas (see chapter 12). These efforts led to another unexpected consequence of regulatory planning—a quickly forming gas "bubble" (oversupply), which emerged in the early 1980s and didn't pop. With adequate supplies of new domestically produced, low-priced gas, none of the high-cost supplemental fuel projects except those that received substantial government subsidies such as the Great Plains project had a chance of success.

The legacy of the 1970s gas industry was a lesson in basic market economics. National gas supply was clearly responsive to federal gas pricing policy. The time lag between the Phillips decision (1954) and the 1970s shortages was due in part to the tremendous demand for gas in the intervening years. Even stringent price controls could not dull explosive industry growth. But with the emergence of a national pipeline grid and the maturation of the industry, the gas supply problem emerged. Exacerbating problems in the complexly structured industry, pipeline firms invested huge sums of money in supplemental gas projects, which in historical perspective represented pipeline firms' last gasp of retaining merchant status, or their ability to allocate through managerial decision making both national gas flow and public policy.

PART 5

Restructuring, 1978–2000

12

Deregulation, Consolidation, and the Environment

NATURAL GAS SHORTAGES plagued the industry, agitated policy makers, and disrupted the nation in the 1970s. The shortages reminded Americans that natural resources are limited. No longer was energy simply abundant. Permanent natural gas depletion in the future was now a possibility. Conservation became an integral part of Americans' lives on an industrial and residential scope. Americans learned that conservation meant reducing energy bills, protecting the environment, and not wasting fuel. While the shortages were temporary, they occurred during an era of increasing environmental awareness, and this theme permeated energy policy during the last two decades of the twentieth century.

Both industry and government responded in dramatic fashion to the 1970s shortages. As we saw in chapter 11, gas companies spent billions of dollars on supplemental fuel projects only to see nearly all them fail by the early 1980s. They failed not because the technology was inadequate but because policy makers began deregulating the gas industry (and prices), making the new projects comparably much too expensive. Pipeline firms had sponsored most of the supplemental fuel projects, and these large investments essentially placed the pipelines in double jeopardy. Lacking gas in the late 1960s and early 1970s due to restrictive wellhead gas-pricing regulations, they had poured tremendous sums of money into these new and expensive projects. The federal government encouraged companies to develop new gas supplies while it simultaneously began the process of deregulating the industry. Deregulation and concurrent efforts to conserve domestic energy in the late 1970s resulted in a "gas bubble" by the early 1980s. With ample supply for domestic consumption, natural gas prices fell. Supplemental projects no longer appeared as heroic corporate efforts to achieve energy independence. Instead, they were sometimes described as unreasonably expensive projects designed to enrich their sponsors and gouge the public in a time of crisis.

The solution was deregulation, which led to relaxed price and entry regulations. These actions not only resulted in a weakened regulatory system, but they also led to significant gas industry restructuring. Policy makers, economists, and gas firms heralded the return of "market forces" as gas firms emerged from decades of strict pricing regulations and restructured operationally and administratively. Instead of the "visible hand" of regulators, market forces would soon play a larger role in determining gas availability and price.

Along with price deregulation, policy makers focused on the role of interstate gas pipelines. From the consumers' perspective, the regulated, merchant-oriented interstate gas pipelines had not performed well. Their regulated economic function of purchasing gas on one end of the system and selling it at the other had caused problems. The pipelines' merchant function was essentially that of a middleman who bought and then resold a product, unnecessarily complicating the relationship between producer and distributor or large industrial end user. Correcting this apparent market defect resulted in new regulations during the last decade of the twentieth century, which transformed pipelines into virtual common carriers presumably for the benefit of both gas consumers and the industry. One consequence of this policy appeared in the early 1990s, when the American public began to see once again the formation of large gas and electric corporations with nationwide—even international—reach. Not since the 1930s had utility firms with such scale and scope operated in the United States.

Before gas and electric firms could begin the process of consolidation, federal regulatory policy had to be modified. By the early 1970s, two basic policy issues begged reconsideration: price controls and the economic function of interstate gas pipelines. The focus of attention was first on prices. Price setting in the past had been a kind of high art, almost a practice of market divination, but its practitioners had failed to satisfy everyone and in some cases anyone. In the era of deregulation, prices had to reflect market conditions, operating costs, and consumers' abilities to pay while promoting continued exploration and development efforts. Throughout the 1970s and into the 1980s, price setting evoked considerable controversy. The second controversy was the Federal Energy Regulatory Commission's determination to change the economic function of interstate pipelines from gas merchants to contract carriers.

Deregulating the Gas Industry

James Earl Carter campaigned for the presidency in 1976 and pledged the "moral equivalent of war" on the energy crisis. He promised to make changes in energy policy that would lead to greater national energy independence. Following through on his promise, he created the Department of Energy to oversee the nation's energy situation. Carter tackled the natural gas availability problem, and he supported efforts to revitalize the coal industry, subsidize synfuel projects, and encourage foreign gas imports. All these measures were designed to improve the U.S. energy supply outlook.[1]

The Carter administration actively supported the revision of federal natural gas regulations to stimulate exploration and production efforts, put more gas in the market, and lower prices. These programs were applauded by industry and economists, including Alfred Kahn, who said, "I was one of the 'architects' of regulation, but I think it's bankrupt now. If we had deregulated, we would have had more gas; we also would have had more customers hooked up with that gas. We would not have had the restrictions that we've had in the last few years."[2] Earlier, Kahn had opposed talk of deregulation, believing that it would benefit producers at the expense of consumers.[3]

Deregulation commenced with congressional passage of the National Energy Act (1978) that included five parts. Two of these parts were the Natural Gas Policy Act (NGPA) and the Public Utility Regulatory Policies Act of 1978, which in part discouraged natural gas use by electric utilities and large industrial firms.[4] Congress also renamed the Federal Power Commission as the Federal Energy Regulatory Commission (FERC), which assumed most of the FPC's responsibilities.

The FERC's primary responsibility regarding natural gas was managing the implementation of nine major new natural gas price categories, each containing subcategories, based on well depth, vintage, and source. Newly discovered on-shore gas received a price of $1.75 per Mcf, plus an inflation escalator remaining in effect until January 1, 1985. On that date, all new gas produced for interstate and intrastate commerce would be deregulated. Gas in production before 1978 would be priced in three tiers ranging from $.29 through $1.45, plus inflation, and remain regulated indefinitely.[5] (See table 12.1.)

TABLE 12.1 Gas Prices Before and After Deregulation

Year	Wellhead ($/Mcf†)	City Gate* ($/MMBtu†)	Cost to the Ultimate Customer ($/MMBtu†)
1966	0.157	0.333	0.612
1968	0.164	0.328	0.607
1970	0.171	0.354	0.641
1972	0.186	0.429	0.730
1974	0.304	0.573	0.953
1976	0.580	0.984	1.599
1978	0.905	1.466	2.184
1980	1.588	2.414	3.134
1982	2.457	3.598	4.456
1984	2.655	3.890	5.128
1986	1.942	3.579	4.602
1988	1.690	3.243	4.312
1990	1.710	3.542	4.588
1992	1.740	3.475	4.661
1994	1.830	2.225	5.222

Source: American Gas Association, *Gas Facts* (Arlington: AGA, 1988), 112.
Note: Mcf = thousand cubic feet.
*Resale prices approximate city-gate prices.
†Mcf and MMBtu are roughly comparable. On a MMBtu basis, the wellhead price would be slightly less.

The NGPA marked the official beginning of U.S. natural gas deregulation, but it was roundly criticized. Richard Vietor stated that as a solution to the shortages, the NGPA "could not have been more inept."[6] The new law was a political compromise between consumer-oriented regulatory policy and federally mandated price controls. The NGPA did stimulate gas production, but it did not do the same for demand. By the early 1980s, even residential gas customers were abiding calls for conservation and using less gas. Texas's electric utilities, which led the nation in gas use for generating electricity, also began burning less gas, although California's began using more. The result of the NGPA, combined with conservation efforts, led to an unexpected gas surplus, which emerged in the early 1980s. While deregulation was supposed to result in increased supplies, the lack of a comprehensive and coordinated policy for the entire industry meant that the gas bubble would benefit consumers price-wise but result in financial problems for the industry. Natural gas prices rose initially in the early 1980s when some gas companies were still investing heavily in supplemental fuel projects. But after consumption began to decline, gas prices unexpectedly fell following the 1985 removal of wellhead price controls on new gas production. The overall increased supply and drop in prices ensured the permanent demise of all remaining 1970s supplemental gas projects. Natural gas energy consumption was lower in the 1980s compared to the 1970s, but it increased again in the 1990s.

An equally significant industry-wide problem related to the long-term take-or-pay contracts (typically 20 years in duration) that bound many gas pipelines to producers. These contracts required pipelines to pay for a minimum amount of contract gas whether it was actually taken or not. Many of these contracts had been signed during the 1970s when prices were high and supply uncertain, but the long-term contracts provided assurance to pipelines and their LDC (local distribution company) customers of a long-term, stable supply. As lower-priced gas became available on the market, major utility companies objected to purchasing expensive natural gas under long-term contract when market prices had fallen to significantly lower levels. Utilities petitioned the FERC and state regulatory commissions for permission to break their gas purchase contracts with pipelines so they could purchase lower-priced, newly produced gas. It was this regulated market dysfunction that led to the transformation of gas pipelines from merchants to transporters.

Restructuring the Gas Industry

The FERC began the process of transforming interstate natural gas pipelines into contract carriers during the early 1980s. In siding with consumers, the agency began allowing LDCs to purchase lower-cost natural gas despite the long-term contracts between pipeline and distributor. First, the commission issued "blanket certificates" to pipelines allowing them to transport gas for distributors and industrial consumers.[7] A more formalized policy followed; this policy encouraged pipelines to form Special Marketing Programs through which they could buy, sell, and transport short-term "spot market" gas for customers.[8]

While some pipeline firms adopted aggressive gas transportation programs that accommodated the utilities determined to break their gas purchase contracts with pipelines, other pipelines were accused of forcing customers to continue purchasing high-priced gas. In one instance, the Central Light Company of Illinois accused Panhandle Eastern, its sole natural gas supplier, of not allowing it to buy spot gas. The dispute intensified in early 1984 when the Illinois attorney general filed an antitrust suit against Panhandle. Philip O'Connor, chairman of the Illinois Commerce Commission, proposed to Congress his solution to the "virtual havoc in the natural gas industry. . . . Immediately change natural gas interstate pipeline status to common carriage."[9]

This sentiment seemed to underlay FERC policy initiatives in the 1980s and early 1990s. The U.S. gas industry was a nationwide network of interconnected pipeline systems connecting producers with consumers. With such an infrastructure in place, it was no longer necessary for pipelines to have a specific economic function other than transporting natural gas. A national transportation grid existed, so market demand should dictate price and allocation rather than a pipeline firm's management. Recall the debate about imposing common-carrier status much earlier in the century (see chapter 5) when Senator Foraker of Ohio argued against this policy since it might discourage the construction of new gas lines. Entrepreneurial efforts in subsequent years had been unhampered by intrusive regulation and had succeeded in creating a gas transportation gird. The existence of this grid, according to current regulatory policy, now justified removal of the pipeline's merchant status.

To create a national gas market in which consumers contracted directly with producers for gas supply, the restrictive gas sales and purchase contracts that included minimum bills, escalator clauses, and take-or-pay agreements had to be dismantled. The FERC supported efforts to quickly reduce gas costs for consumers. In May 1984, the agency issued Order 380, which eliminated the "minimum bill" provision in gas purchase contracts requiring purchasers to pay for minimum purchase volumes whether the gas was actually taken or not.[10] This allowed distributors to abandon higher-cost pipeline supplies and buy more and more gas on the growing spot market. By early 1985, gas purchased by utilities directly from producers accounted for approximately 14 percent of the nation's gas sales.[11]

While utility firms could break their contracts with pipelines and transact directly with producers, the take-or-pay contracts between pipelines and producers remained in full force. This meant that gas pipelines were obligated to continue purchasing expensive gas even though they could not sell it.[12] The FERC acted slowly to relieve gas pipelines of their take-or-pay contracts while seeking to make gas transportation a distinct business function. FERC mandated pipelines to provide voluntarily open-access, nondiscriminatory gas transportation services. The order also authorized the agency to review take-or-pay buyouts

Modern gas pipeline construction.

Photo by Keith R. Schmidt. Courtesy, Duke Energy.

for pipelines adhering to the Order 436 gas transportation guidelines. From the perspective of pipeline companies, the order required pipelines to maintain responsibility for acquiring long-term gas supply while allowing utility customers to reduce their existing contract demand to zero over a five-year period.[13] Pipeline companies complained bitterly that Order 436 did not satisfactorily deal with the take-or-pay issue, and

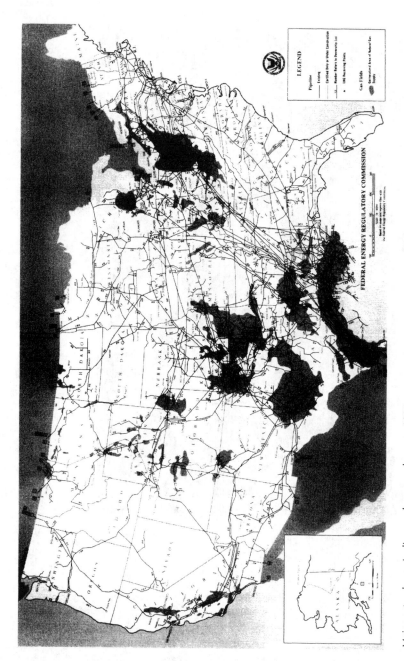

Major natural gas pipelines and gas supply areas, 1997.

Federal Energy Regulatory Commission.

they took FERC to court about it. The D.C. Court of Appeals heard a case brought against the FERC regarding Order 436, and during June 1987 the Court remanded the Order back to the Commission because it did not address the take-or-pay issues.[14]

The disputed take-or-pay contracts were serious business. By 1987, U.S. take-or-pay liability exceeded $10 billion; several pipelines had individual liabilities reaching more than $1 billion. Some companies attempted to exercise various legalistic provisions of their gas purchase contracts such as "market-out" clauses or "force-majeure" (a superior force such as war or weather) to avert paying for gas not taken. Producers continued to press for pipelines to abide by their contracts. The only solution was further regulatory action.

The FERC responded in August 1987 with the first of several versions of Order 500, which finally dealt with the take-or-pay issue. This order allowed a pipeline to transport a particular volume of gas for a producer in return for an equal volume of credit against that producer's take-or-pay claims against the same pipeline. This new regulation also provided a formula for take-or-pay liability resolution. If a pipeline absorbed 25 percent of its take-or-pay liability, it could charge the remaining in its rates (25 percent in its commodity rate and 50 percent in its demand rate). Order 500 was not entirely satisfactory to the gas industry, and FERC worked to devise a long-lasting solution to the industry's confused state.[15]

The solution was Order 636 of April 1992. FERC chairman Martin L. Allday explained that "Order No. 636 will signal the end of the seemingly endless transition period the gas industry has been in. . . . [Order 636] is the next and hopefully last major step in the Commission's efforts to allow competition rather than regulation to govern how pipelines function."[16] Order 636 resolutely "unbundled" traditional natural gas pipeline merchant service. This meant in effect that services including transportation, gathering, and storage could be contracted individually based on market conditions rather than regulatory policy. Order 636 also mandated that interstate pipelines operate as nondiscriminatory open-access transportation services, or contract carriers. Pipelines had traditionally made more money buying and selling gas than transporting it, but Order 636 prompted gas firms to significantly enlarge their arm's length marketing services, including purchasing, gathering, and processing gas.[17] To keep track of gas flow and pipeline allocations, the Order required pipelines to post on Electronic Bulletin Boards information necessary for others to contract their transportation services. Order 636 also called for interstate gas companies to support increased natural gas availability for electric generation.[18]

Modern gas control room.

Courtesy, Duke Energy.

The effects of deregulation on gas industry restructuring are evident in statistics. In 1983, about 5 percent of all interstate natural gas was delivered under contract directly between producer and consumer; 95 percent of that gas was bought and then resold by pipelines. By 1994, the statistics were reversed; virtually all interstate gas was contracted directly between producers and consumers (see table 12.2). The FERC had converted gas pipelines into virtual common carriers with the express purpose of allowing the "market" to operate more effectively by balancing supply with demand. The "middleman," or merchant gas pipeline, could no longer confuse the market with its own economic decisions and self-interest.

While pipeline firms were regulated into virtual common-carrier status, utility corporations sought other ways to profit from buying and selling gas. In the early 1980s, small, entrepreneurial-oriented gas-marketing firms emerged to begin buying gas from producers, selling it to consumers, and arranging for transportation through a pipeline. As it became clear in the late 1980s that "open access" would become permanent, gas pipelines created their own marketing affiliates; as long as these marketing divisions remained physically separated (located in a

TABLE 12.2 Natural Gas Transported by Interstate
Pipelines (as a percentage of transportation to sales)

Year	% Transported
1983	5
1984	8
1985	17
1986	37
1987	56
1988	63
1989	71
1990	79
1991	84
1992	87
1993	90
1994	100

Source: Derived from INGAA, "Carriage through
1993," Report no. 94-2, June 1994.

separate office building) from the pipeline division, an energy corporation could own both a pipeline and marketer. By 1993, gas marketers
brokered 43 percent of all natural gas transported through interstate
pipelines. A gas firm's financial officer reflected on this change from
merchant to common carrier: "We went from dealing with sales to 80
customers with $5 billion worth of revenues and now we've got $2 1/2 billion in revenues and we've probably got 5,000 customers."[19] There were
thousands of gas transportation service bills to collect each month and a
new need for marketing capabilities.[20]

Deregulation of gas prices led to the imposition of contract carrier
status on gas pipelines. The industry is not free from regulation, but
deregulation has changed the industry's structure. While the gas industry
of the late 1990s appears to be operating effectively, changing economic
conditions in the future will certainly bring more change to energy policy. As one executive noted, regulatory systems reflect "the continual ten-
sion of one group of people to exert jurisdiction over another group of
people. And it's a very delicate balance to make the thing work and make
it produce the desired results."[21] The future will tell whether the industry
remains in balance or not.

By the end of the twentieth century, the term "open architecture" might well describe the gas industry.[22] The phrase suggests both the concept of open access and, perhaps, rampant competition as well as overall industry change. In fact, rapid change in policy, industry structure, and even technology seems to be a defining feature of the late twentieth-century gas industry. Certainly, the transformation of pipelines into virtual common carriers, and opening local distribution company markets to competition, has shifted power and control to marketers instead of the infrastructure's owners.

Reemergence of Utility Combines

Perhaps one unintended consequence of natural gas deregulation is the reemergence of the public utility combine through merger and acquisition. In 1996, the combined value of mergers, acquisitions, and asset sales in the U.S. gas and electric industry reached $70 billion. New combinations in the natural gas, communications, and electric utility sectors are occurring with seemingly increasing frequency. By the late 1990s, the 20 largest gas pipeline firms accounted for 85 percent of interstate natural gas movement. Order 636's call for a closer relationship between gas and electric supply is also reflected in industry structure, as several gas and electric power firms have in the last decade of the twentieth century consolidated into single corporate structures.

Large gas and electric power firms with a national reach once again appear to dominate the public utility landscape. Enron Corporation, the self-described first U.S. "Natural Gas Major," controls several major pipelines including Northern Natural, Transwestern, and Florida Gas Transmission, numerous smaller systems, Portland General Electric (an electric utility operating in Oregon), and other energy-related businesses. Another utility combine is Duke Energy, a large electric utility operating principally in North Carolina, which purchased Panhandle Eastern, Trunkline, and the Texas Eastern pipelines. The Coastal Corporation controls the former NGPL and Colorado Interstate system. These and other firms are also involved in international utility ventures as well.

In some respects, the 1990s utility industry resembles the utility industry of the 1920s and 1930s, when a few huge public utility holding companies dominated their industry. Important differences exist as well, but the general outlines are relatively similar in scale and scope. Whether or not the sheer size and increasingly international characteristics of these firms contributes to future economic dysfunction that requires government intervention is a question (if not a prediction) for the future.

Will these massive public utilities be charged again, rightly or wrongly, with abusing the public's trust? At the very least, this question suggests that historical relationships between government controls and market capitalism exist in an ever-shifting yet not entirely unpredictable balance.

With these structural changes in the utility industry, it is not surprising that there has been increasing debate in recent years about the efficacy of the Public Utility Holding Company Act. Since the mid-1980s, the SEC, which oversees implementation of the act's provisions, has conducted studies of it geared toward either repealing or dramatically reforming this legislation. Congress has debated bills that would either repeal or modify the PUHCA, but the law remains in effect for now.[23] Indeed, the law's opponents argue that the original act is antiquated, impeding the transition to competition, and restricts utilities from entering into new business activities. Those supporting repeal believe that the combination of state regulatory commissions, FERC, U.S. Department of Justice, and antitrust laws are significant to protect the national and consumer interest.[24]

Deregulation did not stop at the wholesale energy market; similar developments are occurring in the residential market. Individual states are passing new laws allowing residential consumers to begin choosing their own gas and electric suppliers in the same fashion as they now choose their own long-distance telephone service. The economic problem is that consumers will be expected to make rational decisions based on a potentially huge amount of information in order to chose a particular supplier. Marketers are unlikely to make cost comparisons for packaged services easy for consumers to make.

The best example of this new market structure is exemplified by AMWAY Corporation's entry into the gas business. In November 1998, AMWAY Corporation, a company famous for selling household products through pyramid sales schemes, announced that it will soon add natural gas and electricity to its product line. AMWAY's 1 million–strong sales force will sell natural gas for the Columbia Energy Group, a large natural gas distribution company based in Virginia. These partners will first sell gas to residential customers in Georgia and then gradually expand their marketing efforts across the nation.[25]

Americans have tolerated for years television, radio, direct mail, and telephone call appeals to switch long-distance telephone service providers. It appears that the gas industry will follow the same path. Even Alfred Kahn, one of the leading modern proponents of deregulation, has expressed some concern about this situation when he stated that, "conceivably, . . . the burden on consumers of digesting such information and choosing may outweigh the benefits of competition." The social costs of deregulation are yet to be calculated.[26]

Legacy of the Past

During the late twentieth century, environmental awareness has influenced natural gas policy and the manner in which the public perceives this fuel. The environment is both a cultural phenomenon and a physical one, and in both cases the gas industry provides cogent examples of the new environmental awareness. Perhaps one of the most intriguing recent examples of the gas industry's cultural significance relates to the Big Inch and Little Big Inch pipelines, originally called the War Emergency Pipelines, currently known as the Texas Eastern Transmission Corporation, which is now owned and operated by Duke Energy. Due to the historical significance of the Big Inch and Little Big Inch pipelines and the fact that they are currently more than 50 years old, these gas lines are eligible for inclusion on the National Register of Historic Places. When Duke Energy began to replace segments of the line—a project that required a FERC certificate, the company was obligated to follow National Environmental Policy Act and National Historic Preservation Act guidelines. Duke was consequently required to conduct a thorough survey of the gas line and "mitigate" the changes made to this historic property. As part of the mitigation, Duke chose to produce a video about the Inch Line's history.[27] It is both remarkable and now very much understandable that a buried and therefore invisible gas pipeline could hold such historical significance.

It is also remarkable that the American manufactured gas industry, which first provided fuel for lighting, is largely forgotten, indeed invisible, in studies of American history and technology. Any technology that produced light and heat through a locally networked system when none existed before is certainly a socially and culturally significant historical episode. At the end of the twentieth century, the remains of the plants that once produced manufactured gas are becoming known for another reason. There are an estimated 3,000 former manufactured gas plant sites in the United States, and these pose potentially serious environmental problems.[28]

The large amounts of coal funneled through manufactured gas plants created coal tar and by-product chemicals often dumped in wastewater lagoons and coal tar pits. The Environmental Protection Agency (EPA) reported that typical manufactured gas plant waste products discovered at Superfund assessment and remediation projects included high concentrations of benzene, toluene, sulfur compounds, and cyanide compounds, as well as some volatile phenolic compounds. These chemicals are typically part of the coal tar waste deposited in the pits surrounding the plants. Some coal tar waste pits were more than 20 feet deep. One concern is that these chemicals may contaminate groundwater as well as subsurface soil.

In contrast to the environmental legacy of coal gas, natural gas is a relatively clean-burning fuel. In particular, nitrogen and sulfur oxide emissions are substantially less from natural gas and therefore its utilization contributes less than that of other fossil fuels to ozone production and the resulting greenhouse effect. Thus, natural gas use conforms to modern environmental laws such as the Clean Air Act and its amendments. Compared to the common gasoline engine, for example, compressed natural gas and liquefied natural gas produce 65 to 90 percent less carbon monoxide, fewer reactive hydrocarbons, and virtually no particulates. Industrial use of natural gas is environmentally preferable to coal, although new methods to reduce undesirable emissions from coal are increasingly effective. While methane itself contributes to the greenhouse effect, completely burned methane produces lower levels of carbon dioxide. Thus, natural gas utilization contributes less to the greenhouse effect than any other fossil fuel.[29]

Natural gas is utilized primarily in homes and businesses for heat production, by utilities for electric power production, and in industrial heat processes (see table 12.3); it is also becoming a realistic fuel for motor vehicles. Gas-powered engines are not new. In France during 1860, Etienne Lenoir built an engine fueled by coal gas stored in a rubber bladder. Two years later, he built a moving vehicle powered by a coal gas engine. By the late twentieth century, gas-powered vehicles are still used more widely outside of the United States; the Energy Policy Act of 1992 required that federal, state, and some private fleets begin purchasing vehicles powered by alternative fuel (including natural gas). By the mid-1990s, there were as many as 300,000 natural gas–powered vehicles operating in Italy and 250,000 in the former Soviet Union compared to approximately 40,000 in the United States. Many of these are utility company fleet vehicles and transit buses.[30] In 1996, about 20 percent of transit buses purchased in the United States were powered by natural gas. However, by 1998, of the 50,000 transit buses in operation, only about 4 percent were powered by an alternative fuel such as compressed natural gas, liquefied natural gas, and methanol.

While natural gas is highly regarded for its environmental characteristics, the gas industry has had to deal with environmental problems of its own. For many years, pipeline companies used oils, which contained PCBs (polychlorinated biphenyls). PCBs were widely used as coolants and lubricants in part for their insulating and nonflammable characteristics. In 1976, federal law greatly limited PCB utilization, and the EPA

TABLE 12.3 Market Share of Natural Gas Appliances
in the United States (1995)

Appliance	Market Share (%)
Gas Furnaces	51
Gas Ranges	36
Gas Water Heaters	52
Gas Clothes Dryers	23

Source: Derived from American Gas Association, Gas
Facts (Arlington: AGA, 1997).

subsequently banned PCB manufacture. But it had been routine practice
at many compressor station sites for PCBs to be buried in nearby waste
pits. PCBs are recognized as carcinogenic, so sites require cleanup, and
groundwater contamination has been a serious problem.

The history of gas includes not only the social utility of this fuel but
the dangers of using it. Throughout its history as we have seen, both
manufactured and natural gas have injured and killed people through
asphyxiation and explosion. In late the twentieth century, a 36-inch gas
pipeline in Edison, New Jersey, exploded dramatically. An 80-foot length
of the line, buried seven feet, blew up near an apartment complex and
created a massive crater measuring 60 feet deep and 120 feet wide.
Although 128 nearby apartments were destroyed, no person was killed
by the blast, but a 32-year-old women died of an apparent heart attack
during the melee.[31] Accidents will undoubtedly continue to occur, but
safety measures should limit them to rarities.

Estimates of the availability of natural gas, or methane, vary widely
from hundreds to thousands of years. Such estimates depend upon technology that must be developed to drill for gas in more difficult geographical conditions and actually finding gas where it is expected to be.
Methane can also be extracted from coal, peat, and oil shale, and if these
sources can be successfully utilized for methane production the world's
methane supply will be extended another 500 or more years.[32]

In one sense, there has not been two gas industries, one that manufactured gas from coal and another that produced and distributed gas
from the earth. While the chemical composition of each gas was not the
same, nor was their heating content, the idea of using flammable gas
first for light and then heat relied on the similar characteristics of both
gases; consumers have used each fuel in comparable ways. The natural

one proved more efficient than the synthetic in the late nineteenth and twentieth centuries, but as natural gas supply diminishes in the future synthetically produced methane may well become society's best fuel choice.

For the foreseeable future, natural gas will continue to be used primarily for residential and commercial heating, electric power generation, and industrial heat processes. The market for methane as a transportation fuel will undoubtedly grow, but eventual improvements in electric vehicles may well dampen any dramatic increase in natural gas–powered engines. The environmental characteristics of natural gas will certainly retain this fuel's position at the forefront of all fossil fuels. Yet, in a period of a few hundred or even a thousand years, human society will have burned as fuel for lighting, cooking, and heating the remains of a very large percentage of many millions of years of living organisms. Natural resources are limited. Even in an era of relative fuel abundance we should not forget the lessons of the past as we use energy today and plan policy for the future.

CHRONOLOGY

ca. 1609   Van Helmont gives the name "gas" to vapors from heated coal.
1684   John Clayton records detailed observations of an experiment with coal gas (published in 1739).
1770   George Washington observes a "burning spring" on the Kanawah River in West Virginia.
1792   William Murdock uses gas lighting at his home in Redruth, Cornwall.
1796   M. Ambroise & Company, an Italian fireworks manufacturer, reportedly exhibits some form of gaslights in Philadelphia.
1801   Gaslight demonstration by Philippe Lebon at the Hotel Seignelay in Paris.
1802   Benjamin Henfrey demonstrates his "thermo-lamp" coal gas lighting method in Pennsylvania.
1806   David Melville lights his house in Newport, Rhode Island, using coal gas.
1812   The National Light and Heat Company (London) receives its charter and is renamed the Gas Light and Coke Company.
1814   Rubens Peale installs gaslights at Charles Willson Peale's museum in Philadelphia, but the system is soon removed.
1815   Friedrich Christian Accum publishes the first textbook on gas lighting.
1816   Rembrandt Peale illuminates his Baltimore museum with gaslights.
1817   Gas Light Company of Baltimore, the first U.S. gas company, is incorporated.
1821   A natural gas well is dug in Fredonia, New York.
1822   Boston Light Company receives its charter (gas service begins in 1829).
1823   New York Gas Light Company is granted a charter (gas service begins in 1825).
1828   New York City's "Great White Way" is illuminated with manufactured gaslights.

1849   Chicago Gas Light and Coke Company is formed. Gas service begins in 1850.
1858   Fredonia Gas Light and Water Works Company is one of the first incorporated natural gas companies in the United States.
1859   The first issue of the *American Gas-Light Journal* is published on July 1.
1859   Edwin Drake discovers oil in Titusville, Pennsylvania.
1870s   Kerosene begins taking a share of the lighting market.
1872   Gas pipeline transports gas from nearby field to Titusville, Pennsylvania.
1873   Theodore Lowe invents carbureted water gas manufacturing process.
1880   The Bradford Gas Company at Rixford, Pennsylvania, begins using the first natural gas compressor. It is a duplex compressor powered by a 580-horsepower steam engine capable of compressing 5 MMcf/d.
1882   Thomas Edison's Pearl Street electric power generating station begins producing electricity for lighting.
1883   Chartiers Valley Gas Company formed to produce, gather, and transport gas to Pittsburgh industrial plants.
1884   Carl Auer von Welsbach at the Robert Bunsen laboratory in Germany develops the Welsbach mantle, which permits burning low-Btu gas for lighting.
1885   A high-pressure manufactured gas transmission line is installed between Oakland and Almeda under the San Francisco Bay.
1887   S. R. Dresser develops improved pipe coupling using rubber rings.
1889   Automatic gas water heater built by Fuel Gas and Electric Engineering Company.
1908   Wisconsin Railroad Commission orders gas companies to use British thermal units as new heating measurement standard.
1913   Los Angeles receives natural gas transported from Buena Vista gas fields located 120 miles distant.
1918   American Gas Association is formed through consolidation of smaller gas organizations.
1918   Panhandle gas field is discovered in Potter County, Texas.
1920s   Electric welding replaces acetylene welding.
1922   First well of Hugoton gas field is discovered in southwestern Kansas. This massive field comprises acreage in Kansas, Texas, and Oklahoma.
1928   The Federal Trade Commission commences massive investigation of the nation's utility industry.

1929– Organization and construction of Panhandle Eastern,
1931   Northern Natural and Natural Gas Pipeline Company of America deliver Southwestern gas to Midwestern markets.

1938   Congress enacts the Natural Gas Act.

1940s   Manufactured gasworks rapidly convert to natural gas.

1942   Congress modifies Section 7(c) of the Natural Gas Act.

1944   The U.S. Supreme Court rules in the lawsuit *FPC v. Hope Natural Gas Company* that "just and reasonable" rates can be based on original cost of constructing facilities less depreciation.

1944   Tennessee Gas begins delivering gas produced in the Southwest to Appalachia.

1946   The FPC conducts hearings in its Natural Gas Investigation to examine problems in all segments of the natural gas industry.

1946   Tennessee Gas temporarily leases the Big Inch and Little Big Inch to deliver natural gas to Appalachia.

1947   Texas Eastern Transmission Corporation purchases the Big Inch and Little Big Inch and begins the process of converting them to natural gas.

1949   First natural gas deliveries to New York City area arrive at Staten Island through New York & Richmond Gas Company.

1954   The U.S. Supreme Court affirms in *Wisconsin v. Phillips Oil Company* FPC authority to regulate wellhead gas prices.

1960   The FPC institutes area rates for wellhead pricing.

1968   Domestic gas production dedicated for interstate sale declines.

1973   Arab oil embargo leads to oil shortages and oil prices increase.

1978   Iranian revolution results in a second oil embargo against the United States.

1978   Congress passes the Natural Gas Policy Act.

1984   FERC Order 380

1985   FERC Order 436

1987   FERC Order 500

1992   FERC Order 636 completes the process begun in early 1980s to convert gas pipelines into open-access carriers.

NOTES AND
REFERENCES

Chapter 1

1. For an overview of gas lighting technology see Van Rensselaer Lansingh, "Gas as an Illuminant," in *Lectures Delivered at the Centenary Celebration of the First Commercial Gas Company to Sell Gas as an Illuminant* (New York: American Gas Institute, 1912), 126–42.

2. Malcolm W. H. Peebles, *Evolution of the Gas Industry* (New York: New York University Press, 1980), 5; and Alfred M. Leeston, John A. Crichton, and John C. Jacobs, *The Dynamic Natural Gas Industry: The Description of an American Industry from the Historical, Technical, Legal, Financial, and Economic Standpoints* (Norman: University of Oklahoma Press, 1963), 3–4.

3. Jean Baptiste van Helmont, *Van Helmont's Workes: Containing his most excellent Philosophy, Chirurgery, Physick, Anatomy* (London: for Lodowick Lloyd, 1664), 106.

4. Arthur Elton, "Gas for Light and Heat," in *A History of Technology: The Industrial Revolution, 1750–1850,* ed. Charles Singer et al. (New York: Oxford University Press, 1958), 4:258–59.

5. The Reverend John Clayton, *A Parson with a Scientific Mind: His Scientific Writings and Other Related Papers,* ed. Edmund Berkeley and Dorothy Smith Berkeley (Charlottesville: University of Virginia Press, 1965), 138.

6. Ibid., 139.

7. Ibid., 140.

8. Elton, "Gas," 4:260.

9. Ibid., 261–62, 264.

10. R. J. Forbes, "Power to 1850," in *A History of Technology: The Industrial Revolution, 1750–1850,* ed. Charles Singer et al. (New York: Oxford University Press, 1958), 4:162. Also, Sir Eric Roll, *An Early Experiment in Industrial Organization: Being a History of the Firm of Boulton & Watt, 1775–1805* (London: Frank Cass, 1968), 4.

11. Hugh Barty-King, *New Flame* (Tavistock, U.K.: Graphmitre Limited, 1984), 16–17.

12. Elton, "Gas," 4:265.

13. William Murdock, "An Account of the Application of the Gas from Coal to Economical Purposes," read before the Royal Society on 25 February 1808 and printed in the Philosophical Transactions for that year.

14. Elton, "Gas," 4:263.

15. Also see Murdock, "Application of the Gas from Coal."

16. Elton, "Gas," 4:268.

17. A. Clow and N. L. Clow, "The Chemical Industry: Interaction with the Industrial Revolution," in *A History of Technology: The Industrial Revolution, 1750–1850,* ed. Charles Singer et al. (New York: Oxford University Press, 1958), 4:252.

18. Barty-King, *New Flame,* 20; and Elton, "Gas," 4:268–69.

19. Barty-King, *New Flame,* 34–36.

20. Elton, "Gas," 4:268–69, 271.

Chapter 2

1. *Federal Gazette and Baltimore Daily Advertiser,* March 11, 1802, quoted in George T. Brown, *The Gas Light Company of Baltimore: A Study of Natural Monopoly* (Baltimore: Johns Hopkins Press, 1936), 9–10.

2. Erlick, "The Peales and Gas Lights in Baltimore," *Maryland Historical Magazine,* Spring 1985, 9–10; Malcolm W. H. Peebles, *Evolution of the Gas Industry* (New York: New York University Press, 1980), 9; Thomson King, *Consolidated of Baltimore, 1816–1950: A History of Consolidated Gas Electric Light and Power Company of Baltimore* (Baltimore: Consolidated of Baltimore, 1950), 8–9.

3. David Melville's patent, March 18, 1813, National Archives and Records Administration. Also see Peebles, *Evolution of the Gas Industry,* 8; and King, *Consolidated of Baltimore,* 9–10.

4. Quoted in William E. Worthington Jr., "Beyond the City Lights: American Domestic Gas Lighting Systems," *An Exhibit at the National Museum of American History,* October 17, 1985–April 20, 1986 (Washington, D.C.: Smithsonian Institution, 1985), 3.

5. See Charles Coleman Sellers, *Mr. Peale's Museum: Charles Willson Peale and the First Popular Museum of Natural Science and Art* (New York: W. W. Norton, 1980); and Charles Coleman Sellers, *Charles Willson Peale* (New York: Charles Scribner's Sons, 1969), 212–24.

6. Lillian B. Miller, *Rembrandt Peale, 1778–1860: A Life in the Arts* (Philadelphia: Historical Society of Philadelphia, 1985), 13.

7. Miller, *Rembrandt Peale,* 13; Eugenia Calvert Holland, Romaine Stec Somerville, Stiles Tuttle Colwill, and K. Beverley Whiting Young, *Four Generations of Commissions: The Peale Collection* (Baltimore: Maryland Historical Society, 1975), 59.

8. Wilbur Harvey Hunter Jr., *Rendezvous for Taste: Peale's Baltimore Museum, 1814–1830* (Baltimore: Peale Museum, n.d.), 4; Erlick, "The Peales ," 9.

9. Lillian B. Miller, *In Pursuit of Fame: Rembrandt Peale, 1778–1860* (Seattle: National Portrait Gallery, Smithsonian Institution in conjunction with the University of Washington Press, 1992), 124.

10. Erlick, "The Peales ," 10; also see Charles Coleman Sellers, *Charles Willson Peale: Later Life, 1790–1827,* (Philadelphia: American Philosophical Society, 1947), 2:300–301.

11. Elton, "Gas," 4:268.

12. Joel Tarr, "Transforming an Energy System: The Evolution of the Manufactured Gas Industry and the Transition to Natural Gas in the United States, 1807–1954," in *The Governance of Large Technical Systems,* ed. Oliver Coutard (London: Routledge, 1999), 21.

13. Erlick, "The Peales," 11; Sellers, *Charles Willson Peale: Later Life,* 301–2; Sellers, *Mr. Peale's Museum,* 229.

14. Quoted in Erlick, "The Peales," 12.

15. Ibid., 12.

16. Hunter, *Rendezvous for Taste,* 3.

17. Miller, *Rembrandt Peale,* 124.

18. Rembrandt Peale, "On Gas Lights," *The Portico: A Repository of Science and Literature* 1, no. 6 (June 1816): 529.

19. King, *Consolidated of Baltimore,* 13.

20. Miller, *Rembrandt Peale,* 124.

21. Miller, *Rembrandt Peale,* 125; Erlick, "The Peales," 13–14.

22. George T. Brown, *The Gas Light Company of Baltimore: A Study of Natural Monopoly* (Baltimore: Johns Hopkins University Press, 1936), 18–19; King, *Consolidated of Baltimore,* 24.

23. Erlick, "The Peales," 14.

24. King, *Consolidated of Baltimore,* 25; see also Louis Stotz and Alexander Jamison, *The History of the Gas Industry* (New York: Stettiner Bros., 1938), 14.

25. Quoted in Miller, *Rembrandt Peale,* 125; Erlick, "The Peales," 14; *A History of the Baltimore Gas and Electric Company, 1816–1987* (unpublished manuscript by the company, September 14, 1988), 14.

26. Erlick, "The Peales," 15.

27. Ibid.

28. Miller, *Rembrandt Peale,* 207; *Rembrandt Peale v. The Gas Light Company of Baltimore,* in Chancery, September Term 1831 (Maryland Hall of Records: Chancery Papers); Erlick, "The Peales," 15–16.

29. Quoted in Erlick, "The Peales," 16.

30. Sellers, *Charles Willson Peale: Later Life,* 2:385–86.

31. *A History of the Baltimore Gas and Electric Company, 1816–1987* (unpublished manuscript by the company, September 14, 1988), 20.

32. Erlick, "The Peales," 14; Stotz and Jamison, *Gas Industry,* 15; Roger W. Moss, *Lighting for Historic Buildings: A Guide to Selecting Reproductions* (Washington, D.C.: Preservation Press, 1988), 100.

33. Alfred Lief, *Metering for America: 125 Years of the Gas Industry and American Meter Company* (New York: Appleton-Century-Crofts, 1961), 3, 6.

34. King, *Consolidated of Baltimore, 1816–1950,* 33.

35. Ibid., 22.

36. *History of the Baltimore Gas and Electric Company,* 24.

37. Lief, *Metering for America,* 4–6.

38. Ibid., 6–7.

39. Erlick, "The Peales," 17.

40. Quoted in George B. Cortelyou, "Commercial and Financial Aspects of the Gas Industry," in *Lectures Delivered at the Centenary Celebration of the First Commercial Gas Company to Sell Gas as an Illuminant* (New York: American Gas Institute, 1912), 75.

41. Ibid., 75–76.

42. Quote from Philadelphia Gas Works, "Tracing PGW History," *Newsline* (February 1986), 7. See S. V. Merrick, "Report Upon an Examination of Some of the Gas Manufactures in Great Britain, France, and Belgium," in *Reports of the Trustees of the Philadelphia Gas Works to the Select and Common Councils of the City of Philadelphia* (Philadelphia: Philadelphia City Councils, 1838), 59–102.

43. Philadelphia Gas Works, "PGW History," 17; Stotz and Jamison, *Gas Industry,* 93–95. Also see Charles A. Howland, *Philadelphia's Gas Problem* (Philadelphia: Bureau of Municipal Research of Philadelphia, 1926).

44. Frederick L. Collins, *Consolidated Gas Company of New York: A History* (New York: Consolidated Gas Company of New York, 1934), 18–23.

45. Collins, *Consolidated Gas,* 22–24. Also see Tarr, "Transforming an Energy System."

46. Collins, *Consolidated Gas,* 41.

47. Stotz and Jamison, *Gas Industry,* 22–23, 33–34; Collins, *Consolidated Gas,* 59; Robert Friedel and Paul Israel, *Edison's Electric Light: Biography of an Invention* (New Brunswick, N.J.: Rutgers University Press, 1986), 192.

48. George G. Foster, *New York by Gas-Light and Other Urban Sketches,* ed. Stuart M. Blumin (Berkeley: University of California Press, 1990), 69.

49. Quoted in Frederick Penzel, *Theatre Lighting before Electricity* (Middletown, Conn.: Wesleyan University Press, 1978), 50–51, quoting George C. D. Odell, *Annals of the New York Stage* (New York: Columbia University Press, 1928).

50. Collins, *Consolidated Gas,* 66–71.

51. Ibid., 92–95.

52. Quoted in Allen Strunk, *History of the Cincinnati Gas and Electric Company, 1837–1956* (Cincinnati Gas and Electric, n.d.), 2.

53. Ibid., 3.

54. Ibid., 6.

55. Ibid., 6, 14.

56. Wallace Rice, *Seventy-five Years of Gas Service in Chicago: The Peoples Gas Light and Coke Company* (Chicago: Peoples Gas Light and Coke, 1925), 3–6; Stotz and Jamison, *Gas Industry*, 100.

57. Quoted in Rice, *Seventy-five Years*, 7.

58. Ibid., 10.

59. Ibid., 20–23.

60. Charles M. Coleman, *PG&E of California: The Centennial Story of Pacific Gas and Electric Company, 1852–1952* (New York: McGraw-Hill, 1952), 9–10.

61. Ibid., 11–15.

62. "San Francisco by Gas-Light," *Daily Alta California*, February 12, 1854.

63. Stotz and Jamison, *Gas Industry*, 6.

64. "Cars Lighted by Gas," *New York Times*, April 2, 1858, 5.

65. "Gas-Light for Railroad Cars," *American Gas-Light Journal* (July 1, 1859): 10.

66. "Gas-Light—Progress of the Manufacture of Gas," *New York Times*, November 23, 1855, 6.

67. Darwin H. Stapleton, *The Transfer of Early Industrial Technologies to America* (Lawrence, Kans.: Allen Press for the American Philosophical Society, 1987), 22.

Chapter 3

1. Christian Le Clercq, *First Establishment of the Faith in New France*, trans. John Gilmary Shea (1881; reprint, New York: AMS Press, 1973), 1:270.

2. Orasmus H. Marshall, *The First Visit of De La Salle to the Senecas, made in 1669* (n.p., 1874), 22–23.

3. Adolph B. Benson, *Peter Kalm's Travels in North America* (New York: Dover Publications, 1964), 2:608.

4. Lockwood R. Doty, ed., *History of the Genesee Country (Western New York): Comprising the Counties of Allegany, Cattaragus, Chautauqua, Chemung, Erie, Genesee, Livingston, Monroe, Niagara, Ontario, Orleans, Schuyler, Stuben, Wayne, Wyoming and Yates* (Chicago: S. J. Clarke, 1925), 2:1062.

5. Donald Jackson, ed., *The Diaries of George Washington* (Charlottesville: University Press of Virginia, 1976), 2:309.

6. Thomas Jefferson, *Notes on the State of Virginia*, ed. William Peden (Chapel Hill: University of North Carolina Press, 1955), 36.

7. *Memoirs of the American Academy of Arts and Sciences: To the End of the Year 1783* (Boston: Adams and Nourse, 1785), 1:372.

8. Stotz and Jamison, *Gas Industry,* 69–70.

9. For the popularized version of the Lafayette story, see Stotz and Jamison, *Gas Industry,* 70.

10. A. Levasseur, *Lafayette in America in 1824 and 1825 (or, Journal of a Voyage to the United States),* trans. John D. Goodman (New York: Research Reprints, 1970), 2:185.

11. "Reception at Fredonia," *Fredonia Censor,* June 8, 1825. Quoted in Andrew W. Young, *History of Chautauqua County, New York* (Buffalo, N.Y.: Matthews & Warren, 1875), 141.

12. Levasseur, *Lafayette in America,* 166.

13. "What Village Can Compare with Fredonia?" *Fredonia Censor,* August 31, 1825.

14. *Fredonia Censor,* November 29, 1826, p. 2, col. 4.

15. Stotz and Jamison, *Gas Industry,* 70.

16. Harold F. Williamson and Arnold R. Daum, *The American Petroleum Industry: The Age of Illumination, 1859–1899* (Evanston: Northwestern University Press, 1959), 18–22.

17. Martin V. Melosi, *Coping with Abundance: Energy and Environment in Industrial America* (New York: Alfred A. Knopf, 1985), 36.

18. Williamson and Daum, *American Petroleum Industry,* 72–75.

19. Ibid., 78–79.

20. Daniel Yergin, *The Prize: The Epic Quest for Oil, Money, and Power* (New York: Simon & Schuster, 1991), 14, 37, 46, 50.

21. Tarr, "Transforming an Energy System," 22.

22. Leeston, Crichton, and Jacobs, *Dynamic Natural Gas Industry,* 6.

23. Stotz and Jamison, *Gas Industry,* 70.

24. Ibid., 78.

25. Ibid., 77–78.

26. Leeston, Crichton, and Jacobs, *Dynamic Natural Gas Industry,* 6.

27. Charles A. Ashburner, "The Geology of Natural Gas," *The Petroleum Age* 4, no. 12 (January 1886): 1195.

28. Benjamin J. Crew, *A Practical Treatise on Petroleum* (Philadelphia: Baird, 1887), 233–34.

29. Hax McCullough and Mary Brignano, *The Vision and Will to Succeed: A Centennial History of the Peoples Natural Gas Company* (n.p.: Peoples Natural Gas, n.d.), 8–10.

30. Ibid., 14–15.

31. Ibid., 16–17.

32. "The Natural Gas Industry at Pittsburgh, Pennsylvania," *Scientific American Supplement,* no. 627 (January 7, 1885): 10012.

33. Ibid.

34. Darwin Payne, *Initiative in Energy: Dresser Industries, Inc., 1880–1978* (New York: Simon & Schuster, 1979), 60–78

35. "The Philadelphia Company and Its Gas Lines," *American Manufacturer and Iron World,* November 12, 1886, 12.

36. "Natural Gas Industry at Pittsburgh," 10,013.

37. Ibid.

38. J. G. Crowther, *Six Great Engineers* (London: Hamish Hamilton, 1959), 85; Henry G. Prout, *A Life of George Westinghouse* (New York: Arno Press, 1972), 227.

39. "The Philadelphia Company and Its Gas Lines," 12.

40. Crowther, *Six Great Engineers,* 85–87; Prout, *George Westinghouse,* 224–29, 334–36, 362–65.

41. "Killed by Natural Gas," *New York Times,* February 1, 1885, 1.

42. "The Effort to Utilize Natural Gas," *New York Times,* July 8, 1884, 4; John L. Cowan, "The Beginning of the Use of Natural Gas for Fuel," *Mining and Scientific Press* (July 9, 1910): 45; Crew, *Petroleum,* 235–36.

43. Crew, *Petroleum,* 235–36.

44. Charles E. Munroe, "By-Products in Gas Manufacture," *Lectures Delivered at the Centenary Celebration of the First Commercial Gas Company to Sell Gas as an Illuminant* (New York: American Gas Institute, 1912), 39.

45. The six companies were the Philadelphia Company, Chartiers, Manufacturers, Pennsylvania, Washington, and Peoples.

46. "Natural Gas Wells Supplying Pittsburgh," *American Manufacturer and Iron World,* natural gas supplement (November 12, 1886): 12.

47. "The Mileage and Sizes of Natural Gas Pipes in Pittsburgh," *American Manufacturer and Iron World,* natural gas supplement (November 12, 1886): 12.

48. "Natural Gas: Its Occurrence and Application in Pittsburgh," *Engineering News* (September 17, 1887): 198–200.

49. Crew, *Petroleum,* 230–34.

50. Ibid.

51. John H. Newell, *The Origin and Founders of the Hope Natural Gas Company* (n.p.: Hope Natural Gas Company, ca. 1960), 33.

52. McCullough and Brignano, *Vision and Will,* 14.

53. "Natural Gas, Its Occurrence and Application in Pittsburgh," *Engineering News* (September 17, 1887): 198–200.

54. Crew, *Petroleum,* 226–27.

55. "The Future of Natural Gas," *New York Times,* July 26, 1888, 2:2.

56. Stotz and Jamison, *Gas Industry,* 80–81.

Chapter 4

1. "Our First Subscriber," *American Gas-Light Journal* (July 1, 1859): 8.

2. "Our First Number," *American Gas-Light Journal* (July 1, 1859): 1.

3. *American Gas-Light Journal* (March 1, 1886).

4. "An Act to Provide for the Inspection and Sealing of Gas Meters, and for the Protection of Consumers of Illuminating Gas," passed April 14, 1859, quoted in *American Gas-Light Journal* (July 1, 1859): 12.

5. "Gas Dogs," *New York Times,* January 22, 1885, 4:5.

6. Ibid.

7. Collins, *Consolidated Gas Company,* 95.

8. "Gas," *New York Daily Times,* February 22, 1856, 4.

9. Collins, *Consolidated Gas Company,* 97, 103.

10. Ibid., 111–12.

11. Collins, *Consolidated Gas Company,* 163–65.

12. Eugene B. Block, *Above the Civil War: The Story of Thaddeus Lowe, Balloonist, Inventor, Railway Builder* (Berkeley, Calif.: Howell-North, 1966), 126, 159. Lowe later formed the New Lowe Gas System to maintain and repair gasworks. The company was later acquired by Pacific Gas & Electric.

13. Werner Troesken, *Why Regulate Utilities? The New Institutional Economics and the Chicago Gas Industry, 1849–1924* (Ann Arbor: University of Michigan Press, 1996), 28; and American Gas Association (AGA), *Gas Rate Fundamentals,* 4th ed. (Arlington, Va.: AGA, 1987), 3. Also see Werner Troesken, "The Institutional Antecedents of State Utility Regulation: The Chicago Gas Industry, 1860–1913," in *The Regulated Economy: A Historical Approach to Political Economy,* ed. Claudia Goldin and Gary D. Libecap (Chicago: University of Chicago Press, 1994), 59.

14. Collins, *Consolidated Gas Company,* 180.

15. Ibid., 167.

16. See "Rapid Advance in Electric Lighting," *New York Times,* January 1, 1886, 4:5; Henry Schroeder, *History of Electric Light* (City of Washington: Smithsonian Institution, 1923).

17. Robert Friedel and Paul Israel, *Edison's Electric Light: Biography of an Invention* (New Brunswick, N.J.: Rutgers University Press, 1986), 67.

18. Robert Silverberg, *Light for the World: Edison and the Power Industry* (Princeton, N.J.: D. Van Nostrand, 1967), 91.

19. Quoted in Harold C. Passer, "The Electric Light and the Gas Light: Innovation and Continuity in Economic History," *Explorations in Enterprise,* ed. Hugh G. J. Aitken (Cambridge: Harvard University Press, 1965), 212.

20. Silverberg, *Light for the World,* 93–94; Neil Baldwin, *Edison: Inventing the Century* (New York: Hyperion, 1995), 137.

21. Silverberg, *Light for the World*, 105; Floyd A. Lewis, *The Incandescent Light* (New York: Shorewood, 1961), 32.

22. Reese V. Jenkins, ed., *The Papers of Thomas A. Edison* (Baltimore: Johns Hopkins University Press, 1994), 3:411, 431; Silverberg, *Light for the World*, 106.

23. Silverberg, *Light for the World*, 108. Also see *New York Times*, January 18, 1881, 4; "Possibilities of Electricity," *New York Times*, January 1, 1882, 6.

24. "Doubts about the Electric Light," *New York Times*, January 6, 1880, 2.

25. "The Electric Light in the British Museum," *New York Times*, December 18, 1879, 2.

26. Quoted in Silverberg, *Light for the World*, 163.

27. Passer, "Electric Light and Gas Light," 211.

28. Martin V. Melosi, *Thomas A. Edison and the Modernization of America* (Glenview, Ill.: Scott, Foresman/Little, Brown Higher Education, 1990), 72–73. Arthur A. Bright Jr., *The Electric-Lamp Industry: Technological Change and Economic Development from 1800–1947* (New York: MacMillan, 1949), 76. For a brief summation of the transition from gas to electric lighting in New York's theaters, see "In and About the City: To Displace Gas in Theatres," *New York Times*, March 16, 1889, 8:3. Also see Terence Rees, *Theatre Lighting in the Age of Gas* (London: Society for Theatre Research, 1978) and Frederick Penzel, *Theatre Lighting before Electricity* (Middletown, Conn.: Wesleyan University Press, 1978).

29. "New Device for Lighting Gas," *New York Times*, January 4, 1884, 8:2.

30. Passer, "Electric Light and Gas Light," 217.

31. Ibid., 216.

32. Ibid., 218–19.

33. *New York Times*, June 25, 1884, 4:6; *New York Times*, November 18, 1882, 4:7.

34. See "An Ever-Present Danger," *New York Times*, April 21, 1889, 12:5–6; "Electric Light Wire Nuisance," *New York Times*, December 1, 1883, 8:3; "Excited Property Owners," *New York Times*, April 6, 1883, 2:7; "Electric Progress," *New York Times*, January 5, 1883, 4:5, 6; "The Poles and Wires to Stay," *New York Times*, March 2, 1884, 10:2; "The Risks of Electric Lighting," *New York Times*, March 26, 1882, 8:4; "Safe Electric Lights," *New York Times*, December 31, 1889, 1:4.

35. "Papers by Men of Science," *New York Times*, September 10, 1882, 6:5.

36. Stotz and Jamison, *Gas Industry*, 20–66.

37. Troesken, *Why Regulate Utilities*, 29.

38. Rice, *Seventy-five Years*, 30.

39. Troesken, *Why Regulate Utilities*, 36–37.

40. Harold L. Platt, *The Electric City: Energy and the Growth of the Chicago Area, 1880–1930* (Chicago: University of Chicago Press, 1991), 90; Troesken, *Why Regulate Utilities*, 25–50.

41. Douglas R. Littlefield and Tanis C. Thorne, *The Spirit of Enterprise: The History of Pacific Enterprises from 1886 to 1989* (Los Angeles: Pacific Enterprises, 1990), 14–27. For additional information on gas lighting in California, see James C. Williams, *Energy and the Making of Modern California* (Akron, Ohio: University of Akron Press, 1997), 61–69.

42. John Stock, "Carl Auer von Welsbach and the Development of Incandescent Gas Lighting," *Journal of Chemical Engineering* 68, no. 10 (October 1991): 801–3; Roger Moss, *Lighting for Historic Buildings: A Guide to Selecting Reproductions* (Washington, D.C.: Preservation Press, 1988), 100; Bright, *Electric-Lamp Industry,* 126–27; "Something New in Gaslight," *New York Times,* June 6, 1888, 5:3.

43. Denys Peter Myers, *Gaslighting in America: A Pictorial Survey, 1815–1910* (New York: Dover Publications, 1978), 206–7.

44. Bright, *Electric-Lamp Industry,* 212–13.

45. "A Word for Gas Companies," *New York Times,* October 21, 1886, 5:3; Thomas K. McCraw, *Prophets of Regulation* (Cambridge: Harvard University Press, Belknap Press, 1984), 58. Also see Gabriel Kolko, *The Triumph of Conservatism: A Re-interpretation of American History, 1900–1916* (New York: Free Press, 1963).

Chapter 5

1. See Alfred D. Chandler Jr., *The Visible Hand: The Managerial Revolution in American Business* (Cambridge: Harvard University Press, Belknap Press, 1977), 331–39; and Naomi R. Lamoreaux, *The Great Merger Movement in American Business, 1895–1904* (Cambridge: Cambridge University Press, 1985).

2. Chandler, *Visible Hand,* 339.

3. Quoted in Ralph W. Hidy and Muriel E. Hidy, *Pioneering in Big Business, 1882–1911* (New York: Harper & Brothers, 1955), 173.

4. Williamson and Daum, *American Petroleum Industry,* 452.

5. Ibid., 605–6.

6. Newell, *Hope Natural Gas Company,* 12–14.

7. McCullough and Brignano, *Vision and Will,* 34, 42.

8. *Hepburn Bill* (House Committee on Interstate and Foreign Commerce), H.R. 12987, 59th Cong., 1st sess., *Congressional Record* (May 4, 1906): 6362.

9. Ibid., 6371.

10. Henrietta M. Larson, Evelyn H. Knowlton, and Charles S. Popple, *New Horizons: History of Standard Oil Company (New Jersey) 1927–1950* (New York: Harper & Row, 1971), 100.

11. "Gas and Electricity Combining," *New York Times,* February 22, 1887, 5:4.

12. Ibid.

13. Coleman, *PG&E,* 82.

14. Ibid., 85–87.

15. Ibid., 229.

16. Albert F. Dawson, *Columbia System: A History* (New York: J. J. Little and Ives, 1938), 14–20; Strunk, *Cincinnati Gas and Electric,* 193.

17. Dawson, *Columbia System,* 31,

18. Stotz and Jamison, *Gas Industry,* 121.

19. William Donohue Ellis, *On the Oil Lands with Cities Service* (n.p.: Cities Service Oil and Gas Corporation, 1983), 60–61.

20. Mark H. Rose, *Cities of Light and Heat: Domesticating Gas and Electricity in Urban America* (University Park: Penn State University Press, 1995), 43–45.

21. Ellis, *On the Oil Lands,* 70.

22. Ibid., 72–73.

23. Rose, *Cities of Light,* 7.

24. Platt, *Electric City,* 66–68.

25. Forrest McDonald, *Insull* (Chicago: University of Chicago Press, 1962), 159–60.

26. Platt, *Electric City,* 230. Also see McDonald, *Insull,* 209–12.

27. McDonald, *Insull,* 274–75.

28. McCraw, *Prophets of Regulation,* 58.

29. Quoted in Douglas D. Anderson, *Regulatory Politics and Electric Utilities: A Case Study in Political Economy* (Boston: Auburn House, 1981), 45.

30. Quoted in Anderson, *Regulatory Politics,* 42.

31. Ibid., 56.

32. R. H. Fernald, "Service Regulations for Gas," *State Regulation of Public Utilities: The Annals of the American Academy of Political and Social Science* 53, no. 142 (May 1914): 272.

33. Fernald, "Service Regulations," 275–76; Judson C. Dickerman, "Some Notes on the Regulation of Gas Service," *State Regulation of Public Utilities: The Annals of the American Academy of Political and Social Science* 53, no. 142 (May 1914): 280–81.

34. Melosi, *Coping with Abundance,* 91.

35. For a description of the U.S. economy during World War I, see Robert D. Cuff, *The War Industries Board: Business-Government Relations during World War I* (Baltimore: Johns Hopkins University Press, 1973).

36. John G. Clark, *Energy and the Federal Government: Fossil Fuel Policies, 1900–1946* (Urbana: University of Illinois Press, 1987), 89–90.

37. Ibid., 91, 92 (quote).

38. Collins, *Consolidated Gas Company,* 356–57.

39. Ibid., 360–61.

Chapter 6

1. Arlon R. Tussing and Connie C. Barlow, *The Natural Gas Industry: Evolution, Structure, and Economics,* (Cambridge, Mass.: Ballinger, 1984), 33.

2. Robert W. Gilmer, "The History of Natural Gas Pipelines in the Southwest," *Texas Business Review* (May–June 1981): 130–31. Also see Ralph E. Davis, "Natural Gas Pipe Line Development during Past Ten Years," *Natural Gas* 16, no. 12 (December 1935): 3.

3. M. Elizabeth Sanders, *The Regulation of Natural Gas: Policy and Politics, 1938–1978* (Philadelphia: Temple University Press, 1981), 25.

4. AGA, *Gas Rate Fundamentals,* 13.

5. Gilmer, "Natural Gas Pipelines," 132.

6. Larson, Knowlton, and Popple, *New Horizons,* 103.

7. Gilmer, "Natural Gas Pipelines," 131–32; Stotz and Jamison, *Gas Industry,* 309–89; Larson, Knowlton, and Popple, *New Horizons,* 101–5.

8. Coleman, *PG&E,* 303–5.

9. John H. Herbert, *Clean Cheap Heat: The Development of Residential Markets of Natural Gas in the United States* (New York: Praeger, 1992), 45–47.

10. Insull and the development of gas and electric power have been the subject of numerous studies. See McDonald, *Insull;* Platt, *Electric City;* and Rice, *Seventy-five Years.*

11. Carl D. Thompson, *Confessions of the Power Trust,* (New York: Arno Press, 1976), xvii–xviii. Senators George Norris (Nebraska) and Thomas Walsh (Montana) were strong proponents of public power and initiated legislative attempts to impose governmental control over the public utility industry.

12. Federal Trade Commission, *Report to the Senate on Public Utility Corporations,* 70th Cong., 1st sess., 1936, S. Doc. 92, pt. 84-A (hereafter referred to as FTC Report).

13. Larson, Knowlton, and Popple, *New Horizons,* 105–8.

14. Stotz and Jamison, *Gas Industry,* 381–82.

15. Ibid., 214–18.

16. Ibid.

17. Ibid., 214.

18. Christopher J. Castaneda and Clarance M. Smith, *Gas Pipelines and the Emergence of America's Regulatory State: A History of Panhandle Eastern Corporation, 1928–1993* (New York: Cambridge University Press, 1996), 22.

19. FTC Report, pt. 82:168–69.

20. Castaneda and Smith, *Gas Pipelines,* 24.

21. FTC Report, pt. 84-1:155.

22. See Alfred D. Chandler Jr. and Stephen Salsbury, *Pierre S. Du Pont and the Making of the Modern Corporation* (New York: Harper & Row, 1971); and Daniel Gross, "Ross Perot's $100-Million Disaster," *Audacity*, Summer 1994, 7. Francis du Pont later founded the F. I. Du Pont & Company brokerage firm.

23. Robert Sobel, *The Big Board: A History of the New York Stock Market* (New York: Free Press, 1965), 242.

24. William K. Klingaman, *The Year of the Great Crash—1929* (New York: Harper & Row, 1989), 175–76. Also see Thomas P. Hughes, *Networks of Power: Electrification in Western Society, 1880–1930* (Baltimore: Johns Hopkins University Press, 1983) for an analysis of energy systems building.

25. FTC Report, pt. 84-A:434–39; and FTC Report, pt. 84-1: 158.

26. FTC Report, pt. 84-A:436.

27. FTC Report, pt. 83:542.

28. Castaneda and Smith, *Gas Pipelines*, 35.

29. Panhandle Eastern Pipe Line Company, *Minutes*, February 18, 1930.

30. Castaneda and Smith, *Gas Pipelines*, 38.

31. FTC Report, pt. 82:302; and FTC Report, pt. 83:290.

32. FTC Report, pt. 82:180.

33. Panhandle Eastern Pipe Line Company, *Minutes*, April, 28, 1930.

34. FTC Report, pt. 82:307.

35. FTC Report, pt. 82:298–300.

36. "M-K's Pipe," *Time*, June 9, 1930, 43–44. Also see "Natural Gas," *Time*, March 17, 1930, 50.

37. FTC Report, pt. 84-A:439.

38. FTC Report, pt. 82:195–96, 313.

39. FTC Report, pt. 82:310.

40. FTC Report, pt. 82:315; and FTC Report, pt. 84-1:161; and "Vote Wide Inquiry on Short Selling," *New York Times*, March 5, 1932. Christy Payne also served as a director of Columbia Gas & Electric Corporation from 1931 through 1933.

41. FTC Report, pt. 84-A:440.

42. "Curb Prices Drop under Powerful Bear Selling," *Chicago Herald and Examiner*, June 17, 1930.

43. The closing date for the transaction was October 23, 1930.

44. FTC Report, pt. 84-A:272–73.

45. C. E. Mitchell to Henry L. Doherty, September 23, 1930, in FTC Report, pt. 84-A:273.

46. Henry L. Doherty to Charles E. Mitchell, September 23, 1930, and C. E. Mitchell to Henry L. Doherty, September 24, 1930, in FTC Report, pt. 84-A:273–74.

47. FTC Report, pt. 83:139–90, 1018–20; and FTC Report, pt. 84-1:161.

48. FTC Report, pt. 83:158.

49. "Pipes Link the East with Gas in Texas," *New York Times*, August 21, 1931, 24.

50. FTC Report, pt. 83:47–64. Also see "Utilities Hearing Told of 'Spy' Role," *New York Times*, November 16, 1935. After Walker testified, a Cities Service official implied that the espionage was only for identifying those high-level employees that Parish was attempting to hire for his own organization so that Cities Service could keep them on its payroll.

51. Castaneda and Smith, *Gas Pipelines*, 66–67. Also see "Hints More Utility Suits," *New York Times*, February 17, 1932; "U.S. Eyes Mo-Kan," *Chicago Evening American*, January 18, 1932; and "Columbia Gas Sued for $180,000,000," *New York Times*, July 19, 1935.

52. Castaneda and Smith, *Gas Pipelines*, 66.

53. "35,000,000 Fraud in Stocks Laid to 4," *New York Times*, March 25, 1932; and "Frank Parish Indicted," March 24, 1932, (Chicago) paper unknown. Mo-Kan director Francis I. du Pont owned about 3,000 shares, which he finally sold in 1934 when the stock was worth very little.

54. Castaneda and Smith, *Gas Pipelines*, 68. Insull, who was also indicted on a charge of mail fraud stemming from the collapse of his huge public utility empire, had fled the country in June 1932.

55. "Record Fraud Charged," *New York Times*, April 4, 1935, p. 8.

56. "Parish Tells His Meteoric Rise into Big Money," *Chicago Daily Tribune*, April 25, 1935; Castaneda and Smith, *Gas Pipelines*, 69. Also see numerous articles about the trial found in the following newspapers throughout April 1935: *Chicago Herald and Examiner, Chicago Daily Tribune, Chicago Daily American, Chicago Daily News*.

Chapter 7

1. AGA, *Gas Rate Fundamentals*, 14.

2. Sanders, *Regulation of Natural Gas*, 24.

3. See Thompson, *Confessions*.

4. Herbert, *Clean Cheap Heat*, 69.

5. "Greatest Blessings," *Time*, March 29, 1937, 24; and "500 Pupils and Teachers are Killed in Explosion of Gas in Texas School," *New York Times*, March 19, 1937, 1.

6. For an account of another public power facility, see Thomas K. McCraw, *TVA and the Power Fight, 1933–1939* (Philadelphia: Lippincott, 1971). Also see Federal Trade Commission, *Investigation of Concentration of Economic Power*, no. 36, published as Temporary National Economic Committee Report no. 76-3 (Washington, D.C.: GPO, 1940).

7. See J.R. 329, 68th Cong., 2nd sess., 1925; and "Electric Power Industry, Control of Power Companies," 69th Cong., 2nd sess., 1927, S. Doc. 213 (issued on February 21).

8. Thompson, *Confessions,* xix.

9. *Congressional Record,* 70th Cong., 1st sess., 1928, 69, pt. 3:3054; U.S. Senate, S.R. 83, 70th Cong., 1st sess., 1928, as extended by J.R. 115, 73rd Cong., 2nd sess., 1934. Also see FTC Report, pt. 84-A (all); and William E. Leuchtenburg, *The Perils of Prosperity, 1914–32* (Chicago: University of Chicago Press, 1958), 190–91.

10. Ellis Hawley, *The New Deal and the Problem of Monopoly* (Princeton, N.J.: Princeton University Press, 1966), 326.

11. Ibid., 326–27. Also see Federal Trade Commission, *Investigation of Concentration of Economic Power,* no. 36, published as Temporary National Economic Committee Report no. 76-3 (Washington, D.C.: GPO, 1940).

12. Hawley, *New Deal,* 330.

13. Ibid.

14. FTC Report, pt. 84-A:615–16.

15. FTC Report, pt. 84-A:591, 611.

16. FTC Report, pt. 84-A:611.

17. FTC Report, pt. 84-A:609.

18. FTC Report, pt. 84-A:593.

19. FTC Report, pt. 84-A:616–17.

20. Ibid.

21. For a very readable account of the emergence of regulation, and the men who guided several regulatory agencies, see: McCraw, *Prophets of Regulation.* For a review of the origins of trucking regulation, see William R. Childs, *Trucking and the Public Interest: The Emergence of Federal Regulation, 1914–1940* (Knoxville: University of Tennessee Press, 1985). Also see McCraw, *TVA,* for a study of public power during the presidency of Franklin Roosevelt.

22. M. L. Ramsay, *Pyramids of Power: The Story of Roosevelt, Insull, and the Utility Wars* (Indianapolis: Bobbs-Merrill, 1937); and Stephen Raushenbush, *The Power Fight* (New York: New Republic, 1932).

23. See McDonald, *Insull;* and Francis X. Busch, *Guilty or Not Guilty* (Indianapolis: Bobbs-Merrill, 1952).

24. D. B. Hardeman and Donald C. Bacon, *Rayburn: A Biography* (Austin: Texas Monthly Press, 1987), 172. See *Congressional Record,* January 4, 1935, 116–18.

25. Francis X. Welch, "Functions of the Federal Power Commission in Relation to the Securities and Exchange Commission," *George Washington Law Journal* 46, no. 4 (1956): 81. For a discussion of the early history of the SEC, see Joel Seligman, *The Transformation of Wall Street: A History of the Securities and Exchange Commission and Modern Corporate Finance* (Boston: Houghton Mifflin, 1982), 1–100. For a general discussion of regulation in America, see Thomas K. McCraw,

"Regulation in America: A Review Article," *Business History Review* 44, no. 2 (Summer 1975): 159–83.

26. Hardeman and Bacon, *Rayburn*, 167.

27. For an account of the struggle for passage of the PUHCA, see Hardeman and Bacon, *Rayburn*, 167–99.

28. Press Release, Representative Sam Rayburn (Texas), NBC radio address, August 30, 1935. Sam Rayburn Papers, Center for American History, University of Texas at Austin.

29. Ibid.

30. Kenneth J. Lipartito and Joseph A. Pratt, *Baker and Botts in the Development of Modern Houston* (Austin: University of Texas Press, 1991), 142. See pages 141–47 for a discussion of this law firm's work for EBASCO in conflict with the PUHCA. Also see Hawley, *New Deal*, 336.

31. Hawley, *New Deal*, 337.

32. Richard W. Hooley, *Financing the Natural Gas Industry: The Role of Life Insurance Investment Policies* (New York: Columbia University Press, 1961), 45.

33. U.S. 52 Stat. 821 (1938).

34. *Congressional Record*, 75th Cong., 1st sess., August 19, 1937, 81, pt. 8:9316.

35. Dozier A. DeVane, "Highlights of the Legislative History of the Federal Power Act of 1935 and the Natural Gas Act of 1938," *George Washington Law Journal* 14 (December 1945): 30–41; Donald J. Libert, "Legislative History of the Natural Gas Act," *Georgetown Law Journal* 44, no. 4 (June 1956): 695–723. Also see House Committee on Interstate and Foreign Commerce, *Hearings on the Natural Gas Act*, 74th Cong., 2nd sess., April 1936, 156–58; and Gerald R. Nash, *United States Oil Policy, 1890–1964* (Westport: Greenwood Press, 1976), 214.

36. Sanders, *Regulation of Natural Gas*, 36, 49.

37. House Committee on Interstate and Foreign Commerce, *Public Utility Holding Companies: Hearings on H.R. 5423*, 74th Cong., 1st sess., 1935, pt. 3:1050.

38. Ibid., 1054.

39. Ibid., 1053.

40. Clark, *Energy and the Federal Government*, 280.

41. House Committee on Interstate and Foreign Commerce, *Hearings on the Natural Gas Act*, 74th Cong., 2nd sess., April 1936, 77. Also see House, Committee on Interstate and Foreign Commerce, *Hearings on the Natural Gas Act*, 75th Cong., 1st sess., March 1937, 122.

42. U.S. 52 Stat. 821 (1938).

43. Sanders, *Regulation of Natural Gas*, 50. Also see Hooley, *Natural Gas Industry*.

44. Richard H. K. Vietor, *Energy Policy in America since 1945: A Study of Business-Government Relations* (Cambridge: Cambridge University Press, 1987), 70–72.

45. House, Committee on Interstate and Foreign Commerce, *Hearings on the Natural Gas Act*, 75th Cong., 1st sess., March 1937, 134. Also see Sanders, *Regulation of Natural Gas*, 49–50.

46. U.S. 52 Stat. 825 (1938).

47. *Congressional Record*, 75th Cong., 1st sess., April 22, 1937, 81, pt. 6:3771.

48. Clyde L. Seavey, "Federal Regulation of the Transportation and Sale of Natural Gas in Interstate Commerce," in *American Gas Association Proceedings* (New York: AGA, 1938), 126–29.

49. Richard H. K. Vietor, *Contrived Competition: Regulation and Deregulation in America* (Cambridge: Harvard University Press, Belknap Press, 1994), 100.

50. Ibid.

51. Larson, Knowlton, and Popple, *New Horizons*, 749.

52. "Natural Gas," *Fortune*, August 1940, 56.

53. Ibid.

54. Ibid., 96.

Chapter 8

1. John W. Frey and H. Chandler Ide, *A History of the Petroleum Administration for War, 1941–1945* (Washington, D.C.: GPO, 1946), 227.

2. D. P. Hartson, "The Appalachian," *Proceedings of the American Gas Association* (New York: AGA, 1941), 132.

3. Frey and Ide, *Petroleum Administration*, 229.

4. Ibid.

5. J. French Robinson, "Demand and Supply of Natural Gas after the War," *Proceedings of the American Gas Association* (New York: AGA, 1942), 30.

6. Harold L. Ickes, *Fightin' Oil* (New York: Alfred A. Knopf, 1943), vii.

7. Quoted in Christopher James Castaneda, *Regulated Enterprise: Natural Gas Pipelines and Northeastern Markets, 1938–1954* (Columbus: Ohio State University Press, 1993), 37.

8. ALCOA to the Office of Production Management, "Letters from-to L. C. Tonkin in Support," November 14, 1941, RG 253, box 2924, National Archives.

9. Memorandum of Minutes of Conference on Natural Gas Supply in Appalachian Area, "Hope Natural Gas Co., Cornwell, W. VA, to Perryvill, LA, original application," RG 253, box 294, National Archives.

10. Frey and Ide, *Petroleum Administration*, 230.

11. J. A. Krug to J. S. Knowlson, no date. In folder "Natural Gas-L-31," RG 179, box 6, "L" Orders. National Archives.

12. Memorandum by General H. K. Rutherford, January 13, 1942. "Natural Gas-L-31," RG 179, box 6, WPB "L" Orders, National Archives.

13. Limitation Order L-31, "Natural Gas-L-31." RG 179, box 6, National Archives.

14. Ernest R. Acker, "The Gas Industry in War," in *Proceedings of the American Gas Association* (New York: AGA, 1942).

15. Frey and Ide, *Petroleum Administration,* 229.

16. Kenneth S. Davis, *FDR: The Beckoning of Destiny, 1882–1928: A History* (New York: G. P. Putnam's Sons, 1971), 799; and Kenneth S. Davis, *FDR: The New Deal Years, 1933–1937: A History* (New York, Random House, 1986), 165–66, 341, and 618.

17. In 1946, the company's name changed slightly to Tennessee Gas Transmission Company.

18. Castaneda, *Regulated Enterprise,* 41.

19. Ibid.

20. Ibid., 42.

21. *Public Utilities Reports,* "Re: Tennessee Gas and Transmission Co," Docket no. 2506, vol. 40, (September 11, 1941), 131.

22. House Committee on Interstate and Foreign Commerce, *Hearings on Natural Gas Amendments,* 77th Cong., 1st sess., July 1941.

23. Also see Seavey, "Transportation and Sale of Natural Gas," 126.

24. *Public Utilities Reports,* "Re: Tennessee Gas and Transmission Co.," Docket no. 2506, vol. 40, (September 11, 1941), 137–38.

25. House Committee on Interstate and Foreign Commerce, *Hearings on Natural Gas Amendments,* 77th Cong., 1st sess., July 1941, 1, 5.

26. Federal Power Commission, "Staff Report on the Natural Gas Investigation," *Administration of the Certification Provisions of Section 7 of the Natural Gas Act* (Washington, D.C.: GPO, January 1947), 3.

27. Ibid., 3.

28. House Committee on Interstate and Foreign Commerce, *Hearings on Natural Gas Amendments,* 77th Cong., 1st sess., July 1941, 2–3, 5; Sanders, *Regulation of Natural Gas,* 52–53.

29. J. A. Krug to Curtis B. Dall, February 20, 1942, RG 138, box 147, folder 70-53, National Archives.

30. Federal Power Commission, "Staff Report," 6.

31. Ibid., 9.

32. As of April 24, 1942, the FPC and WPB agreed to coordinate their activities to meet war-related problems of the natural gas industry.

33. Federal Power Commission, "The Ohio Fuel Gas Company and the Panhandle Eastern Pipeline Company," *Federal Power Commission Reports,* Dockets G-408 and G-410, vol. 3 (1942): 301–9. (References to the *Federal Power Commision Reports* will hereafter be cited as [vol. no.] FPC [page no.] [date]).

34. 3 FPC 442–48 (1944).

35. Ibid.

36. Ibid.

37. Ibid., 446.

38. Castaneda, *Regulated Enterprise,* 53.

39. 3 FPC 578 (1944).

40. Ibid.

41. 3 FPC 574 (1944).

42. Reconstruction Finance Corporation Minutes, November 13, 1943, vol. 142, National Archives. Also see Reconstruction Finance Corporation Minutes, February 12, 1944, vol. 145, National Archives; and Castaneda, *Regulated Enterprise,* 57–58.

43. Richard Austin Smith, "Tennessee Gas Transmission vs. El Paso: They Play Rough in the Gas Business," *Fortune,* January 1965, 134.

44. Frank H. Love, "Construction Features of the Tennessee Gas and Transmission Company Pipe Line," *The Petroleum Engineer* 16, no. 2 (November 1944): 121–44. Also see Tenneco, Inc., "Tenneco's First 35 Years," 1978.

45. Tennessee Gas and Transmission Company, *Annual Report* (1945), 2.

46. Reconstruction Finance Corporation Minutes, "Memorandum describing telephone call between Jesse H. Jones and Richard Wagner," December 21, 1944, vol. 155, National Archives.

47. 4 FPC 294 (1946). Also see Defense Plant Corporation Minutes, Roll 98, March 2, 1945, vol. 114, National Archives.

48. Ibid., 295–96. Also see Defense Plant Corporation Minutes, February 21, 1945, vol. 960, National Archives; and Defense Plant Corporation Minutes, March 23, 1945, vol. 1240, National Archives.

49. 4 FPC 302 (1946).

50. Ibid.

51. Ibid., 304.

52. Sanders, *Regulation of Natural Gas,* 86–87.

Chapter 9

1. Quoted in Castaneda, *Regulated Enterprise,* 67.

2. House Special Committee Investigating Petroleum Resources, *Hearings on War Emergency Pipe-Line Systems and Other Petroleum Facilities,* 79th Cong., 1st sess., November 15–17, 1945.

3. Arthur M. Johnson, *Petroleum Pipelines and the Public Policy, 1905–1959* (Cambridge: Harvard University Press, 1967), 326.

4. Ibid., 345.

5. Sidney A. Swensrud, "A Study of the Possibility of Converting the Large Diameter War Emergency Pipe Lines to Natural Gas Service after the

War" (paper presented at the Petroleum Division of the American Institute of Mining and Metallurgical Engineers, New York City, February 24, 1944).

6. Castaneda, *Regulated Enterprise*, 68. Also see Otto Scott, *The Exception: The Story of Ashland Oil and Refining Company* (New York: McGraw Hill, 1968), 325.

7. Reconstruction Finance Corporation Release, September 14, 1945.

8. House Special Committee Investigating Petroleum Resources, *Hearings on War Emergency Pipe-Line Systems and Other Petroleum Facilities*, 79th Cong., 1st sess., November 15–17, 1945, 3. See also Jesse J. Jones, *Fifty Billion Dollars: My Thirteen Years with the RFC* (New York: MacMillan, 1951), 402.

9. Surplus Property Administration, *Government-Owned Pipelines*, Report of the Surplus Property Administration to the Congress (Washington, D.C.: GPO, 1946).

10. Ibid., 2.

11. House Select Committee to Investigate Disposition of Surplus Property, *Second Interim Report*, 79th Cong., 2nd sess., August 1946, pp. 3–4.

12. War Assets Administration, *Government Owned Pipelines: Report of the War Assets Administration to the Congress* (Washington, D.C.: GPO, December 18, 1946), 4.

13. Ibid.

14. AP Wire Service, July 30, 1946.

15. War Assets Administration, *Transcript of Proceedings: Proposals to Buy or Lease the Big and Little Big Inch Pipe Lines* (Washington, D.C.: GPO, July 31, 1946).

16. "Former Big Names in Government Are Involved in Bids for Pipelines," *Washington Daily News*, October 17, 1946. Harold L. Ickes, " 'Uncle Jesse's' Bid for Oil Pipelines Seen Loaded Two Ways for Monopoly," *Evening Star*, October 2, 1946, A-11.

17. Ibid.

18. Harold L. Ickes, "WAA Administrator Urged to Sell 'Inch' Pipe Lines Now, and for Cash," *Evening Star*, October 28, 1946. Also see Harold L. Ickes, "WAA Seen Yielding to Machinations of John L. Lewis on Natural Gas," *Evening Star*, October 30, 1946; and Editorial, "The New Lewis Threat," *News*, October 24, 1946.

19. "Lewis Home Uses Gas," *Washington Post*, December 6, 1946.

20. Department of the Interior Press Release, "Big Inch and Little Big Inch Conferences Held," November 30, 1946. Also see letters from Charles H. Smith, President, Big Inch Oil, Inc., to General Robert M. Littlejohn, WAA, November 29, 1946, and November 30, 1946.

21. Castaneda, *Regulated Enterprise*, 85–87.

22. War Assets Administration, *Government-Owned Pipelines*, 9.

23. Statement of Congressman Francis E. Walter on Disposition of Big Inch Lines before House Committee on Interstate and Foreign Commerce, January 20, 1947.

24. War Assets Administration, *Transcript of Proceedings: Proposals for Purchase of War Emergency Pipe Lines Commonly Known as Big and Little Big Inch Pipe Lines* (Washington, D.C.: GPO, February 10, 1947).

25. John W. Welker, "Fair Profit?" *Harvard Business Review* 26, no. 2 (March 1948), 207. For a detailed discussion of the bid episode, see Joseph A. Pratt and Christopher J. Castaneda, *Builders: Herman and George R. Brown* (College Station: Texas A&M University Press, 1999) and Castaneda, *Regulated Enterprise.*

26. James T. Howard, "Swing $143 Million Deal with $150,000," *PM,* November 11, 1947; H. Walton Cloke, "Huge Paper Profit for Pipeline Group," *New York Times,* November 11, 1947; Welker, "Fair Profit?" 207–15; and Joseph Stagg Lawrence, "Profits and Progress," *Harvard Business Review* 26, no. 4 (July 1948): 480–91.

27. "Duff Doubts Pipeline Curb," *Philadelphia Bulletin,* February 15, 1947.

28. "A Need for Speed," *GAS,* March 1947.

29. House Committee on Interstate and Foreign Commerce, *Hearings on Amendments to the Natural Gas Act,* 80th Cong., 1st sess., April–May 1947.

30. Nicholas B. Wainwright, *History of the Philadelphia Electric Company: 1881–1961* (Philadelphia Electric Company, 1961), 320.

31. Ibid., 321–23.

32. Paul L. Howell and Ira Royal Hart, "The Promoting and Financing of Transcontinental Gas Pipe Line Corporation," *Journal of Finance* 6, no. 3 (September 1951): 311–24.

33. C. A. Williams, "The Story of Transcontinental Gas Pipe Line Corporation," *Oil and Gas Journal* (May 4, 1950). For the quote, see Transcontinental Gas Pipe Line, *Annual Report, 1950,* p. 2.

34. Joseph A. Pratt, *A Managerial History of Consolidated Edison, 1936–1981* (New York: Consolidated Edison, 1988), 166.

35. Martin Toscan Bennet, "The 'Safest Inch,' " *Engineering News-Record* (September 14, 1950).

36. "Texas Gas Comes Through," *New York Times,* January 22, 1951.

37. Pratt, *Consolidated Edison,* 163.

38. Ibid.

39. Ibid., 169.

40. Ibid., 171.

41. David F. Grozier, "The Brooklyn Union Natural Gas Conversion: Biggest Changeover in the World," *Gas Age* (Janaury 1, 1953): 32–33.

42. Ibid., 33–34.

43. Ibid., 30.

44. John Osborne, "A Brawling, Bawling Industry," *Life*, March 10, 1952, 107.

45. Texas Eastern Transmission Corporation, *Annual Report, 1949*, 16; *1951*, 13.

46. "Key Dates in Northeastern's History," Algonquin Calendar, 6 (pamphlet prepared by Public Relations Department, Eastern Gas and Fuel Associates).

47. 12 FPC 210–15 (1958).

48. "Time Clock," *Time*, August 17, 1953, p. 79.

49. "FPC Lets Natural Gas Company Ship to Canada," *Business Week*, September 5, 1953, 30.

50. Algonquin Gas Transmission Company, *Minutes*, January 15, 1954.

51. Osborne, "Brawling, Bawling Industry," 101–8.

Chapter 10

1. Herbert, *Clean Cheap Heat*, 110.

2. Michigan representative John Lesinski blasted MichCon for its monopolistic practices. See *Congressional Record*, 79th Cong., 1st sess., February 12, 1945, 91, pt. 26:1056–1060.

3. Quoted in Castaneda and Smith, *Gas Pipelines*, 119. Also see *Detroit Times*, May 31, 1952.

4. *Panhandle Eastern Pipe Line Co. v. Michigan Public Service Commission*, 486 U.S. (1951). Also see "State Upheld on Gas Sales," *Detroit News*, October 11, 1950.

5. Castaneda and Smith, *Gas Pipelines*, 121. Also see "State Loses Point on Gas," *Milwaukee Journal*, December 13, 1951. The Michigan-Wisconsin line proposed serving utility customers in Wisconsin (8), Michigan (3), Iowa (4), and Missouri (1). Wisconsin discouraged natural gas use through the imposition of a tax. In 1943, the state government set a $.07 per Mcf tax on natural gas; this tax was repealed in 1947. See Wisconsin Laws of 1943, c. 339; Wisc. stat. 76.55 (1943).

6. See *Detroit News*, February 21, 1945, April 3, 1945, June 22, 1945, September 20–21, 1945, and March 4, 1947; *Detroit Free Press*, February 22–24, 1945, April 3, 1945, September 24, 1945, May 16, 1946, September 24, 1946; and *Detroit Times*, April 2, 1945, May 16, 1946, and September 24, 1946.

7. House Committee on Interstate and Foreign Commerce, *Fuel Investigation*, 80th Cong., 2nd sess., 1948, 477. For an informative discussion of competition in the natural gas industry, see John T. Miller Jr., "Competition in Regulated Industries: Interstate Pipelines," *Georgetown Law Journal* 48, no. 2 (Winter 1958): 224.

8. Castaneda and Smith, *Gas Pipelines*, 121–22.

9. 6 FPC 37–50, 74–91 (1949).

10. Ibid.

11. American Light & Traction became American Natural Gas on June 15, 1949. 9 SEC 833, 856 (1941).

12. 11 FPC 172 (1957); and 6 FPC 91 (1949). Also see 236 F. 2d 289 and 335 U.S. 854.

13. 6 FPC 17 (1949).

14. SEC, "In the Matter of the United Light & Railways Company, American Light & Traction Company et al.," November 13, 1947 (File no.s 59–11; 59–17; 54–25), tr 31–1832, 31–1850–1.

15. 10 FPC 317 (1953).

16. Ibid., 313.

17. Ibid., 317.

18. Ralph Nelson, "Gas Firm's Buying Influence with Jobs?" *Detroit Free Press*, May 10, 1951.

19. 10 FPC 246 (1953).

20. Vernon W. Thomson to Thomas Burke, May 1, 1952, In folder "Texas-Michigan Pipeline Co., 1950–1951–1952," box 189B6, Panhandle Eastern Historical Archives.

21. *Phillips Petroleum Company v. State of Wisconsin,* 374 U.S. 672 (1954). Also see Raymond N. Shibley and George B. Mickum III, "The Impact of Phillips upon the Interstate Pipelines," *Georgetown Law Journal* 44, no. 4 (June 1956): 628.

22. Panhandle Eastern, *Annual Report, 1954,* 5.

23. Vietor, *Energy Policy,* 83. Also see Panhandle Eastern, *Annual Report, 1954,* 11.

24. 13 FPC 76 (1961). Also see 13 FPC 53–54 (1961) and 13 FPC 59–77 (1961).

25. Panhandle Eastern, *Annual Report, 1952,* 14.

26. *Congressional Record,* 83rd Cong., 2nd sess., March 29, 1954, 100, pt. 57.

27. 230 F. 2(d) 810.

28. Vietor, *Energy Policy,* 84.

29. Panhandle Eastern, *Annual Report, 1956,* 5.

30. Vietor, *Energy Policy,* 87–89. A Senate investigation of the alleged bribe revealed that Superior Oil Company had paid Senator Case $2,500. The oil company later paid a $10,000 fine for not registering its lobbyists. See David Howard Davis, *Energy Politics,* 2nd ed. (New York: St. Martin's Press, 1978), 122–23.

31. "Management's Report on the Gas Bill Veto," *Panhandle Lines,* February 1956. Also see "Presidential Message, February 17, 1956," Box 726, file 140-C, White House Official File, Dwight D. Eisenhower Presidential Library.

32. Panhandle Eastern, *Annual Report, 1959,* 19.

33. 24 FPC 546 (1964).

34. 24 FPC 547 (1964).

35. For sources that trace the Trunkline project, see "New Company Headed by Davies Plans Wholesale Gas Line," *Oil and Gas Journal* (March 29, 1947): 184–85; 8 FPC 250–61 (1952).

36. Castaneda and Smith, *Gas Pipelines*, 128–32. For an analysis of life insurance company financing of gas pipelines after World War II, see Hooley, *Natural Gas Industry*.

37. See Frank Mangan, *The Pipeliners* (El Paso: Guynes Press, 1977).

38. American Gas Association, *Historical Statistics of the Gas Industry* (New York: AGA, 1961), 231 B.

39. Richard Austin Smith, "T.G.T. vs. El Paso: They Play Rough in the Gas Business," *Fortune,* January 1965.

40. Mangan, *Pipeliners*, 260–64.

41. "Back Door to California: The Great Pipeline Battle," *Forbes,* December 15, 1961, 30.

42. David Rulison Palmer, "American Politics and Policies in the Regulation of Mexican Natural Gas Imports" (Ph.D. diss., University of California–Berkeley, 1982).

43. Smith, "T.G.T. vs. El Paso," 135.

44. Ibid., 230.

45. Ibid., 231–33.

Chapter 11

1. Stephen G. Breyer and Paul W. MacAvoy, *Energy Regulation by the Federal Power Commission* (Washington, D.C.: Brookings Institution, 1974), 73.

2. See William D. Smith, "Natural Gas: Short, and Getting Shorter," *New York Times,* September 28, 1975, p. 2, col. 1.

3. "Swidler Confesses Error on Gas Supply," *Oil and Gas Journal* (September 27, 1971): 70.

4. Sanders, *Regulation of Natural Gas,* 127.

5. Richard Vietor argued that "the concrescence of these three trends—depletion, concentration, and environmentalism—nearly overshadowed a polity already shaken by a broader crisis of a confidence that stemmed from the Vietnam War" (Vietor, *Energy Policy,* 194). Also see Steven Rattner, "Gas Crisis Has Complicated Origins," *New York Times,* January 30, 1977; Edward Cowan, "Natural Gas Allocation Dilemma," *New York Times,* February 23, 1975; and Edward Cowan, "Northeast Warned It Faces Winter Natural Gas Crisis," *New York Times,* September 15, 1974.

6. See Tussing and Barlow, *Natural Gas Industry,* 113–14.

7. Sanders, *Regulation of Natural Gas,* 125.

8. Ibid., 131.

9. Vietor, *Energy Policy*, 278. Also see Pipeline Production Area Rate Proceeding (Phase I), FPC Opinion no. 326, 42 FPC 738 (1976). This opinion was affirmed in the case *City of Chicago v. FPC*, 458 F. 2d 731 (D.C. Cir., 1971). Also see 405 U.S. 1074 (1972).

10. Richard Vietor states that a combination of economic factors contributed to determining the timing of the shortage. "However, short-sighted public policies, consumerism, and business decision-making affected the timing, severity, and economic impact that made transition from abundance to scarcity a crisis" (Vietor, *Energy Policy*, 194). For an overview of the international repercussions of the rise of OPEC, see Peter Odell, *Oil and World Power*, 8th ed. (New York: Penguin, 1986); and John G. Clark, "The Energy Crises of 1919–1924 and 1973–1975," in *Energy Systems and Policy* (New York: Taylor & Francis, 1980), 4:239–271. In "Energy: A Federal Oil Firm," *Time*, February 24, 1975, xx, it was reported that independent marketers "suspect the major oil companies have contrived the shortage to force them out of business."

11. Vietor, *Energy Policy*, 289–90. *Consumer Federation of America v. FPC*, 515 F. 2d 347.

12. Tussing and Barlow, *Natural Gas Industry*, 112. The first emergency rules for transportation were issued in Order 533, 54 FPC 21 (1975).

13. Tussing and Barlow, *Natural Gas Industry*, 110; Vietor, *Energy Policy*, 278.

14. Panhandle Eastern, *Annual Report, 1977*, 2.

15. FPC Opinion no. 699, 51 FPC 2212 (June 21, 1974), set a single national ceiling price for natural gas.

16. National Rates for Jurisdictional Sales of Natural Gas, Docket no. RM75–14, FPC Opinion no. 770 (1976); Vietor, *Energy Policy*, 282, 287. Also see McCraw, *Prophets of Regulation*, 235; Vietor, *Contrived Competition*, 114; Alfred E. Kahn, "Economic Issues in Regulating the Field Price of Natural Gas," *American Economic Review* 50 (May 1960): 507–13; and FPC Opinion no. 468, 34 FPC 159–434 (1969). Kahn, who had earlier suggested implementation of a two-tier pricing structure, one price for old gas and one for new, was not at this time in favor of natural gas decontrol. In 1974, while serving on the New York State Public Service Commission, Kahn stated that gas production was "inexorably declining" and that decontrol would only transfer "tens of billions of dollars" from the producers to the consumers (Sanders, *Regulation of Natural Gas*, 148). Although the regulatory tide was now swinging in favor of the producers, debate intensified on the best methods to stimulate production while preventing prices from skyrocketing.

17. Mel Horwitch, "Coal: Constrained Abundance," in *Energy Future*, ed. Robert Stobaugh and Daniel Yergin (New York: Random House, 1979), 80.

18. Horwitch, "Constrained Abundance," 79–80. Also see Edmund Faltermayer, "Clearing the Way for the New Age of Coal," *Fortune*, May 1974, 215–38.

19. Vietor, *Energy Policy*, 294.

20. Jack Schomaker provided a detailed account of the origin and plans for WyCoalGas. Other pipeline firms considered the possibility of engaging in coal gasification projects as early as 1973. The first modern project was designed by El Paso Natural Gas in conjunction with Consolidation Coal, a subsidiary of Continental Oil; see Vietor, *Energy Policy,* 293. Christopher J. Castaneda and Joseph A. Pratt, *From Texas to the East: A Strategic History of Texas Eastern Corporation* (College Station: Texas A&M University Press, 1993), 213–16; and Vietor, *Energy Policy,* 294. Also see Federal Energy Administration, *Final Task Force Report on Coal Project Independence* (Washington, D.C.: GPO, November 1974); James K. Harlan, *Starting with Synfuels* (Cambridge, Mass.: Ballinger, 1982); and Ernest J. Yanarella and William C. Green, eds., *The Unfulfilled Promise of Synthetic Fuels: Technological Failure, Policy Immobilization, or Commercial Illusion* (New York: Greenwood Press, 1987).

21. Panhandle Eastern, *Annual Report, 1970,* 16; Panhandle Eastern 1977 proxy statement, 38; and Panhandle Eastern, *Annual Report, 1972,* 15.

22. William F. Nicholson, "SASOL: From South Africa to Kentucky," *Owenboro Messenger-Inquirer,* October 5, 1980.

23. Castaneda and Smith, *Gas Pipelines,* 190.

24. Ibid.

25. Panhandle Eastern, *Annual Report, 1988,* 4. Panhandle sold North Antelope to Peabody in 1989.

26. Vietor, *Energy Policy,* 324.

27. Sabrina Willis, "The Synthetic Fuels Corporation as an Organizational Failure in Policy Mobilization," in *The Unfulfilled Promise of Synthetic Fuels: Technological Failure, Policy Immobilization, or Commercial Illusion,* ed. Ernest J. Yanarella and William C. Green (New York: Greenwood Press, 1987), 71–73. Willis argues that "the problems of the Synthetic Fuels Corporation have been so many and so serious that it is difficult to determine exactly why the corporation failed to come close to achieving the goals set for it by Congress in the Energy Security Act."

28. Tussing and Barlow, *Natural Gas Industry,* 72–73.

29. "SFC Aid Needed for N.M. Gas Plant," *Synfuels Week,* December 20, 1982, 3.

30. See Castaneda and Pratt, *From Texas to the East,* 215.

31. "Synfuels: Once a Flame, Now a Flicker," *Courier and Press* (Evansville, Indiana), May 23, 1982.

32. Tussing and Barlow, *Natural Gas Industry,* 74–78.

33. Tussing and Barlow, *Natural Gas Industry,* 78–86; and Vietor, *Energy Policy,* 297–99. Also see Christopher Gibbs and Richard Vietor, "The Alaskan Natural Gas Pipeline" (Boston: Harvard Business School, Case 9-381-195, 1981); and 58 FPC 810–1548 (1981).

34. Edward R. Leach, "Arctic Energy: In Search of a Route," *Pipeline and Gas Journal* (July 1971): 52.

35. Nicholas P. Biederman, "Arctic Gas: Potential Looks Good, Many Are Studying How to Move It," *Pipeline and Gas Journal* (July 1972): 21–23.

36. "Panhandle Eastern Corp.," *Houston Post,* January 20, 1983. For a review of early U.S. and Canadian relations regarding natural gas imports, see Ralph S. Spritzer, "Changing Elements in the Natural Gas Picture," *Regulation of the Natural Gas Producing Industry,* ed. Keither C. Brown (Baltimore: Johns Hopkins University, Resources for the Future, 1972), 114–16.

37. For background, see "Is LNG the Answer?" *The American Legion Magazine,* August 1977, 20–38; Les Gajay, "LNG-Import Limits and Project Subsidies Are Likely to Be Axed in Carter Proposal," *Wall Street Journal,* April 14, 1977; James P. Sterba, "Gas Shortage a Fundamental, Long-Term Economic Threat to U.S. Experts Say," *New York Times,* February 22, 1977; and Tim Metz, "Gas Shortages Give Some New Ammunition to LNG Advocates," *Wall Street Journal,* February 14, 1977.

38. Tussing and Barlow, *Natural Gas Industry,* 63.

39. Edward Faridany, "Marine Operations and Market Prospects for Liquefied Natural Gas," in *LNG: 1974–1990* (London: Economist Intelligence Unit, 1974), 20. For a valuable analysis of the international context of energy use, see John G. Clark, *The Political Economy of World Energy: A Twentieth-Century Retrospective* (Chapel Hill: University of North Carolina Press, 1990), 274–311.

40. Nick Kotz and Nick Mintz, "Houston Gas Exec's Gifts to Nixon's Drive Probed," *Houston Chronicle,* July 1, 1973, 1.

41. Castaneda and Pratt, *From Texas to the East,* 206–8.

42. William Beecher, "Politics Derail U.S.-Soviet Deal," *Boston Globe,* November 3, 1978.

43. Vietor, *Contrived Competition,* 120.

44. Ibid.

45. Ibid., 130.

46. FPC Opinion no. 796, 58 FPC 726 (1981); and FPC Opinion no. 796-A, 58 FPC 2935–46 (1981).

47. Panhandle Eastern, *Annual Report, 1979,* 14; and Panhandle Eastern, *Annual Report, 1981,* 18.

48. Ibid. In 1980, Trunkline estimated that the initial price of regasified LNG placed into its pipeline system would be $6.62 per MMBtu for deliveries made before July 1, 1981. The price of Trunkline's regasified LNG was based on three elements: (1) the LNG delivered cost (FOB) to the LNG tankers at the Algerian port, (2) the costs of transporting the LNG across the ocean by tanker, and (3) the capital and operating costs of the Lake Charles facilities.

49. "Customers Balk at High-Price LNG," *Energy News,* August 16, 1982.

50. Sam Fletcher, "Expensive Gas Imports Stop," *The Houston Post,* December 15, 1983; "Panhandle Eastern Halts Its Purchases of Algerians' Gas," *Houston Chronicle,* December 15, 1983.

51. Quoted in Castaneda and Smith, *Gas Pipelines*, 230 n. 47.

52. "Pact for Costly Algerian Gas Upheld," *Victoria Advocate*, February 24, 1983.

53. "Washington Roundup," *Platt's Oilgram*, December 1, 1983. In November 1983 Congress passed legislation providing that "the United States Government should move immediately to promote lower prices and fair market conditions for imported natural gas." Also see Panhandle Eastern, *Annual Report, 1984*, 46.

Chapter 12

1. James E. Carter, *Keeping Faith: Memoirs of a President* (Toronto: Bantam, 1982); Davis, *Energy Politics*, 136–38; Vietor, *Energy Policy*, 322.

2. Castaneda and Smith, *Gas Pipelines*, 212.

3. Sanders, *Regulation of Natural Gas*, 148.

4. The resulting gas glut forced Congress to rescind the provisions of this act, which discouraged natural gas use.

5. *Natural Gas Policy Act of 1978*, Public Law 95-621, 95th Cong., 2nd sess. (November 1978); Senate Committee on Energy and Natural Gas Resources, *Natural Gas Pricing Proposals of President Carter's Energy Program* (Part D of S. 1469), 95th Cong., 1st sess., June 1977, 235–45; *Congressional Record*, 95th Cong., 1st sess., 1977, S15322–S15365 and S15595–S15604. Also see Vietor, *Energy Policy*, 311.

6. Vietor, *Energy Policy*, 312.

7. Order 319, 3 FERC 30,477 (1983).

8. A court decision subsequently disbanded the Special Marketing Programs. Panhandle Eastern, *Annual Report, 1983*, 9; and Panhandle Eastern, *Annual Report, 1984*, 8–9. *Maryland People's Counsel v. FERC*, 761 F.2d 768 (D.C. Cir. 1985)

9. *State of Illinois v. Panhandle Eastern Pipe Line Company*, Central District of Illinois, "Motion of Defendant Panhandle Eastern Pipe Line Company for Award of Attorney's Fees and Imposition of Sanctions," 2; *State of Illinois v. Panhandle Eastern Pipe Line Company*, Central District of Illinois, "Memorandum in Support of Defendant Panhandle Eastern Pipe Line Company for Award of Attorney's Fees and Imposition of Sanctions," 3.

10. FERC, Docket RM83–71–000, Order 380, Final Rule, May 25, 1984, 11–4.

11. Vietor, *Contrived Competition*, 146.

12. For background on direct sales, see Robert C. Means and Robert S. Angyal, "The Regulation and Future Role of Direct Producer Sales," *Energy Law Journal* 5.1 (1984): 1–46.

13. Vietor, *Constrained Competition*, 149–50. See pages 147–49 for background on FERC Order 436. Also see FERC Order 436, Stats. & Regs. 30,665 (November 1985), 31,467–68; 50 Fed. Reg. 42,408 (October 18, 1985).

14. "Court Rejects Key Provisions of FERC Order 436," *Oil and Gas Journal,* (June 29, 1987): 18.

15. Vietor, *Contrived Competition,* 158; Castaneda and Pratt, *From Texas to the East,* 252. FERC Order 500, Fed. Reg. vol. 52, no. 157 (August 14, 1987), 30334–57. "FERC Trying to Solve Problems in Order 500," *Oil and Gas Journal* (October 26, 1987): 30.

16. See FERC, *Fact Sheet,* Remarks of FERC Chairman Allday, April 8, 1992.

17. Charles Trabandt, "A Revolution of Details: Order 636," *Electric Perspectives* 17, no. 5 (September 1993): 30. Also see Daniel Macey, "Preparing for the Worst under Order 636," *Gas Daily's NG* (Winter 1993): 32–36.

18. Trabandt, "Revolution of Details," 30.

19. Quoted in Castaneda and Smith, *Gas Pipelines,* 267.

20. "The Brave New World of FERC Order 636 Opens New Frontiers," *PipeLines* (November-December, 1993).

21. Quoted in Castaneda and Smith, *Gas Pipelines,* 268.

22. Arlon Tussing and Bob Tippee, *The Natural Gas Industry: Evolution, Structure, and Economics,* 2nd. ed. (Tulsa, Okla.: Pennwell Books, 1995), 266.

23. See S. 1317, Public Utility Holding Company Act of 1995, introduced on October 12, 1995, by Republican senator Alphonse D'Amato of New York; H.R. 3601, Public Utility Holding Company Act of 1996, introduced on June 6, 1996, by Republican congressman W. J. Tauzin of Louisiana; and S. 621, "The Public Utilities Holding Company Act of 1997," introduced by Senator D'Amato.

24. I would like to thank Martin Edwards and Skip Horvath of INGAA for discussing the PUHCA with me.

25. AMWAYUSA, *Press Release: Columbia Energy and Amway Launch Retail Energy Program,* November 9, 1998.

26. Alfred E. Kahn, "Deregulation: Looking Backward and Looking Forward," *Yale Journal on Regulation* 7, no. 2 (Summer 1990): 352.

27. Thanks to John W. Pepper of Duke Energy for providing information about this project.

28. Ronald F. Lewis, "Thermal Desorption at Gas Plants," *Tech Trends* (June 1995).

29. Ernest J. Oppenheimer, *Natural Gas: The Best Energy Choice* (New York: Pen & Podium, 1989), 138; Tussing and Tippee, *The Natural Gas Industry,* 52.

30. "Fuel and Vehicle History Characteristics," http://www.energy.ca.gov/afvs/ngv/ngvhistory.ht (11/24/98, 8:57 A)

31. " 'Nuclear holocaust' rocks N.J.," *Houston Chronicle,* March 25, 1994, 1; Adrienne Knox, "Witness Recounts Escape from Flames," *Houston Chronicle,* March 26, 1994, 17A; "Tetco Gas Blast Levels Buildings;

Long-Term Effect on Pipes Eyes," *Natural Gas Week* 10, no. 13 (March 28, 1994): 1.

32. Oppenheimer, *Natural Gas,* 36, 55–58; Tussing and Tippee, *The Natural Gas Industry,* 34–36.

SELECTED
BIBLIOGRAPHY

Accum, Friedrich Christian. *Description of the Process of Manufacturing Coal Gas, for the Lighting of Streets, Houses, and Public Buildings,* with Elevations, Sections, and Plans of the most improved sorts of apparatus now employed at the gas works of Great Britain. London: Thomas Boys, 1819.

———. *A Practical Treatise on Gas-Light.* London: R. Ackerman, 1815.

American Gas Association. *Gas Facts.* New York: American Gas Association, 1945–1997.

———. *Gas Rate Fundamentals.* 4th ed. Arlington: American Gas Association, 1987.

American Gas Institute. *Lectures Delivered at the Centenary Celebration of the First Commercial Gas Company to Sell Gas as an Illuminant.* New York: American Gas Institute, 1912.

Barty-King, Hugh. *New Flame: How Gas Changed the Commercial, Domestic and Industrial Life of Britain between 1813 and 1984.* Tavistock, U.K.: Graphmitre Limited, 1984.

Block, Eugene B. *Above the Civil War: The Story of Thaddeus Lowe, Balloonist, Inventor, Railway Builder.* Berkeley, Calif.: Howell-North Books, 1966.

Bragdon, Earl D. "The Federal Power Commission and the Regulation of Natural Gas: A Study in Administrative and Judicial History." Ph.D. diss., Indiana University, 1962.

Breyer, Stephen G., and Paul W. MacAvoy. *Energy Regulation by the Federal Power Commission.* Washington, D.C.: Brookings Institution, 1974.

Brignano, Mary, and Hax McCullough. *The Spirit of Progress: The Story of the East Ohio Gas Company and the People Who Made It.* N.p.: East Ohio Gas Company, 1988.

Brown, George T. *The Gas Light Company of Baltimore: A Study of Natural Monopoly.* Baltimore: Johns Hopkins University Press, 1936.

Bush, George. *Future Builders: The Story of Michigan's Consumers Power Company.* New York: McGraw-Hill Company, 1973.

Castaneda, Christopher James. *Regulated Enterprise: Natural Gas Pipelines and Northeastern Markets, 1938–1954.* Columbus: Ohio State University Press, 1993.

Castaneda, Christopher J., and Joseph A. Pratt. "New Markets, Outmoded Manufacturing: The Transition from Manufactured Gas to Natural Gas by Northeastern Utilities after World War II." In *Business and Economic History* 18 Williamsburg, Va.: Business History Conference at the Department of Economics, College of William and Mary, 1989.

————. *From Texas to the East: A Strategic History of Texas Eastern Corporation.* College Station: Texas A&M University Press, 1993.

Castaneda, Christopher J., and Clarance M. Smith. *Gas Pipelines and the Emergence of America's Regulatory State: A History of Panhandle Eastern Corporation, 1928–1993.* New York: Cambridge University Press, 1996.

Clark, James A. *The Chronological History of the Petroleum and Natural Gas Industries.* Houston: Clark Book Co., 1963.

Clark, John G. *Energy and the Federal Government: Fossil Fuel Policies, 1900–1946.* Urbana: University of Illinois Press, 1987.

Clegg, Samuel, Jr. *A Practical Treatise on the Manufacture and Distribution of Coal-Gas.* London: J. Weale, 1841.

Coleman, Charles M. *PG&E of California: The Centennial Story of Pacific Gas and Electric Company, 1852–1952.* New York: McGraw-Hill, 1952.

Collins, Frederick L., *Consolidated Gas Company of New York: A History.* New York: Consolidated Gas Company of New York, 1934.

Cooper, Thomas. *Some Information Concerning Gas Lights.* Philadelphia: John Conrad, 1816.

Davis, Ralph E. "Natural Gas Pipe Line Development during Past Ten Years." *Natural Gas* 16, no. 12 (December 1935): 3–8.

————. *Stories of Natural Gas.* N.p.: Ralph E. Davis, 1964.

Dawson, Albert F. *Columbia System: A History.* New York: J. J. Little and Ives, 1938.

DeVane, Dozier A. "Highlights of the Legislative History of the Federal Power Act of 1935 and the Natural Gas Act of 1938." *George Washington Law Review* 14 (December 1945).

De Vany, Arthur S., and W. David Walls. *The Emerging New Order in Natural Gas: Markets versus Regulation.* Westport, Conn.: Quorum, 1995.

Elton, Arthur. "Gas for Light and Heat." In *A History of Technology: The Industrial Revolution, 1750–1850.* Edited by Charles Singer, E. J. Holmyard, A. R. Hall, and Trevor I. Williams. New York: Oxford University Press, 1958.

Erlick, David P. "The Peales and Gas Lights in Baltimore." *Maryland Historical Magazine,* Spring 1985, 9–18.

Frey, John W., and H. Chandler Ide. *A History of the Petroleum Administration for War, 1941–1945.* Washington, D.C.: GPO, 1946.

Friedel, Robert, and Paul Israel. *Edison's Electric Light: Biography of an Invention.* New Brunswick: Rutgers University Press, 1986.

Gilmer, Robert W. "The History of Natural Gas Pipelines in the Southwest." *Texas Business Review* (May–June 1981): 130–35.

Grozier, David F. "The Brooklyn Union Natural Gas Conversion: Biggest Changeover in the World." *Gas Age,* January 1, 1953.

Hale, Dean. "Diary of an Industry." *American Gas Journal* (October 1966): 43–74.

Hawley, Ellis. *The New Deal and the Problem of Monopoly.* Princeton, N.J.: Princeton University Press, 1966.

Herbert, John H. *Clean Cheap Heat: The Development of Residential Markets for Natural Gas in the United States.* New York: Praeger, 1992.

Hershman, Robert R., and Edward T. Stafford. *Growing with Washington: The Story of Our First Hundred Years.* Edited by Albert W. Atwood. Washington, D.C.: Judd & Detweiler, 1948.

Hidy, Ralph W., and Muriel E. Hidy. *Pioneering in Big Business, 1882–1911.* New York: Harper & Brothers, 1955.

Hooley, Richard W. *Financing the Natural Gas Industry: The Role of Life Insurance Investment Policies.* New York: Columbia University Press, 1961.

Howell, Paul L., and Ira Royal Hart. "The Promoting and Financing of Transcontinental Gas Pipe Line Corporation." *Journal of Finance* 6, no. 3 (September 1951): 311–24.

Huitt, Ralph K. "National Regulation of the Natural-Gas Industry." In *Public Administration and Policy Formation,* edited by Emmett S. Redford. Austin: University of Texas Press, 1956.

Johnson, Arthur M. *Petroleum Pipelines and the Public Policy, 1905–1959.* Cambridge: Harvard University Press, 1967.

King, Thomson. *Consolidated of Baltimore, 1816–1950: A History of Consolidated Gas Electric Light and Power Company of Baltimore.* Baltimore: Consolidated of Baltimore, 1950.

Leeston, Alfred M., John A. Crichton, and John C. Jacobs. *The Dynamic Natural Gas Industry: The Description of an American Industry from the Historical, Technical, Legal, Financial, and Economic Standpoints.* Norman: Oklahoma University Press, 1963.

Lief, Alfred. *Metering for America: 125 Years of the Gas Industry and American Meter Company.* New York: Appleton-Century-Crofts, 1961.

Littlefield, Douglas R., and Tanis C. Thorne. *The Spirit of Enterprise: The History of Pacific Enterprises from 1886 to 1989.* Los Angeles: Pacific Enterprises, 1990.

Mangan, Frank. *The Pipeliners.* El Paso: Guynes Press, 1977.

Marcus, Kenneth Karl. *The National Government and the Natural Gas Industry, 1946–56: A Study in the Making of National Policy.* New York: Arno Press, 1979.

McCullough, Hax, and Mary Brignano. *The Vison and Will to Succeed: A Centennial History of the Peoples Natural Gas Company.* N.p.: Peoples Natural Gas Company, n.d.

Melosi, Martin V. *Coping with Abundance: Energy and Environment in Industrial America.* New York: Alfred A. Knopf, 1985.

Miller, Lillian. *Rembrandt Peale, 1778–1860: A Life in the Arts.* Philadelphia: Historical Society of Philadelphia, 1985.

Mitchell, Edward J., ed. *The Deregulation of Natural Gas.* Washington, D.C.: American Enterprise Institute, 1983.

Morgan, Jerome J. *Manufactured Gas: A Textbook of American Practice.* New York: Jerome J. Morgan, 1928.

Myers, Denys Peter. *Gaslighting in America: A Pictorial Survey, 1815–1910.* New York: Dover Publications, 1978.

Nash, Gerald D. *United States Oil Policy, 1890–1964.* Westport, Conn.: Greenwood Press, 1976.

Neuner, Edward J. *The Natural Gas Industry: Monopoly and Competition in Field Markets.* Norman: University of Oklahoma Press, 1960.

Norman, Oscar E. *The Romance of the Gas Industry.* Chicago: A. C. McClurg, 1922.

Osborne, John. "A Brawling, Bawling Industry." *Life,* March 10, 1952.

Palmer, David Rulison. "American Politics in the Regulation of Mexican Natural Gas Imports." Ph.D. diss., University of California–Berkeley, 1982.

Passer, Harold C. "The Electric Light and the Gas Light: Innovation and Continuity in Economic History." In *Explorations in Enterprise,* edited by Hugh G. J. Aitken. Cambridge, Harvard University Press, 1965.

Peebles, Malcolm W. H. *Evolution of the Gas Industry.* New York: New York University Press, 1980.

Platt, Harold L. *The Electric City: Energy and the Growth of the Chicago Area, 1880–1930.* Chicago: University of Chicago Press, 1991.

Pratt, Joseph A. *A Managerial History of Consolidated Edison, 1936–1981.* N.p.: Consolidated Edison of New York, 1988.

Pratt, Joseph A., and Christopher J. Castaneda, *Builders: Herman and George R. Brown.* College Station: Texas A&M University Press, 1999.

Ramsay, M. L. *Pyramids of Power: The Story of Roosevelt, Insull, and the Utility Wars*. Indianapolis: Bobbs-Merrill, 1937.

Rice, Wallace. *Seventy-five Years of Gas Service in Chicago: The Peoples Gas Light and Coke Company*. Chicago: Peoples Gas Light and Coke, 1925.

Rose, Mark H. *Cities of Light and Heat: Domesticating Gas and Electricity in Urban America*. University Park: Pennsylvania State University Press, 1995.

Rose, Mark H., and John G. Clark. "Light, Heat, and Power: Energy Choices in Kansas City, Wichita, and Denver, 1900–1935," *Journal of Urban History* 5 (May 1979): 340–64.

Sanders, M. Elizabeth. *The Regulation of Natural Gas: Policy and Politics, 1938–1978*. Philadelphia: Temple University Press, 1981.

Sellers, Charles Coleman. *Mr. Peale's Museum: Charles Willson Peale and the First Popular Museum of Natural Science and Art*. New York: W. W. Norton, 1980.

Silverberg, Robert. *Light for the World: Edison and the Power Industry*. Princeton, N.J.: D. Van Nostrand, 1967.

Smith, Richard Austin. "Tennessee Gas Transmission vs. El Paso: They Play Rough in the Gas Business." *Fortune*, January 1965, 134.

Stock, John. "Carl Auer von Welsbach and the Development of Incandescent Gas Lighting." *Journal of Chemical Engineering* 68 (October 1991), 801–3.

Stotz, Louis, and Alexander Jamison. *History of the Gas Industry*. New York: Stettiner Brothers, 1938.

Tarr, Joel. "Transforming an Energy System: The Evolution of the Manufactured Gas Industry and the Transition to Natural Gas in the United States, 1807–1954." In *The Governance of Large Technical Systems*, edited by Olivier Coutard. London: Routledge, 1998.

Thompson, Carl D. *Confessions of the Power Trust*. New York: Arno Press, 1976.

Troesken, Werner. *Why Regulate Utilities? The New Institutional Economics and the Chicago Gas Industry, 1849–1924*. Ann Arbor: University of Michigan Press, 1996.

Tussing, Arlon R., and Connie C. Barlow. *The Natural Gas Industry: Evolution, Structure, and Economics*. Cambridge, Mass.: Ballinger Publishing, 1984.

Tussing, Arlon R., and Bob Tippee. *The Natural Gas Industry: Evolution, Structure, and Economics*. 2nd ed. Tulsa, Okla.: Pennwell, 1995.

U.S. Federal Power Commission. *Natural Gas Investigation—Leland Olds and Claude Draper Report*. Washington, D.C.: GPO, 1948.

————. *Natural Gas Investigation—Nelson Lee Smith and Harrington Wimberly Report*. Washington, D.C.: GPO, 1948.

U.S. Federal Trade Commission. *Report to the Senate on Public Utility Corporations*. 70th Cong., 1st sess. S. Doc. 92. (Published in 96 vols., summary recommendations in pt. 84-A, 1935).

Vietor, Richard H. K. *Energy Policy in America since 1945: A Study of Business-Government Relations*. Cambridge: Cambridge University Press, 1987.

————. *Contrived Competition: Regulation and Deregulation in America*. Cambridge: Harvard University Press, Belknap Press, 1994.

Wainwright, Nicholas B. *History of the Philadelphia Electric Company, 1881–1961*. Philadelphia Electric Company, 1961.

Waters, L. L. *Energy to Move: Texas Gas Transmission Corporation*. N.p.: Texas Gas Transmission Corporation, 1985.

Williams, James C. *Energy and the Making of Modern California*. Akron, Ohio: University of Akron Press, 1997.

Williams, Trevor I. *A History of the British Gas Industry*. Oxford, U.K.: Oxford University Press, 1981.

Williamson, Harold F., and Arnold R. Daum. *The American Petroleum Industry: The Age of Illumination, 1859–1899*. Evanston: Northwestern University Press, 1959.

Wilson, John F. *Lighting the Town: A Study of Management in the North West Gas Industry, 1805–1880*. London: Paul Chapaman, 1991.

Yergin, Daniel. *The Prize: The Epic Quest for Oil, Money, and Power*. New York: Simon & Schuster, 1991.

INDEX

THE AUTHOR

CHRISTOPHER J. CASTANEDA is Associate Professor of History and Associate Director of the Capital Campus Public History Program at California State University, Sacramento. He has published *Regulated Enterprise: Natural Gas Pipelines and Northeastern Markets, 1938–1954; Gas Pipelines and the Emergence of America's Regulatory State: A History of Panhandle Eastern Corporation, 1928–1993* (with Clarance M. Smith); *From Texas to the East: A Strategic History of Texas Eastern Corporation* (with Joseph A. Pratt); and *Builders: Herman and George R. Brown* (with Joseph A. Pratt) as well as other works on the gas and oil industry.

THE EDITOR

DR. KENNETH J. LIPARTITO is professor of history at Florida International University of Miami, Florida. He holds a Ph.D. in history from the Johns Hopkins University and has published extensively in the field of economic and business history. He is the author of *The Bell System and Regional Business: The Telephone in the South* and *Baker and Botts in the Development of Modern Houston*. His work has appeared in leading journals, including the *American Historical Review*, the *Journal of Economic History*, the *Business History Review*, and *Industrial and Corporate Change*. Dr. Lipartito was appointed Newcomen Fellow at the Harvard Business School for the year 1989 to 1990. In 1995 he was awarded the IEEE Life Members Award for the best article in the history of electrical technology, as well as the Newcomen Society Award for Excellence in Business History Research and Writing by the Business History Conference.